Influence and Interests in the European Union:
The New Politics of Persuasion and Advocacy

Influence and Interests in the European Union: The New Politics of Persuasion and Advocacy

Edited by Alex Warleigh and Jenny Fairbrass

FIRST EDITION

 Europa Publications
Taylor & Francis Group

LONDON AND NEW YORK

First Edition 2002

ISBN 185743 163 4

Development Editor: Cathy Hartley
Assistance: John Bailie

100394-5802.

Typeset by Bibliocraft Ltd, Dundee
Printed and bound by TJ International Ltd, Trecerus Industrial Estate,
Padstow, Cornwall

Acknowledgements

This book almost failed to see the light of day, because so many of the contributors to it were seriously ill, or changed jobs, or both, during the time in which it was written. Thus, more than usual, we owe thanks to our contributors, who managed to rework and rethink their papers despite very demanding and otherwise full schedules.

Most of the chapters here were initially written as papers for a conference co-sponsored by the University Association for Contemporary European Studies (www.uaces.org) and the University of Reading Politics Department, held at the University of Reading in February 2001. We would like to express our thanks to both organizations for their support.

We would like to thank Cathy Hartley at Europa for her support for our project and enthusiasm.

We would also like to thank all those who have contributed to the process of making, and studying, European Union public policy, creating a fascinating field of study to which this book seeks to add.

Alex Warleigh and Jenny Fairbrass, October 2002

Dedication

Alex Warleigh: To my family, which is almost as multi-layered and complex as the European Union, but far better at letting its hair down.

Jenny Fairbrass: To Jack Greenleaf and Neil Harding.

Contents

The Editors

Alex Warleigh is Reader in European Governance, and Deputy Director of the Institute of Governance, Public Policy and Social Research at Queen's University Belfast. His publications include (as editor) *Understanding European Union Institutions* (Routledge, 2001), and as co-editor *Citizenship and Governance in the European Union* (Continuum, 2001) as well as monographs entitled *The Committee of the Regions: Institutionalising Multi-level Governance?* (Kogan Page, 1999) and *Flexible Integration: Which Model for the European Union?* (Continuum, 2002).

Jenny Fairbrass is a Senior Research Associate at the Centre for Social and Economic Research on the Global Environment (CSERGE) at the University of East Anglia. She is currently working on the impact of devolution on environmental decision-making at the subnational, national, European Union and wider international levels. She has published primarily on British and European Union (EU) environmental policy in a number of peer-reviewed academic journals and books.

The Contributors

David Earnshaw is Head of Office at Oxfam International, Brussels, and a freelance consultant on EU interest representation. Previously Head of EU Campaigns for GlaxoSmithKline, he has also worked in the European Parliament and as a university lecturer. He currently teaches for the Open University in Brussels. He has published widely in academic journals on the European Parliament and the EU decision-making process.

Rebekka Goehring is a member of the graduate programme 'The New Europe' at the Humboldt and Free Berlin Universities. She is currently completing her doctoral dissertation on 'Shaping the New Europe: Integration through Representation'.

Justin Greenwood is Jean Monnet, and University, Professor of European Public Policy at the Robert Gordon University, Aberdeen. He has led nine book projects in nine years on his career research specialism of interest representation in the EU, including his single authored books *Inside the EU Business Associations* (January 2002, Palgrave), and *Representing Interests in the European Union* (Macmillan, 1997).

Andrew Jordan is Lecturer in Environmental Politics at the University of East Anglia and a research fellow of the UK ESRC's Centre for Social and Economic Research on the Global Environment (CSERGE). He is currently working on two ESRC grant funded projects. He has published widely in peer-reviewed academic journals and books, and is a contributing author of the latest Inter-governmental Panel on Climate Change (IPCC) report.

Campbell McPherson, formerly Senior Lecturer in European Studies at the University of Lincoln, is currently an independent consultant in the satellite communications sector.

Irina Michalowitz is Assistant Professor at the Institute for Advanced Studies in Vienna, and has previously been a lecturer at the United Business Institutes (Brussels). She has also worked in the public affairs offices in Bonn and Brussels of the tourism company Preussag AG.

Nieves Pérez-Solórzano Borragán is Lecturer in Politics at the School of Economic and Social Studies, University of East Anglia. She previously taught at the University of Exeter. She has undertaken consultancy work for EUROCHAMBRES and SBRA under the aegis of TAIEX and CAPE II (November 1999–December 2000).

Carlo Ruzza teaches Migration Studies and European Studies at the University of Trento, and has previously taught at the universities of Essex and Surrey. He is co-ordinator of an EU-funded project involving 10 countries entitled 'Organized Civil Society and European Governance' (2003–05).

Kerry Somerset is currently reading for a PhD at the University of Loughborough, having formerly worked as a consultant on issues of enlarging the EU and as an official in the UK Department of Trade and Industry. Between 1996 and 1999 she was a 'detached' National Expert in the European Commission, specializing in issues of EU enlargement and international trade.

Josephine Wood is an experienced EU lobbyist. She is currently Director of European Union Relations at GlaxoSmithKline, whose Brussels office she runs. She was previously employed in European government affairs at SmithKline Beecham, and has also worked both as a consultant and in the European Commission.

Abbreviations

AEPOC	Association Européenne pour la Protection des Œuvres et Services Cryptés
BEUC	European Bureau of Consumers' Associations
CAMs	Conditional Access Modules
CCP	Common Commercial Policy
CEEC	Central and Eastern European Countries
CEFIC	European Chemical Industry Federation
CEO	Chief Executive Officer
CEOR	Central and Eastern European Office of Representation
CLA	Countryside Landowners Association
COGECA	General Committee for Agricultural Co-operation in the European Union
COM	Commission Document
CONECCS	Consultation, the European Commission and Civil Society
COPA	Committee of Professional Agricultural Organizations in the European Community
COREPER	Committee of Permanent Representatives
CPRE	Council for the Protection of Rural England
DG	Directorate-General (of the European Commission)
DoE	Department of the Environment (United Kingdom)
DTI	Department of Trade and Industry (United Kingdom)
DTH	direct to home
EC	European Community
ECE	East and Central Europe/European
ECJ	European Court of Justice
EC	European Community
ECSC	European Coal and Steel Community
ECT	Treaty establishing the European Community
ECU	European Currency Unit
Ed(s)	Editor(s)
EDF	Electricité de France
EEA	European Environment Agency
EEC	European Economic Community
EFTA	European Free Trade Association
e.g.	exempli gratia (for example)
EIA	Environmental Impact Assessment
EMU	Economic and Monetary Union
EP	European Parliament
ERT	European Round Table

ESC	Economic and Social Committee
et al.	*et alii* (and others)
etc.	et cetera
ETUC	European Trade Union Confederation
EU	European Union
EURATOM	European Atomic Energy Community
EUROCHAMBRES	Association of European Chambers of Commerce and Industry
EUROFER	European Confederation of Iron and Steel Industries
GAC	General Affairs Committee
GATS	General Agreement on Trade in Services
GATT	General Agreement on Tariffs and Trade
GMOs	Genetically Modified Organisms
i.e.	id est (that is to say)
ibid.	*ibidem* (in the same source)
IGC	Intergovernmental Conference
IR	international relations
ITO	International Trade Organization
m.	million
MACs	Movement Advocacy Coalitions
MAFF	Ministry of Agriculture, Fisheries and Food (United Kingdom)
MEP	Member of the European Parliament
NAB	Non-attributable Source
NFU	National Farmers' Union (United Kingdom)
NGO	non-governmental organization
OECD	Organisation for Economic Co-operation and Development
OEEC	Organisation for European Economic Co-operation
RSPB	Royal Society for the Protection of Birds
SBRA	Slovenian Business and Research Association
SEA	Single European Act
SEM	Single European Market
SMEs	Small- and Medium-Sized Enterprises
TENs	Trans-European Networks
TRIPS	Trade-related Aspects of Intellectual Property Rights
UK	United Kingdom
UNICE	Union of Industrial and Employers' Confederations of Europe
US	United States
USA	United States of America
v	versus
WTO	World Trade Organization
WWF	World Wide Fund for Nature

Chapter 1: Introduction

The New Politics of Persuasion, Advocacy and Influence in the European Union

Jenny Fairbrass and Alex Warleigh

INTRODUCTION

This chapter introduces the volume by furnishing a common framework for the chapters that follow. The focal point of the book is provided by the subject of interest representation in the European Union (EU). The volume comprises contributions from both academics and practitioners. Together the chapters build on an extensive body of existing literature in the selected field by providing fresh empirical data and advancing the theoretical debate. The volume reports on and evaluates recent and novel developments in the activities, practices and strategies of those (be they state or non-state actors) who wish to be 'represented' to those who 'govern' in the EU. Additionally, some of the future challenges (e.g. the impact of EU enlargement) to the relationship between 'state' and 'society' in the EU, as mediated by or through a variety of structures and institutions, are examined. In sum, this chapter explores what is meant by the new politics of persuasion, advocacy and influence in the EU context.

A NOTE ON TERMINOLOGY

There are a number of key terms used throughout this volume. Pivotal to it is the notion of 'interest representation'. Conventionally, the idea has tended to be associated with that process, usually found in representative democracies, whereby those who are 'governed' (i.e. civil society) convey their wishes, demands, views and opinions to those who 'govern' them (i.e. elected representatives and those who form the 'administration' or the 'state'). In much of the academic literature on the subject, the term interest representation refers to *collective activity* undertaken by organizations such as 'pressure' or 'interest' groups rather than actions on the part of *individuals* (who would normally express their preferences by voting in elections at the local, regional, national or European levels).

Recent literature on the subject of interest groups has typically employed one of several terms to refer to *group* activities. These include our preferred term 'representation' (e.g. Greenwood 1997; Grant 2000). In addition, words such as 'lobbying' (e.g. Mazey and Richardson 1993; Coen 1998) and 'mobilization' (see Marks 1992) are used. However, both terms – lobbying and mobilization[1] – are problematic. The word lobbying has acquired some unfortunate connotations (i.e. that lobbying confers an unfair advantage on those that can afford to carry it out and therefore runs counter to the notion of democracy). Similarly, the word mobilization has limitations. In other earlier academic literature the term mobilization, and specifically 'resource-mobilization', was used in a narrow way to examine social protest movements, particularly in an American context (e.g. McCarthy and Zald 1977) and especially in relation to those organizations situated to the left of the political spectrum (e.g. the civil rights movement in the USA). This approach tended to focus on the *internal* features (e.g. resource levels in terms of staff and funding) of protest groups, an approach which omits the *external* political and social environment in which they operate. Subsequent studies of protest movements, which have been loosely based on the 'resource-mobilization' approach, have addressed this shortcoming by considering the external political opportunity structures (Kitschelt 1986). Despite this refinement to the resource-mobilization approach, clearly not all interest groups can (or should) be classified as part of a social protest movement (e.g. most business interest groups are unlikely to think of themselves as social protest groups). Hence our preference for the more neutral terminology: interest representation.

However, in using the term interest representation we depart from earlier academic works in that we do not confine it to the activities of *collective* organizations. Nor do we restrict the discussion to the actions of individual members of *civil society*, but include the strategies and practices of institutions themselves (e.g. the interest representation undertaken by the European Commission). This volume uses the term 'interest representation' to refer to those activities, tactics and strategies utilized by state and non-state actors when they attempt to influence European public policy. It ranges across lobbying, the exchange of information, alliance building, formal and informal contact, planned and unplanned relationships: in other words, all forms of interaction that

---

[1] That is not to say that terms such as 'lobbying' and 'mobilization' are absent from our text. For example, where respondents have used them or where we refer to the work of other authors who employ the terms, we do not eschew them.

are designed to advocate particular ideas, persuade the decision-takers to adopt different positions or perspectives, and ultimately to influence policy.

In a sense, the words we use in this volume reveal something of the basic premise of the work. The book argues that interest representation has become crucial to all those who seek to influence decision-making in the EU, including actors from within the EU institutions and national and sub-national governments themselves. It argues that EU decision making, which rests on complex patterns of often informal politics and network construction (Peterson 1995), is aptly described as a 'hustle' (Warleigh 2000) in which each actor must seek to construct coalitions with others in order to secure his or her objectives. The book also seeks to explore how the evolving agenda of the EU has shaped interest representation practices (and vice versa). In addition, it examines issues such as enlargement to include Central and Eastern European countries and the uses of interest representation in the Europeanization of civil society. This, then, is what we mean by the 'new politics' of EU interest representation: *persuasion and advocacy are the means to secure influence, and interest representation itself is an evolving practice which both shapes and is shaped by the development of the EU.*

WHY STUDY INTEREST REPRESENTATION IN THE EU?

One significant reason for studying interest representation is the academic challenge of discovering patterns of actual political behaviour, tracing their development, and analysing and constructing theories about them. From a practical perspective, there is also the desire to know about and understand how a political system operates, in order to be able to participate (more) effectively within it. From either point of view the task is not a simple one. It is rendered all the more complex in relation to a multi-level system such as the EU, where national and EU politics are no longer separate, but rather 'fused' together in one system (Wessels 1996; 1997). Thus, scholars of public policy-making in general, and interest representation in particular, are likely to find much rewarding material in a study of how these processes work at the EU level, particularly if they are interested in how shifts in patterns of governance towards inter- and transnationalization affect politics and policy-making within a given state. In the context of ongoing European integration, ever-increasing numbers of interest groups find that engaging with the EU to secure the policy outcomes they desire is not only advantageous, but essential, given the EU's increasing competence and scope. This has especially been the case since the Single European Act (SEA), which furnished first the European Communities (EC), then the EU with new, more extensive powers and also reduced the ability of any single government to defend a given interest unilaterally. Thus, even interest groups whose focus is primarily national often find themselves obliged to integrate the EU into their lobbying strategies – often with unanticipated outcomes in terms of their ability to maintain or develop influence over the content of public policy (Marks and McAdam 1996).

In turn, this changing pattern of ability to influence policy has an impact on issues of democracy. In part, this is because actors excluded from, or marginalized in, policy networks at the national level in theory have an opportunity to make good such peripheralization by engaging with the EU: policy deals made at national level may be altered when they are entered into the EU arena and its on-going search for compromise between different actors, institutions, and states (for an overview of this system, see Warleigh 2001b). Indeed, EU interest representation patterns even ask questions of established senses of identity and community in the member states: if all member state nationals are EU citizens (as they have been officially since the ratification of the Maastricht Treaty–the Treaty on European Union), then arguably these citizens may seek to work politically with others who share their views in different member states, rather than solely those in their member state of origin (Warleigh 2001a; see also Goehring, this volume). However, such opportunities are generally best exploited by those actors and groups with the most extensive resources of human and financial capital, which tend to be from the private, rather than public, sector (Balanyá *et al.* 2000).

Studying patterns of interest representation in the EU can also reveal much about the power relationships present in the EU system. Although the EU is a very complex and variegated system (see below), thus making it difficult to generalize between different policy areas and time periods, it is, none the less, possible to develop an understanding of how decisions are made, and by whom, by studying how interest representation patterns shape decisions along the policy chain, and how actors at different stages of the chain impact upon the decisions made and strategies used by each other. Thus, it can show how actors from national and regional or local governments, EU institutions and non-governmental organizations (NGOs) interact with each other within the EU system. By the same token, studying interest representation can reveal much about how the EU's modes of policy-making change over time and according to policy area: it can help to show whether and how different institutional rules and structures constrain and shape actors' capacity to influence policy outcomes.

Following the lead of neofunctionalist scholars such as Ernst Haas (1958; 1964), a number of scholars have specifically linked the evolution of interest representation in the EU with the more general development of the EU. For example, Sidjanski (1967) argued that the creation of new waves of professional groups (e.g. Committee of Professional Agricultural Organizations in the European Community—COPA, Union of Industrial and Employers' Confederations of Europe—UNICE, and others) occurred in four phases, centred on four events: the Marshal Plan; the establishment of the Organisation for European Economic Co-operation (OEEC); the creation of the European Coal and Steel Community (ECSC) and the European Economic Community (EEC); and finally the birth of the European Free Trade Area (EFTA). Similarly, Kirchner and Schwaiger (1981: 5) have pointed to the (then newly created) European Monetary System as providing the motivation for members of UNICE to transfer their loyalties to the Europe-wide group, resulting in an increase in its capability and efficacy. More recently Cowles (1998) and Coen (1997, 1998 and 1999) have traced the development of business associations and linked them to particular events at the EU level. Although these writers may not share the teleological view of the neofunctionalists (who viewed interest representation as vital to the process by which citizens would transfer their loyalties and identity to the EU and away from the member states), it is clear that patterns of interest representation in the EU can impact upon the structures and policies that it develops – and vice versa. Thus, for normative, strategic and policy analysis reasons, the patterns, methods and processes of interest representation in the EU are an important field of study.

REPRESENTING INTERESTS IN THE EU: EVOLVING PATTERNS IN AN EVOLVING SYSTEM

There is now a wealth of academic and practitioner literature about who conducts interest representation in Brussels, and to what effect (see *inter alia* Greenwood 1997; Greenwood and Aspinwall 1998; the pioneering works of Mazey and Richardson, e.g. 1993). Various theoretical frameworks have been put forward to encapsulate this process, perhaps best depicted by Richardson's (2001) application of the 'garbage can' model. Moreover, the study of interest representation (or 'mobilization') by regional and local governments has been a central concern of multi-level governance scholars of the EU since the early 1990s (for the key work, see Marks, Hooghe and Blank 1996; and Hooghe and Marks 2001).

How, though, should the European Union be characterized? Certainly, as an economic, social and political entity it has confounded and intrigued scholars since its inception in the 1950s. For many observers (and participants alike), part of the fascination of the EU lies in trying to explain how an international organization with such modest origins (i.e. the 1951 European Coal and Steel Community) could have evolved into a wide-ranging, highly complex, multi-layered and dynamic polity, currently encompassing most of Western Europe and resting on an extensive body of legislation and policy that impacts on most aspects of life. In responding to this intellectual challenge, for over 40 years scholars have attempted to discover, clarify and analyse the role played by various actors and processes in this development. Significantly, the many and varied theoretical expositions that have been proffered have been, more often than not, at variance with one another (see Rosamond 2000). In part, the very complexity and dynamism of the EU generates uncertainty, a lack of clarity and controversy. Part of the fundamental dispute about the character of the EU (as a political system) concerns the nature of interest representation patterns within it. For neofunctionalists (e.g. Haas 1958) interest representation at the EU level is a vital part of the regional policy-making system. For others (Moravcsik 1998) domestic groups and their behaviour are marginal to the process once it goes beyond national borders, although they can play a key part in deciding the preferences and strategies of the national governments, who enter the EU arena to some degree on their behalf.

We consider that the EU has now developed to the point at which it has acquired the 'policy-making attributes of a modern state' (Richardson 2001: 4) across an increasingly wide range of policy sectors. None the less, it does not have many of the hallmarks of what is traditionally considered 'statehood', at least as understood in the 'Westphalian' model created in Europe in the 17th century. In this view, states are discrete political structures, which each have exclusive control of public power within their borders, the internal monopoly of legitimate violence, a strong bureaucracy which gathers taxes and administers the system, and institutions with the authority and personnel to make binding public decisions (Caporaso 1996: 34–5). The EU, with its intertwining policy networks which stretch from national and sub-national to EU level (and even beyond), cannot match this kind of exclusive control of territory (Peterson 1997). Indeed, it has member states which continue to claim exclusive control of its various component territories. However, the EU does have the ability to make binding decisions, a uniquely powerful body of law, a role in redistributive policy, a currency, a single market and its own nascent defence policy. It also has institutions of its own that are capable of wielding significant influence over the policy it produces (Warleigh 2001b). Consequently the EU is perhaps best marked out as a new kind of political system – an 'objet politique non-identifié' (unidentified political object) (Schmitter 1996: 37), which is part of the reconfiguration of its member states, but not necessarily their replacement (Hix 1999).

Given this novelty, it is no surprise that the EU exhibits 'a unique, fluid decision-making process', in which power relations between even the key institutions are not yet stabilized (Mazey and Richardson 1996: 42). Consequently, the EU's decision-making rules can be vague, contentious, shiftable or negotiable (Peterson and Bomberg 1999: 254). Ultimately, if the EU is a complex and unique policy-making system (Richardson 2001: 5), which is 'multi-national and neo-federal [in] nature' exhibiting 'extreme openness of decision-making', the net effect could be that the EU offers an 'unpredictable and multi-level policy-making environment' for political actors. It is one in which one might reasonably expect to find dynamism and adaptation on the part of those seeking to advocate, persuade, and influence policy and policy makers.

THEMES AND STRUCTURE OF THE BOOK

Thus, the contributors to this volume examine the complexities of a situation in which interest representation is vital for any actor caught in the web of EU policies and policy-making, even though this Europeanization of political practice is primarily pragmatic rather than affective (Warleigh 2001a). We also examine the recourse of decision-makers themselves to lobbying in order to secure their desired outcomes, thereby reversing the usual focus upon institutional actors as mere recipients of interest representation.

This book, therefore, offers two novel and central contentions. First, we argue that lobbying and other forms of interest representation have become crucial to *all* those who seek to influence EU decision making. Thus, it is mistaken to view interest representation simply as a process by which non-institutional or non-state actors such as organized interest groups seek to influence policy makers 'behind closed doors'. Nor is such activism a confession of weakness: given the prevalence of informal politics in the EU system, whose institutions share legislative and executive power in a rather complex manner both between themselves and with institutions in the member states, it is an essential function of the policy entrepreneur at every stage of the legislative chain. Second, we argue that the patterns of interest representation uncovered in the book are of utility in explaining the manner in which the EU is developing – gradually and elliptically, as much by the cumulative impact of policy entrepreneurship on the part of diverse actors as by grand design or intergovernmental bargain. Therefore, this volume is broadly in keeping with ideas normally associated with historical institutionalism (Pierson 1996; Steinmo and Thelen 1992; Peters 1999; Hall and Taylor 1996).

This volume adopts a number of key themes in examining contemporary developments in interest representation in the EU. These are:

- interest representation as *necessary activity* for all actors in EU decision making

- institutional actors as lobbyists
- interest representation, legitimacy and civil society formation
- the Europeanization of interest representation
- novel tactics and strategies employed by those wishing to influence EU policy
- future challenges to interest representation in the EU, e.g. enlargement to include Central and Eastern Europe

These themes are explored throughout the book by an international team of academics and practitioners, all of whom draw on original empirical work and, in some cases, participant observation. The contributors include five current or past practitioners of EU politics, each of whom has experience of interest representation from either institutional, NGO or corporate perspectives.

Accordingly, the book is divided into three parts. The first builds on this Introduction, setting out the 'new politics' of EU interest representation and putting it in historical and theoretical context. Part 2 is devoted to the issue of EU actors as lobbyists, focusing on two of the three main institutions of the EU as 'multi-organizations' and examining how actors in each undertake interest representation to secure their desired outcomes. Part 3 is issue-driven, seeking to uncover how interest representation is playing a role in the management of many of the EU's key issues such as legitimacy-generation, Europeanization of national policy regimes and enlargement.

Part 1: New Bottles for New Wine?

Following the present Introduction comes Chapter 2 (by Justin Greenwood) which surveys the state of the art in studies of EU interest representation, and which calls for refinements in the conventional wisdom about both how interest representation works in the EU and how it should be studied. Greenwood argues that the received notion that interest representation by non-institutional actors is a useful and stable source of influence over policy outcomes is open to question, as the Commission's role in that process has altered. The Commission may no longer be either willing or able to construct supporting constituencies of interest groups. It is important to acknowledge other limits to the success of interest representation by non-institutional actors, for example by accepting that certain institutions (such as the central bank) are more resistant to it than others, and that other institutions may make deliberate choices to be impervious to outside interest representation – at least at certain times and regarding certain groups. Furthermore, it may be that, as 'high politics' issues rise ever higher on the EU agenda, the influence of interest groups will decline as member states exert ever tighter control over the decision-making process, ideas and institutions. In other words, outside interest representation may come to play a lesser role in shaping policy outcomes. In addition, it is possible that the drive for greater transparency may reduce the scope for effective lobbying by a given organized interest. Thus, there are sound reasons to question what we think we know about EU interest representation and, unless academics pay greater attention to both detail and methodological rigour they are in danger of exaggerating both the importance of their particular case studies and the influence of any given set of lobbyists, thereby producing work which generates heat rather than light.

Chapter 3 (by Irina Michalowitz) completes the introductory section, by examining theories of corporatism and pluralism – the two traditional modes of interest representation and regulation – and arguing that neither is a suitable frame for the study of the contemporary EU. Michalowitz argues that posing the question whether the European Union is to be characterized as pluralist or as neocorporatist is superfluous – because it is both, and neither, simultaneously. Approaches which define the EU decision-making system as rather pluralist in character often do so for reasons which are in fact spurious, grounded in an assumption that the EU's large number of lobbying actors and access points must *ipso facto* make it a pluralist system. Other approaches take a closer look and point out the Commission's tendency to consult interest groups or even create them, thus leading towards diagnoses of neocorporatism. However, given that the concepts of pluralism and neocorporatism were developed with regard to the nation-state, they are not likely to be suitable for transfer to EU studies without revision, especially as evidence points towards the coexistence of both models at different parts of the policy chain and in different issue areas. Michalowitz draws on empirical enquiries in the field of consumer policy to detail which aspects of the policy-making chain favour which mode of interest representation and why. Theoretical conclusions are then drawn.

Part 2: European Union Actors and Interest Representation

To begin part two of the volume, Chapter 4 (by Kerry Somerset) poses a number of crucial questions about the EU itself as an actor seeking to represent its interests in matters of international political economy. Why is this particular representative function often entrusted to the Commission and how effective is the latter in pursuit of the goals of the member states? These basic questions are often overlooked in studies of interest representation in the EU, being studied more often as issues of institutional power struggles between the Council and Commission. Somerset helps fill this gap by examining the Commission's work as a lobbyist for the EU at the WTO, arguing that the defence of the single market is causing the Commission to develop a complex set of practices and procedures which mix lobbying and economic diplomacy, adding a new strand to studies of the Commission's role in interest representation.

Chapter 5 (by David Earnshaw, Josephine Wood and Alex Warleigh) focuses on the impact upon and of the European Parliament (EP) in the new politics of EU interest representation. Codecision has made the EP a real legislative force, but in the changing context of EU politics as a whole it is not safe to assume that the EP will be able to exploit its new powers effectively. Earnshaw, Wood and Warleigh argue that the transformation of interest representation practices in the EU over recent years presents new challenges to the EP, itself undergoing a difficult period marked by issues such as the decline of the 'grand coalition' in plenary sessions and leadership struggles between committees and parties, national parties and EP party groups, and committees and plenary. Adapting to the new politics of interest representation will require the EP to develop 'hustling' skills of issue-specific coalition formation in the pursuit of marginal advantage: as a result, the EP may not always profit from a situation of which its own entrepreneurialism has been a major cause.

Part 3: New Issues in EU Interest Representation

Part 3 of the book opens with an examination of how interest representation can help alter the terms in which policy issues are considered, contributing to a changing ideational context which in turn helps condition actor choices. Chapter 6 (by Carlo Ruzza) deploys the concept of 'frame bridging' (a cultural mechanism through which a synthesis emerges between the dominant ideas of social movements and institutions). He argues that the EU's current concern with transparency and the participation of civil society groups in EU policy-making helps engender processes whereby existing EU political ideologies are merged with those of social movements, as a result of lobbying by such groups and resource interdependencies. Ruzza examines key organizations which are representative of three families of Brussels-based social movements (environmental, left-libertarian/anti-racism and ethno-nationalist groups) to identify key variables – both instrumental and ideological – which help or impede such social movements, and thus the process by which 'frame-bridging' can occur.

In chapter 7 (by Rebekka Goehring) the link between interest representation and democratic reform of the EU is examined, in particular the attempt to marry 'new governance' ideas to that of an EU-level '(organized) civil society'. Goehring argues that this linkage, whilst highly topical, is under-specified, and that it results from no coherent or dominant conceptual model. Indeed, plans to use interest representation to help create a 'European' civil society are often wishful thinking rather than concrete proposals, frequently incompletely elaborated and sometimes idiosyncratic. They range from rather unspecific ideas to the concrete institutionalization of a 'civil dialogue'. Goehring first examines the notion of civil society, itself something of a portmanteau term. She then analyses and compares different possibilities for the formation of a European civil society by drawing on the models proposed by the Commission in its recently published White Paper on governance, the discussion of the Economic and Social Committee about establishing a group for organized civil society, and the model on which the present Civil Dialogue in the field of WTO negotiations is based. The chapter closes with a discussion of whether any of these models constitutes a suitable blueprint for the EU, and if so whether it can really help the process of democratization.

Chapter 8 (by Jenny Fairbrass and Andrew Jordan) contributes to the debate about the role of interest groups in EU policy formation by exploring the concept of 'Europeanization' and examining the strategies and actions (e.g. lobbying) of certain non-state actors, their relationship with national and supranational policy-makers, and associated policy outcomes. Fairbrass and Jordan draw on evidence surrounding two strands of EU environmental policy (biodiversity and land use planning) in one member state (the United Kingdom—UK). Their cases reveal that UK environmental policy has become Europeanized. In other words, the EU has had a 'top-down' effect to varying degrees on the UK's environmental policy content, structures and styles. As a result the relationship between UK-based environmental groups and policy makers at the national and EU level has been altered. Explicitly, the EU has created opportunities for interest representation (in contrast to the previous lack of opportunities and considerable threats encountered in the national arena). The modified behaviour of the UK-based environmental groups is explained in terms of strategic decision-making tools and ideas drawn from management science (Fairbrass 2002).

In chapter 9 (by Nieves Pérez-Solórzano Borragán) there is an examination of the changing patterns of interest representation in the Central and Eastern European Countries (CEEC) as a result of both the prospect of accession to the EU and a fourfold process of political, economic and social transition, combined with efforts towards nation-building/civil society construction. Pérez-Solórzano Borragán examines the experiences of the CEEC representative offices in Brussels in coming to terms with the EU lobbying environment. She articulates three main hypotheses. First, the forthcoming EU enlargement, analysed in the context of Europeanization and the long-awaited 'return to Europe' of the Eastern and Central European democracies, affects governance at the national level. Hence, emerging interest groups in Central and Eastern Europe demand a more active role in the interaction with the European arena. Second, the European arena embodies a source of legitimization that the emerging interest groups in the CEEC require in order to strengthen their status *vis-à-vis* their national governments and membership. Third, the European activities of Central and Eastern European interest groups constitute a peculiar case of interest representation, where the exchange and ownership of information appear to be more important than the actual impact on the policy-making process at the supranational level. Drawing on original empirical work, the author concludes that, despite their lack of resources and their relative inexperience of the lobbying game, CEEC interest groups are trying to find their own cluster in an overcrowded European lobbying arena. This search for their own space is accompanied by their increasingly important role not only as lobbyists and advisers but also as agents in the transformation process undertaken by their countries of origin. Thus, the increasing Europeanization of interest politics in Central and Eastern Europe will crucially shape the relationship between the state and interest groups, and between interest groups and political parties at the national level. With the growing involvement of interest groups in day-to-day politics, political parties will have to redefine their areas of activity, while the executives will need to allow for more institutionalized channels of intermediation.

The final chapter of the volume considers the problems faced by small companies in the context of European policy and polity formation as a case study of the EU's ability to include or exclude interest groups from the policy-making process. Chapter 10 (by Campbell McPherson) considers the case of small companies in the context of the EU's development of Directive 98/84/EC on the Protection of Encrypted Services, drawing on a decade of empirical research into this and related matters. The Directive was intended to criminalize the activities of numerous small and micro companies that had developed to meet needs in the satellite television market arising from attempts at market manipulation by content providers. The chapter thus focuses upon the place of small satellite retail enterprises (SSREs) in an environment in which large economic actors, national governments and the European Union were mobilized against their economic *raison d'être* (the supply of pirate reception equipment), a perversion of single market logic which necessitated the skilful construction of new categories of inclusion and exclusion. McPherson argues that, whilst literature on lobbying and policy formation concedes the existence of inequalities between actors in the process, this practical study of the development of a specific Directive reveals patterns of deliberate exclusion and manipulation which are important in two ways. First, it serves as a warning that the Governance White Paper's emphasis on broad consultation is likely to benefit 'big business' rather than currently marginalized groups. Second, it provides useful evidence that the evolution of the EU may well create new kinds of exclusion and marginalization rather than a truly 'level playing field', which will intrigue those seeking to trace the kind of polity that the EU is becoming as a cumulative product of its policies.

REFERENCES

Balanyá, B., Doherty, A., Hoederman, O., Ma'anit, A. and Wesselius, E. (2000): *Europe Inc: Regional and Global Restructuring and the Rise of Corporate Power* (London: Pluto Press).

Caporaso, J. (1996): 'The European Union and Forms of State: Westphalian, Regulatory or Post-Modern?', *Journal of Common Market Studies* 34:1, 29–52.

Coen, D. (1997): 'The evolution of the large firm as a political actor in the EU', *Journal of European Public Policy*, 4:1, 91–108.

Coen, D. (1998): 'The European Business Interest and the Nation State: Large Firm Lobbying in the European Union and Member States', *Journal of Public Policy*, 18:1, 75–100.

Cowles, M. (1998): 'The Changing Architecture of Big Business', in J. Greenwood and M. Aspinwall (eds) *Collective Action in the European Union* (London: Routledge).

Fairbrass, J. (2002): 'Business Interests: Strategic Engagement with the EU Policy Process', Unpublished PhD thesis, University of Essex.

Grant, W. (2000): *Pressure Groups and British Politics* (Basingstoke: Macmillan).

Greenwood, J. (1997): *Representing Interests in the European Union* (London: Macmillan).

Greenwood, J. and Aspinwall, M. (eds) (1998): *Collective Action in the European Union* (London: Routledge).

Haas, E. (1958): *The Uniting of Europe* (Stanford: Stanford University Press).

Haas, E. (1964): *Beyond the Nation State* (Stanford: Stanford University Press).

Hall, P. and Taylor, R. (1996): 'Political Science and the Three New Institutionalisms', *Political Studies* 45, 936–57.

Hix, S. (1999): *The Political System of the European Union* (London: Macmillan).

Hooghe L. and Marks G. (2001): *Multi-level Governance and European Integration* (Lanham: Rowan and Littlefield).

Kirchner, E. and Schwaiger, K. (1981): *The Role of Interest Groups in the European Community* (Farnborough: Gower).

Kitschelt, H. (1986): 'Political Opportunity Structures and Political Protest', *British Journal of Political Science*, 6, 57–85.

Lord, C. (1998): *Democracy in the European Union* (Sheffield: Sheffield Academic Press).

Marks, G. (1992): 'Structural Policy in the European Community', in A. M. Sbragia (ed.) *Euro-Politics: Institutions and Policymaking in the 'New' European Community* (Washington: Brookings Institute).

Marks, G., Hooghe, L. and Blank, K. (1996): 'European Integration from the 1980s: State-centric v Multi-level Governance', *Journal of Common Market Studies*, 34:3, 341–78.

Marks, G. and McAdam, D. (1996): 'Social Movements and the Changing Structure of Political Opportunity in the European Union', *West European Politics* 19:2, 191–212.

Mazey, S. and Richardson, J. (eds) (1993): *Lobbying in the European Community* (Oxford: Oxford University Press).

Mazey, S. and Richardson, J. J. (1996): 'EU policy-making. A garbage can or an anticipatory and consensual policy style?', in Y. Mény, P. Muller and J.-L. Quermonne (eds) *Adjusting to Europe* (London: Routledge).

McCarthy, J. D. and Zald, M. N. (1977): 'Resource Mobilization and Social Movements: A Partial Theory', *American Journal of Sociology,* 82, 1212–1241.

Moravcsik, A. (1998): *The Choice for Europe* (Ithaca, NY: Cornell University Press).

Peters, B. G. (1999): *Institutional Theory in Political Science: The 'New Institutionalism'* (London: Sage).

Peterson, J. (1995) 'Decision-making in the European Union: Towards a Framework for Analysis', *Journal of European Public Policy*, 2:1, 69–93.

Peterson, J. (1997) 'States, Societies and the European Union', *West European Politics*, 20: 4, 1–23.

Peterson, J. and Bomberg, E. (1999): *Decision-making in the European Union* (Basingstoke: Macmillan).

Pierson, P. (1998): 'The Path of European Integration: A Historical Institutionalist Analysis', in W. Sandholtz and A. Stone Sweet (eds) *European Integration and Supranational Governance* (Oxford: Oxford University Press).

Richardson, J. (2001): 'Policy-making in the EU: Interests, Ideas and Garbage Cans of Primeval Soup', in J. Richardson (ed): *European Union – Power and Policy Making* (2nd ed) (London: Routledge).

Rosamond, B. (2000): *Theories of European Integration* (Basingstoke: Macmillan).

Schmitter, P. C. (1996): 'Some alternative futures for the European policy and their implications for European public policy', in Y. Mény, P. Muller, and J.-L. Quermonne, (eds) *Adjusting to Europe* (London: Routledge).

Sidjanski, D. (1967): 'Pressure Groups and the European Economic Community', *Government and Opposition*, 2, 397–416.

Steinmo, S. and Thelen, K. (1992): 'Historical Institutionalism in Comparative Politics', in S. Steinmo, K. Thelen and F. Longreth (eds) *Structuring Politics* (Cambridge: Cambridge University Press).

Warleigh, A. (2000): 'The Hustle: Citizenship Practice, NGOs and "Policy Coalitions" in the European Union – The Cases of Auto Oil, Drinking Water and Unit Pricing', *Journal of European Public Policy* 7:2, 229–43.

Warleigh, A. (2001a): '"Europeanizing" Civil Society: NGOs as Agents of Political Socialisation in the European Union', *Journal of Common Market Studies* 39:4, 619–39.

Warleigh, A. (2001b): 'Introduction: Institutions, Institutionalism and Decision-making in the European Union', in A. Warleigh (ed) *Understanding European Union Institutions* (London: Routledge).

Wessels, W. (1996): 'Institutions of the EU system: models of explanation', in D. Rometsch and W. Wessels (1996) *The European Union and Member States. Towards Institutional Fusion?* (Manchester: Manchester University Press).

Wessels, W. (1997): 'An Ever Closer Fusion? A Dynamic Macropolitical View on Integration Processes', *Journal of Common Market Studies* 35:2, 267–99.

Part 1

New Bottles for New Wine?

Chapter 2

Advocacy, Influence and Persuasion: Has it All Been Overdone?

Justin Greenwood

INTRODUCTION: RECONSIDERING THE ROLE OF INTERESTS

Non-state interests have long been seen by practitioner and analyst alike as playing a key part in the functioning of the European Union (EU) political system, and sometimes in the development of European integration. In classic institutionalist accounts of the integration process, the relationship between non-state interests and political authority provides an explanation of how the EU acquires competencies. In modern institutionalist accounts of integration, the EU political institutions become 'learning spaces' to which private interests respond, and through participation in which they may even form their preferences. In accounts grounded in international relations, non-state actors create influences upon the political behaviour of states that contribute towards explanations of national preference formation. And in accounts of policy-making and the EU policy process, non-state interests and their relationships with decision-making actors, whether cast in pluralist or elite terms, provide a recognizable toolbox to help analysis.

The task of this chapter is to ask whether 'interest/group' type explanations of EU policy-making and integration tend to exaggerate the importance of these factors. In the interests of pleading for a somewhat more measured and cautious approach, and to recast views as to the role of non-state interests in EU policy making and integration, the analysis which follows itself somewhat overplays the 'interest/group explanations have been overdone' scenario.

There is certainly no shortage of case studies claiming that policy-making outputs can be understood as arising from the relationship between EU political institutions and non-state interests. Some of these are plausible, yet some accounts have been somewhat overdone. Some proceed from the unquestioned assumption that 'lobbying' is important, because this is their background and pitch. Some are based on the classic fallacy of assuming there is a causal relationship between action taken by political institutions and the public position of non-state interests. Some take the claims of public affairs based respondents without a critical eye, or fail to take the trouble to check claims that a particular interview respondent from a company or interest group 'wrote a particular Directive'. And, while interest intermediation can add a tool to the analysis of public policy, 'interest' alone does not provide a sufficient explanatory basis. Interest group scholars can be too easily drawn towards those types of explanations because they are concerned with the role of interest groups in public policy. As the debates of the 1950s remind us, not all politics can be reduced to 'interest group politics', while the mine of resources available from the analytical tools grounded in ideas, and institutional analysis, takes much of the edge from 'interest group explanations'.

While private interests can engage in important, sometimes monopolistic, relationships in highly technical fields of 'low politics' and exert some significant influences by virtue of the inability of others to enter these policy spaces, in a number of EU public policy events, particularly those involving 'high politics', interest intermediation is almost peripheral, or absent. And in any event, the fragmented EU policy-making architecture, in which policy-making passes through many different types of arenas which vary greatly in their accessibility to non-state interests, can only ever be a bit story about the role of non-state interests.

In all accounts of European integration, non-state interests are recognized as actors of integration in 'low' politics and in preference formation in domestic politics, though some accounts (where states are seen as the principal sources of integration) see the role of private interests as limited to this. To *some* accounts, the relationship between private interests and the Commission, in particular, provide a key mechanism in the development of European integration/acquisition of new EU competencies and applications. The Commission reflects that it

> ... has always been an institution open to outside input. The Commission believes this process to be fundamental to the development of its policies. This dialogue has proved valuable to both the Commission and to interested outside parties. Commission officials acknowledge the need for such outside input and welcome it (European Commission 1992, p.3).

Non-state private and public interests are the 'natural constituency' of a Commission lacking in resources, support, legitimacy, grass roots contact, and in search of allies to help develop European integration. Many EU interest groups have been 'kick-started' by the Commission in a deliberate attempt to build support constituencies and create demand pressures for, and technical know how in, European integration.

Beyond the technical arena of low politics, some accounts have sought to dramatize the role of interests in the 'high politics' of European integration, and in particular the role of the European Round Table of Industrialists (ERT) in the creation of the single market (Sandholtz, 1989; Green-Cowles 1995; Ruigrok and van Tulder 1995; van Apeldoorn 2001). These studies pass the 'so what?' test beyond which many case studies fail to progress, because they are about the role of non-state interests as a dynamic in the integration process and therefore provide a useful starting point for our analysis, examining whether 'interest group' type explanations have been overdone. The process of becoming interested in the role of an agent like the ERT, and in building a research career around it, tends to result in appraisals of it that are likely cast a significant role for it in European integration. Once colours have been nailed to the mast, it is then difficult to prise them away.

A recent *Financial Times* (FT) article marvelled at the reputation of the ERT in achieving its aim, in view of its relatively humble offices and small secretariat (Betts 2001). The article recites a familiar story of how policy makers, analysts and critics alike have credited the organization with agenda setting many of the big ideas which have come to dominate the EU agenda. The best known of these stories concerns the role of the organization in agenda setting, and helping the European Commission to achieve the shared goal of a European single market project. This story has been extensively used to provide evidence of how the relationship between the European Commission and outside interests can be used to explain the course of European integration.

In support of this account of the role of the ERT in the single market project, the FT article cites Jacques Delors in recalling that 'The ERT was the right vehicle. UNICE [Union of Industrial Employers' Confederations of Europe] could not have done it. Discussions with the ERT were simple and straightforward' (Betts 2001: 16). The clout of the ERT, with its CEO (Chief Executive Officer) involvement from household name firms, undoubtedly made this 'the right vehicle' through which to build the support necessary among member states. Certainly, the relationship between Delors, on the look out for supportive allies, and the ERT, was a close one, with the two partners appearing together at press conferences. Green-Cowles recounts how ERT members worked alongside, cajoled and even threatened member state governments to achieve the necessary political support (Green-Cowles 1995).

According to some sources, this influence has prevailed. The FT article cites a recent description of the ERT by the United Kingdom (UK)

Guardian national newspaper as 'a shadowy lobby group that has, for the past 15 years, exerted an iron grip on policy making in Brussels' (Betts 2001). Similarly, a report entitled 'Misshaping Europe', claiming that 'the political agenda of the EU has to a large extent been dominated by the ERT', is also quoted by the FT article. Assertions in support of these claims include the role of the ERT in agenda setting Trans European Networks (TENs), the benchmarking of EU policies and, most recently, in the development of a ten-year EU economic and social strategy agreed under the 2000 Portuguese presidency (Betts 2001). The ERT's own literature also presents its achievements in setting the climate of ideas from which public policy events have arisen (ERT 2001). Among these are listed: work on lifelong learning and investing in knowledge; information highways; climate change; competitiveness; and 'pressure to help close the Uruguay Round negotiations' in world trade negotiations (www.ert.be). These perceptions appear to have provided much of the inspiration for the creation of an opposing pressure group, Corporate Europe Observatory, whose exposé style literature also contributes to the 'ERT rules OK' model (see Balanyá *et al.* 2000).

Certainly, evidence taken from friend, foe and propaganda alike provides a powerful case for the strength of the ERT. Its consistent role as an ally of the Commission in promoting European integration is reflected in the preamble to its objectives, stating that 'Europeans can only solve their problems by closer co-operation' (www.ert.be). Undoubtedly, the Commission and the ERT have been mutual influences. But it is also easy to over-egg the pudding, and in any event, a good journalist will not let accuracy get in the way of a good story. The ERT participates in the rarefied atmosphere of 'high politics', in which its voice is just one of a number seeking influence upon public policies, alongside forces such as national governments and the international environment. Undoubtedly, it contributes to the climate of debate, and to the influences upon some of these decision-making forces. But the simple connection should not be made between its demands and public policy outcomes. A rival explanation for the arrival of the Single European Act is that of a 'grand state bargain', with 'side payments' to those countries most vulnerable to lose out (Moravcsik 1995). This is a helpful reminder of where the levels of power reside in big EU decision making, and certainly the growth, and pattern of distribution, of EU structural funds since the SEA provide an air of plausibility to Moravcsik's argument. Undoubtedly, the ERT has historically made its presence felt, although it is an open question whether it remains as significant today as the claims made for it at the peak of the Delors period.

The ERT was established at a time of highly favourable circumstances for business interest organizations because the Commission was 'on the march' to create a single market with the backing of member states. The prevailing discourse was a highly favourable one, and a policy entrepreneur, Delors, was about to enter the scene and search for allies to help him deepen European integration. Viscount Davignon reportedly helped put together the ERT by recruiting most of the members of the original group (Sandholtz & Zysman 1989). The ERT was a product of its time and of a specific combination of circumstances. The generalizability of this to the wider process of integration is limited. Groups like the Association for the Monetary Union of Europe (AMUE) have been little more than a background noise in the wider debate.

Studies of the ERT sit alongside a wealth of case studies of EU interest representation. Many of these plausibly describe the role of private interests in helping the Commission to develop policy drafts, or policy solutions, in low politics fields, in conditions favourable to access and influence by non-state actors. But there are good reasons to see the limitations of explanations of EU policy making based upon the role of non-state interests. Indeed, have such claims been overdone?

In Treaty change arenas states are the dominant actors and sources of integration, where private interests are just one among a number of players providing inputs into the calculations and behaviour of these players. Once the policy arrangements are in place, certain arenas, such as the European Central Bank, are designed to be resistant to 'pressure politics'. And even in those cases which do not involve Treaty changes, private interests often take a 'back seat' in integration to those of states and the Commission. One example of this is electricity liberalization.

Electricity liberalization is a dossier that has been driven by the Commission, with intergovernmental highlights, and private interests in the back seat. The issue is one of high politics because the use of energy is highly politicized, while its production, safety and security of supply are matters of national importance, and diversified in ownership across public and private lines. In these circumstances, the politics are colonized by member states, and no one type of interest – industrial producer, industrial consumer, domestic consumer, environmentalist – is able to monopolize the agenda, and to technicalize the agenda and take it away from the public gaze. The policy thrust of liberalization is also one driven by single market ideology of free trade and open competition, and thus one where 'ideas' dominate, sometimes reinforced by the background support of large energy consumers who had most to gain from it. Here, the UK had provided evidence that liberalization could be undertaken successfully. The agenda has been driven forward by the European Commission, skilfully, using the threat of using a wide choice of procedural powers, issuing infringement notices where necessary so as to allay fears among the most recalcitrant actor, Electricité de France (EdF), of an outcome that might be far worse in the European Court of Justice. Over time, EdF has needed to adopt the rhetoric of supporting the principle, if not the detail, of liberalization in its own country. The Commission proved adept at turning the model proposed by EdF to its advantage, ending in a situation in which EdF was isolated.

Events such as the accession of Nordic member states in favour of liberalization have also helped tip the balance of power. A 1996 Directive helped to open ajar a door that the Commission hoped would be kicked open by market forces. Producer interests may have helped influence member state positions (there is some evidence that German industrial consumers, facing the highest electricity prices in Europe, had an impact upon the *volte face* of the German government in 1995 to support it), but interests organized at the European level had a marginal impact. Producer interests were deeply divided for some time within the principal EU electricity association EURELECTRIC, whose position has turned from mainly anti to mainly pro. In part, this is due to variations within the structure of the EU electricity industry. Industrial consumer interests, too, were divided, particularly by the tactic of EdF in buying off resistance through supplying cheap energy to a clutch of key users. Environmental interests organized at the European level have helped to drive some of the detail, but not the principle of liberalization. EU level interest representation played nothing more than a supporting role for events that would have happened anyway. The key players as the story of electricity liberalization has unfolded have been the member states and the European Commission (Greenwood 2002a). Ideas and institutions, not private interests, best explain policy outcomes in this dossier.

NON-STATE INTERESTS: HOW USEFUL ARE ELITE MODELS?

The above factors question the centrality of interest/group-type explanations of integration and public policy outputs. Beyond these are factors which remain focused on the role of interests, but which draw on pluralistic analysis to cast doubt on the extent to which any one type of interest can routinely dominate the EU policy process, and thus the value of the interest/group relationship in casting where influence lies. Naturally, pluralistic analysis continues to provide explanations for policy outputs couched in interest/group terms, such as understanding outputs as arising from competitive pressures.

Multiple arenas of policy making and multiple points of access lead to a 'lobbying free for all' and unpredictable outcomes. Within an institution such as the Commission are multiple identities and interests, with policy co-ordination often weak. These are unpromising circumstances for interests to seek to dominate. Even if one arena can be dominated, the influence gets left behind as policy making enters a new arena, with new rules of the game. For instance, policy drafts shaped in the Commission by business interests move on to the European Parliament where public interests can have a significant impact. The technocratic basis of Commission policy making is a natural arena for business (and all the resources upon which it has to call) to monopolize policy making through exclusive policy communities, whereas the democratic basis of the Parliament ensures that 'behind closed doors' models of policy making are left behind for open, pluralistic arenas. More than this, public interests have a natural advantage in engaging the Parliament because of the popular basis of election and, coupled with the co-decision making powers of the European Parliament, public interest input is given a powerful edge. In addition, in circumstances where permanent coalitions between parties do not operate, every majority has to be built anew. Add to this the possible trade-offs made in Council of Ministers bargaining and decision making, and the sheer complexity of EU politics seems an uncertain place for private and public interests to be. And, adding further to this equation, are the multiple access points for interests that dissent from the common positions of their representative associations. Indeed, one of the features of the 1990s has been the ways in which large companies have come to Brussels, established their own public affairs operations and changed the way in which associations organize as these latter actors respond to being bypassed by large companies in their own sectors.

Grande takes the architectural point further by arguing that the fragmented architecture of the EU leads to its insulation from pressures as institutions play 'two-level' games with interests (Grande 1996). Institutions such as the Commission can insulate themselves by referring to the fact that consent from other public bodies is required, and predicting how those bodies might react to a private interest demand. A more classic strategy that is well recognized by public affairs practitioners themselves is that of playing one off against another in a 'divide and rule' world. This is a task that is made all the easier through the lack of strength of EU business associations, in particular, for which an explanation can also be sought in terms of the institutional architecture of the EU.

Associations derive their strength from their relationship with 'the state' – where there is one. Associations which are 'licensed' with functions by governments become essential organizations for their members to join, and the performance of these functions requires the organization and compliance of members. In these circumstances, associations become intermediaries between their members and state authority, gaining some autonomy from their members. In prewar Germany 50% of industrial production was regulated by controls exercised by trade associations (Schneiberg and Hollingsworth 1991). This type of scenario would not only be impossible because of EU competition policy, it is impossible because the EU is not a 'state' and its fragmented authority structures mean that it does not have the ability to 'licence' associations from which they can then draw their strength.

Without a 'state' as a source of coherence, associations have to turn to specialization as an alternative. My own research, using a composite of the various directories together with my own sources, indicates there are 950 EU business associations from a total of around 1,400 EU interest groups of all types. They include the highly specialist, such as the European Technical Caramel Association, the Alliance on Beverage Cartons and the Environment and the European Association of Flexible Polyurethane Foam Blocks Manufacturers. This high degree of specialization comes at a system-wide cost for business, in that there are often competitive interests across the product chain. Thus, while specialization might be convenient for individual associations, the overall pattern tends to produce competitive politics among business interests. This tendency is exaggerated under conditions of distributive politics, in that, where costs and benefits are narrowly concentrated, competitive interest group politics result (Wilson 1995). The change to open markets inevitably affects different types of interests in different ways. On the whole, large transnational firms with the infrastructure and mass to exploit open borders seek free markets, whereas medium-sized firms, which have most to lose from their previously protected markets being invaded, tend towards protectionist measures. Where associations have tried to bridge the product chain in response to Commission pressures for encompassingness, the results are inevitably disappointing. Thus, Eurocommerce embraces a constituency comprising wholesalers, distributors, and retailers, whose interests sometimes conflict, to the extent that its predecessor, COCCEE, collapsed under the strain of moving beyond lowest common denominator positions.

The average secretariat of an EU business association has less than 5 staff. A sizeable clutch have between 20 and 50, and just one, the 'CEFIC' (European Chemical Industry Association) family, has over 100. Some are even 'virtual' organizations, like the European Modern Restaurants Association. Just about all of them are smaller than their large national counterpart associations, because they were set up with a narrower remit – political representation. They do not undertake the range of functions assumed by national associations, such as training and export promotion. Because they concentrate on political representation, they are highly dependent upon member subscriptions. This over-dependence upon members for resources means that EU associations are often too closely controlled by their members, and are unable to bring value to them by shaping their perceptions as to what their interests are. As one commentator once observed, 'I should prefer my interests to be safeguarded rather than have my more or less shaky opinions prevail' (Burnheim, in Phillips, 1995 p.160).

The sheer openness of EU politics means that most associations find their interests are contested by another interest – whether a non-governmental organization (NGO), a labour union or another business interest. Attempts by the EU to address the 'democratic deficit' are changing the culture of policy-making. For instance, the 2001 White Paper on Governance (WPG—European Commission, 2001), while disappointing on the detail, may have a more lasting effect of cultural change by wedging the door open for citizen interests. Private interests now need to frame their demands in the language of wider public interest. I have already found evidence of changing patterns of consultation by Commission officials, where they prefer to place documents on the internet for responses by anyone who cares to read them, rather than to engage in bilateral consultation with business. The wider agenda of openness and transparency, of which the WPG is a part, has itself made individual interests less reliant upon their associations, in that these are no longer reliant upon their association to access EU information for them.

Some of these perspectives are familiar concerns for business. To the business public affairs practitioner it sometimes seems that public interests 'rule the world', whereas for the latter actor it is business interests that dominate. The battered truth probably lies somewhere in between.

Nonetheless, civic interests do operate within a highly favourable discourse of 'democratic deficit' which opens doors for them. Young and Wallace recently argued that

'civic interests receive greater consideration in the EU than one would expect given its regulatory focus and economic origins ... the imbalance between civic and producer interests may thus not be as great as quantitative comparisons would indicate, because producer interests are often divided and the political dynamics of social regulation often play to the benefit of civic interests, making the outcome more 'balanced' than might otherwise be expected' (Young and Wallace 2000: 28).

Environmental public interest groups, in particular, have a great deal going for them, and, with over 70 staff based in Brussels alone between them, are able to provide a significant counterweight to business. In the social field the funding of interest groups is part of an established pattern of attempts by DG V (now DG Employment and Social Affairs) to agitate for further European integration, but only when the wider discourse is a favourable one, such as gender and disability equality, is this partnership able to make a significant contribution.

To some public interests the reality is that their heyday may already have come and gone. One watershed was the 1998 crisis of funding budget lines, when most of the funding for EU social policy interest associations was brought into question by the ECJ decision of c106/96 (Geyer, 2001). Although a number of these budget lines were later unblocked, some remained frozen, and the enduring insecurity of surviving on unstable project funding remains for many NGOs. Certainly, the Commission's ambitions to develop the NGO sector were somewhat curtailed by the experience. A second watershed may be the White Paper on Governance itself, which, for all its citizen orientation, provides the challenge for NGOs to demonstrate that they are 'representative and accountable'. This is a challenge that few, realistically, can meet. NGOs are groups *for*, not *of*, a particular cause, and cannot demonstrate themselves to be 'representative' in the same way that a business association can claim to represent a proportion of the total potential membership constituency (Halpin 2001). For many NGOs the challenge of accountability is one that remains to be addressed. This issue has been detected by business, which has remorselessly proposed general criteria for 'representativity' and accountability that present it with no difficulty, but which may present NGOs with insurmountable problems. A third watershed has been the failure to achieve a 'civil dialogue' after almost a decade of trying. Not that the 'social dialogue' model to which it aspires is very inspiring. After a decade all that has been achieved are three rather unimportant directives which have hardly taken forward worker rights in many of the Germanic countries, while a far greater number of talks held under its structures have ended in failure.

INTEREST GROUPS AND EUROPEAN GOVERNANCE: LESS BUT BETTER?

To this air of caution towards models of policy-making based on elite relationships can be added a number of other enduring problems facing interest group organization. For instance, the organization of the professions remains, in general, poor because for most professional interests European integration remains more of a threat to their established practices of self-government in the member states and to their modus operandi, than it does an opportunity. Then there is the southern European question. Most European interest groups are dominated by their northern European members, and many have huge gaps in membership from the south of Europe. Finally, there is the problem of system overload. With 1,450 interest groups and, according to some (not implausible) Brussels folklore, an estimated 20,000 lobbyists (around three or four for every Commission policy-making official), EU policy making is approaching paralysis through the sheer weight of interest representation. This puts the framing of 'democratic deficit' and the search for new tiers of democracy by the White Paper on Governance in a somewhat different light. Perhaps the task is to organize the system of EU interest representation so that there are fewer associations, better able to contribute to EU governance. One of the most interesting aspects of the White Paper on Governance process raises questions about how that should be done, with issues about representativity and accountability of interlocuting organizations. The White Paper itself reflects that

> better consultation and involvement . . . will allow (the Commission) to consider much more critically the demands from . . . interest groups for new political initiatives (European Commission 2001, p. 33/4).

While the absence of EU statehood does present problems, a system of accreditation could be the catalyst for consolidation into 'less, but better' associations. This is because accreditation would make associations worthwhile organizations for their members to join, and provide them with some autonomy from the short-term demands of their members through their institutional recognition. This is a system that is successfully used in other transnational organizations, such as the United Nations and the Council of Europe. Some useful criteria have previously been developed in and around the EU institutions for an organized dialogue system with outside interests. The Commission has consistently rejected the idea of accrediting civil society groups on the grounds that it may create a barrier, real or imagined, to democratic input from less organized interests in wider civil society. Nonetheless, it has also taken steps to establish the representativeness of the organizations with which it engages, and particularly those charged with undertaking public policy functions, by seeking to define, establish or promote criteria of representativeness. These include:

- Commission-initiated studies of the representativity of candidate European social partners organizations, with exercises such as COM (93) 600 (Communication concerning the application of the agreement on social policy), and its successor studies such as the September 1999 Report on the Representativeness of European Social Partner Organizations (Institut des Sciences du Travail 1999), in which analysis was undertaken of the ability of candidate organizations to measure up to pre-set criteria. These included measures of membership density, both of the candidate organizations themselves and of each of their members.

- The 1992 Communication from the Commission 'An open and structured dialogue between the Commission and special interest groups' (SEC (92) 2272 final). This gave rise to a family of communications concerned with a number of initiatives, of which one was the regulation of lobbying. In turn, this led to the establishment of representative organizations administering codes of conduct and engaging in dialogue with the EU institutions on behalf of sections of the Brussels public affairs community, and the establishment of criteria to govern the relationship between these parties (Greenwood 1997).

- COM (97) 241, Communication from the Commission on promoting the role of voluntary organizations and foundations in Europe. This communication provided criteria to assist in the appointment of members to a Consultative Committee on Co-operatives, Mutual Societies, Associations and Foundations. A number of structures have developed the concept, including DG Development of the European Commission, the Economic and Social Committee's First Convention on Civil Society (Economic and Social Committee, 1999), and the European Platform of Social NGOs during the period 1998–2001. More recently, the Commission has issued a discussion paper presented by President Prodi and Vice-President Kinnock on 'The Commission and Non-Governmental Organizations: Building a Stronger Partnership' (European Commission 2000), which also identifies and develops some criteria for representativity.

- The White Paper on Governance itself hopes that requirements of interest groups for internal organization 'will prompt civil society organizations to tighten up their internal structures, furnish guarantees of openness and representativity, and prove their capacity to relay information or lead debates in the Member States (European Commission 2001, p. 17). The 'new' Commission database on interest groups (though one has been in existence in various formats since 1996), the database for 'Consultation, the European Commission and Civil Society' (CONECCS),[1] proposed under the terms of the White Paper, establishes a number of criteria before an interest group can be accepted. While the Commission makes it clear that the database does not confer privileged status, the criteria established before a group can be accepted on to the database does represent a de facto form of accreditation (Wincott 2001). These criteria include the number of countries in which the

---

[1] http://europa.eu.int/comm/civil_society/coneccs/index_en.htm

interest is established, the legal foundations of organization, its degree of expertise, and conditions of transparency. There are further questions on the frequency and style of consultation with members, on financing and requests for submission of membership lists and members' addresses.

In reality, the establishment of criteria of representativity lays the groundwork for a system of accreditation. It is a highly suitable system for dialogue with transnational interest organizations because of the number of constituent members from the member state territories involved. While it may not work in a domestic context because of the costs imposed by the impression of a 'two-tier' system of democracy, it is particularly suitable to arenas of fragmented authority, such as the EU political system, where power is highly dispersed. While this creates a 'two-tier' democratic access image problem, 'open-door policies' encourage associations to be bypassed, resulting in democratic overload. Accrediting representative associations as governance partners endows them with the strength they need to be able to participate effectively in governance. In this way associations become part of the solution rather than part of the problem. Instead of contributing to a 'lobby free for all' and democratic overload by their weakness, associations that are supported in this way can help EU governance by providing a systematic link between civil society and political institutions.

The Economic and Social Committee (ESC) might be an organization well placed to evaluate, accredit and monitor interest organizations. While this organization has become a piece of redundant furniture in the architecture of EU policy making, its historical structure embracing the interests of wider civil society has made it the focus of some of the discussion in the White Paper on Governance debate centred on resolving problems of democratic deficit. In one scenario it was seen as having the potential to play a much more significant role as a civil society/EU intermediary, provided it can reform itself to embrace citizen interests fully within its institutional structures of decision making. This means institutional reform of the ESC itself. The obvious way forward would be for professions and other producer interests of Group 3 ('other interests') to merge with Group 1 (employers), with a new Group 3 based wholly on citizen interests. This option has proved a step too far for it, in that employers, concerned about being outflanked by a trade union/civil society alliance, have effectively vetoed the prospect. With it has gone the opportunity for the ESC to become a more significant organization. Beyond this, the ESC needs extended powers – it is presently consulted when policy frameworks are established, whereas if it had powers at the agenda setting stage it would be able to channel the perspectives of civil society. Nonetheless, the organization has represented the opportunity presented to it by the White Paper on Governance and has sought to become engaged in the debate. As part of this, the organization has developed some useful criteria for the accreditation of interest organizations, based on the criteria of accountability and representativeness.

The debate about accreditation proceeds from the basis of the lack of ability of EU-level interest associations to contribute to governance as a result of their structural weaknesses. This brings us back to a debate addressed to the question whether the role of non-state interests in EU policy analysis has been exaggerated. Without doubt there are low politics arenas in which the policy relationship between non-state interests and EU political institutions does help explain how policy initiatives are shaped. Equally, non-state interests are one of the components of the perspectives and behaviour of member states. However, the EU is a *sui generis* political system, and there are major limitations to explanations of both integration, and public policy making and implementation, cast around the role of non-state interests. Firstly, the starting point for EU politics, the high politics of European Treaties, is an arena in which non-state interests are a background component. Indeed, throughout high politics arenas non-state interests provide only one component to policy making. In major dossiers such as electricity liberalization, those who seek 'interest group' type explanations can usually find a degree of credible evidence, but not infrequently more plausible and holistic explanations can be located from the broader ideas which structure policy making, in the actions of member states and in the drive provided by the EU supranational institutions.

As initiatives pass through different policy-making arenas, different rules of the game come into play. The Commission is certainly an arena highly suited to input by non-state interests, but even here the Commission can insulate itself through divide and rule games and by drawing attention to the impact of other political arenas. Thus, the fragmentation of the EU political system is a key factor limiting the impact of non-state interests. For all these preceding reasons, the EU can be a disappointing place for 'interest group scholars' looking for 'interest group type explanations.' These explanations can certainly shape the character of aspects of EU policy making, and go some way towards clarifying who is influential, and how. Once again, fragmentation of political authority is at the heart of the question, providing for unsettled patterns of interest group politics where no one type of interest can routinely dominate. This fragmentation is also a source of weakness for the organization of interests, where the 'logic of membership' triumphs over the 'logic of influence', arising from the lack of statehood of the EU.

While analysis of non-state interests may have limited utility for scholars of European integration, the political arena of the EU does have value for interest scholars. While there is little new to learn about studies of the policy process from an 'interest group focus' on the EU political arena, other than a contribution to the debate about the ways in which the political architecture of institutions limits the role of non-state interests, there is much to learn when the focus is on the organization of interests, and the internal dynamics of interests. This draws from the ways in which the external environment influences internal organizational structures and structures the ways in which members participate in collective action organizations. It helps to understand why interest organizations vary in their ability to unify member interests and to secure goal compliance from them, and how organizations which are already politically active do not face complex issues of incentives to secure their participation (Greenwood 2002b). The evidence for the role of non-state interests in European integration rests considerably on the role of the ERT in a high politics decision, and there are now good grounds to question the generalizability of these findings. Interests may contribute to the 'everyday politics' of the EU, but their role as agents of integration is limited to that of messengers for the Commission's agenda to the doors of member states. Only when the wider discourse is a favourable one are they able to make a direct contribution, and otherwise it is a long-term game of planting and cultivating the seedcorns of ideas. Of course, I have overdone the 'limits' case here myself, but have done so in the interests of ensuring that the more usual, opposite scenario – 'interest groups rule OK' – should not be exaggerated.

REFERENCES

Betts, P. (2001): 'The Quiet Knights of Europe's Round Table, *Financial Times*, 20 March, p. 16.

Balanya B., Doherty A., Hoedeman O., Maanit A. and Wesselius E. (2000): *Europe Inc.* (London: Pluto Press).

Economic and Social Committee (1999): Concise Report of the debates of the First Convention of Civil Society organized at European level, Brussels, Economic and Social Committee, http://www/esc.eu.int.

European Round Table of Industrialists (ERT) (2001): Achievements: Highlights of ERT Activities, www.ert.be/pg/eng_frame.htm.

European Commission (1992): 'An Open and Structured Dialogue Between the Commission and Special Interest Groups'. (Secretariat-General International Coordination, Brussels, 2 December 1992, SEC (92) 2272 final).

European Commission (2000): 'The Commission and Non-Governmental Organizations: Building a Stronger Partnership', Commission Discussion Paper presented by President Prodi and Vice-President Kinnock, http://www.europa.eu.int/comm/secretariat_general/sgc/ong/en/communication.pdf.

European Commission (2001): 'European Governance: A White Paper' (Brussels: Commission of the European Communities, COM(2001) 428).

Geyer, R. (2001): 'Can EU Social NGOs Co-operate to Promote EU Social Policy?', *Journal of Social Policy,* 30, 3, July, pp 477–494.

Grande, E. (1996): 'The State and Interest Groups in a Framework of Multi-Level Decision Making: the case of the EU', *Journal of European Public Policy,* 3, 3, September, pp 318–38.

Green-Cowles, M. G. (1995): 'The European Round Table of Industrialists: The Strategic Player in European Affairs', in J. Greenwood (ed.) *European Casebook on Business Alliances* (Hemel Hempstead: Prentice Hall).

Greenwood, J. (1997): *Representing Interests in the European Union* (Basingstoke: Palgrave).

Greenwood, J. (2002a): 'Electricity Liberalization', in R. Pedler (ed.) *European Union Lobbying: Changes in the Arena* (Basingstoke: Palgrave).

Greenwood, J. (2002b): *Inside the EU Business Associations* (Basingstoke: Palgrave).

Halpin, D. (2001): 'Integrating conceptions of interest groups: Towards a conceptual framework of sectional interest group imperatives', paper prepared for ECPR (European Consortium for Political Research) General Conference, University of Kent, 6–8 September 2001.

Institut des Sciences du Travail (1999): 'Report on the Representativeness of European Social Partner Organizations', undertaken for the European Commission Directorate-General for Employment, Industrial Relations and Social Affairs, Brussels, Commission of the European Communities, http://www.europa.eu.int/comm/employment_social/soc-dial/social/index_en.htm.

Phillips, A. (1995): *The Politics of Presence* (Oxford: Clarendon Press).

Ruigrok, W. and van Tulder, R. (1995): *The Logic of International Restructuring* (London: Routledge).

Sandholtz, W. and Zysman J. (1989): '1992: Recasting the European Bargain', *World Politics,* pp 95–128.

Schneiberg, M. and Hollingsworth, J. R. (1991): 'Can Transaction Cost Economics Explain Trade Associations', in R. M. Czada and A. Windhoff-Heritier (eds), *Political Choice: Institutions, Rules and the Limits of Rationality* (Frankfurt: Campus), pp 199–231.

van Apeldoorn, B. (2001): 'The European Round Table of Industrialists: Still a Unique Player?', in J. Greenwood (ed.) *The Effectiveness of EU Business Associations* (Basingstoke: Palgrave).

Wilson, J. Q. (1995): *Political Organizations* (Princeton: Princeton University Press).

Wincott, D. (2001a): 'Looking forward or Harking Back? The Commission and the Reform of Governance in the EU', Journal of Common Market Studies, 39, 5, December, pp 897–911.

Young, A. and Wallace, H. (2000): *Regulatory Politics in the Enlarging European Union: Weighing Civic and Producer Interests* (Manchester: Manchester University Press).

Chapter 3

Beyond Corporatism and Pluralism: Towards a New Theoretical Framework

Irina Michalowitz

INTRODUCTION AND THEORETICAL BACKGROUND

Making theoretical sense of the European formal and informal systems of decision-making has been, and still remains, one of the most difficult tasks that scholars of European integration undertake. The complexity of and continuous changes in the European project lead to frequent switching between paradigms of analysis, and to disputes over which concepts might be most useful in developing an understanding of European governance. One of the unresolved and protracted arguments concerns the use of the traditional concepts of *pluralism* or *(neo)corporatism*[1], and whether they, or something completely different, should be employed to interpret structures of interest representation at the European level. Many arguments have been put forward for the pluralist interpretation, which states that interest groups compete more or less freely with each other for influence over policy-making, and that access to the institutions is open. However, just as many arguments can be found for the corporatist contention that access is limited because some interest groups receive preferential treatment by the European institutions and are involved in institutionalized formal dialogues with them, whilst others are excluded.

This chapter offers a new perspective. It points to the difficulties that occur when trying to make a definitive assessment, since empirical evidence is found for both interpretations. However, instead of trying to provide watertight evidence for one or the other, it will be demonstrated that both structures co-exist in an intricate way within the legislative system of the European Union (EU), where a range of decision-making procedures can be invoked. Each decision-making process differs in terms of the role played by each of the institutions. Each decision-making

---

[1] In this text, the more recent forms of neopluralism and neocorporatism are treated. In general, the terms pluralism and corporatism are used in recent literature, even when only those current forms are meant.

procedure can be differentiated in terms of the stages that comprise it. Crucially, the different processes and stages within them demand (or permit) different types relationships between the EU institutions and organized interests. Thus, this chapter argues that the main factors that account for the pluralist and/or neocorporatist patterns of behaviour are:

(a) The role played by each individual European institution in any given decision-making process, and in the specific phases of the process. Relationship structures can, therefore, differ *within* and *between* institutions, depending on the process phase.

(b) The type of decision-making process in operation. Depending on whether the Consultation[2], the Co-operation[3] or the Co-decision[4] procedure is applied, certain institutions are less involved, others more so, and the overall character of relations with interest groups varies accordingly.

These contentions will be explored by first outlining the main features of the pluralist and neocorporatist approaches and connecting them to the debate among EU scholars. Next, a close inspection will be carried out of the EU institutions and their individual behaviour in relation to interest groups. This is followed by an empirical illustration: the lobbying activities of the European consumers' association, Bureau Européen des Unions de Consommateurs (BEUC), in relation to the revision of a directive on genetically modified organisms (GMOs) is examined. This chapter is not meant to provide the final word on the question of pluralism or neocorporatism, but it aims at redirecting a discussion that has started to go round in circles.

CONTINUING INTEREST IN AN OLD DISCUSSION

The conceptualization of EU interest intermediation and organized interests has gone through various stages ever since the importance of the European integration process was first recognized by academia. The study of interest representation at the *national level* gave rise to theories of pluralism (concentrating on the input function of interest groups) and later to theories of neocorporatism (stressing steering functions of the state) (Czada 1994: 37). Although, by the mid-1970s, pluralism as a paradigm had already been replaced by neocorporatism and by theories

---

[2] The Parliament possesses only an advisory function

[3] The Parliament has a right of veto but can be overruled by the Council of the European Union

[4] The Parliament plays an almost equal role in the decision-making process: if Council and Parliament cannot find a compromise, a conciliation committee involving equal numbers of representatives from Council and Parliament has to decide.

of political economy, both concepts have remained in use for interpreting specific forms of state-interest group interaction (Kohler-Koch 1992: 1; Schmitter 1979: 14). Since both approaches lacked a sufficient consideration of the potential impact of external environmental factors, a theory of policy networks was developed whose importance in the academic debate has been on the increase (Schubert 1995: 5).[5] However, policy network analysis should not be construed as a replacement for the previous approaches. It is, rather, an umbrella concept, which can redress some of the deficiencies of existing research perspectives. Crucially, whether focusing on micro-level analysis of processes within issue networks or macro-level analysis of state-interest group relations in general, which is what is generally done under policy network analysis, both pluralist and neocorporatist features can be detected. Consequently, neither pluralist nor neocorporatist arguments have entirely lost their value.

It has been widely acknowledged that EU decision making often creates or relies on networks (see e.g. Peterson 1992; Bomberg and Peterson 1999; Pappi and Henning 1999). Controversies emerge when attempts are made to characterize relations between the institutions of the EU and organized interests within these networks as *either* pluralist *or* neocorporatist. A major problem in applying these concepts at all is that the construction of the EU is not comparable to national systems. As has been argued, for instance, by the German constitutional court in its judgment concerning the German ratification of the Treaty of Maastricht in 1993, the concept of a nation state is based on the three elements: *common terrain*, a *common people* and a *common state power*. At the European level, a number of peoples live within a political system characterized by shared power between a supranational and a national level. This structure calls into question the applicability of traditional instruments of analysis which were developed in order to understand the distribution of political power at the national level, because they fail to take into account either the dispersed decision-making levels of the EU or the fact that the EU arena must gradually compose itself as a compromise between the different traditions, systems and practices of its member states. On the other hand, EU-interest intermediation structures are so diverse that the empirical evidence supports almost any kind of interpretation (see Streeck and

---

[5] It assumes an increasing impact as a result of the growth in number of organized interests. Such interests are based on the tendency of sectorization and fragmentation of political decisions, which results in a redistribution of negotiating and implementing resources between governmental and non-governmental actors, leading in turn to the establishment of networks (Schumann 1996:82). Policy network analysis thereby encompasses the complexity of European decision-making to a larger extent than the other approaches.

Schmitter 1994: 185; Gorges 1996: 6ff; Traxler and Schmitter 1994: 53; Pfeifer 1995: 54ff; Greenwood and Ronit 1994: 31).

Before entering the core debate, it is worth recalling the main features of neocorporatism and pluralism in the context of EU interest intermediation structures. The concepts mainly differ in their interpretation of the role of the state, of the role of organized interests and of the relationship between them.

The Role of the State

Neocorporatist contentions focus on *steering* and on *output* aspects of modern political systems, whilst pluralist theories concentrate on the *input* side (Schubert 1995: 2). According to neocorporatism, the state has an *active* role since it incorporates rather than simply meets associations in consultative and decision-making networks (Czada 1994: 46).[6] Institutionalized and contemporary connections are supposed to lead to homogeneous ideas of the 'common will' between participating actors.[7] Finding solutions between a few representatives of an entire sector is easier than obtaining agreements between a large number of diverse actors with equal debating rights. By contrast, according to the pluralist concept, the state is restricted to a *passive* role as a judge between freely competing interests that possess equal rights of debating. The state only provides an arena within which the competition takes place, possibly (from a neopluralist perspective) supporting weak interests insofar as they are provided with equal resources to enter the competition (Schumann 1994: 72).

The Role of Organized Interests

Incorporated groups that are subordinate to the state mediate between individual and state positions, in a system that is stabilized by a few selected groups (Bensch 1996: 113). Drawing on Philippe Schmitter's (1979) concept of the ideal types of corporatism and pluralism, the neocorporatist model depicts a system in which there are a small number of hierarchically structured interest groups that exhibit non-competitive relations, a functional division of labour and a monopoly over governmental relations. This is understood to be the opposite of the pluralist approach in which autonomous, competitive entities are bound to the

---

[6] German wage negotiations, for instance, are led by employers' associations and unions, and the outcome is a legally binding agreement.

[7] Neocorporatism (as well as pluralism) views interest groups as representatives for certain interests or needs within society. The compromise between these groups is thus understood to represent an opinion that might come closest to what all citizens of a state can accept. This is seen as the common will. Neocorporatism is thus based on the selection of certain interest groups as representatives of these groups in order to obtain an idea of the differing opinions in society.

specific interests of their voluntary members, where there is the potential for the control and democratization of associative action (Schmitter 1979: 85–131; Czada 1994: 38). The pluralist approach envisages rivalry for the power to influence the state among a large number of interest groups. For every interest group a counter-interest group is expected to exist.

State–Interest Group Relations

An important feature of neocorporatism is the direct involvement of groups in decision-making processes leading to binding legal results. Pluralist participation is indirect and non-binding. Although interest groups participate in the debate, they are not involved in the final decision-making.[8] Neocorporatist research is mainly differentiated in terms of *macro-* and *meso-corporatism*. Whilst macro-corporatism mainly deals with the relationship between capital and labour, meso-corporatism examines corporatist developments in individual policy fields. Corporatist features at the level of single firms are referred to by the term *micro-corporatism* (Czada 1994: 43). Meso-corporatist structures are the most common forms of corporatism examined in recent literature.[9] Pluralist approaches explore the fragmented, decentralized and unequally distributed power structures of Western systems. It is assumed that not all groups succeed in the same way in raising awareness of their positions, but the possibility is open to all, even those interests that have been marginalized at times. This can potentially lead to greater efforts to participate (Jordan 1990: 293).

The difficulties faced in trying to obtain a clear picture of the nature of the relations between governmental actors and organized interests at the European level originate in the plentiful supply of empirical evidence that can be found for both sides. This indicates that both concepts might have equal weight. Some earlier work concerning the EU decision-making system portrays it as pluralist in character (Mazey and Richardson 1997; Eising and Kohler-Koch 1994). In doing so, such authors adopt a perspective that is focused on the general character of the Union rather than on the specific processes within the system. Such an overview leads

---

[8] This interpretation is contested. The author follows Czada's argumentation: interpreting structures with a lack of direct and binding participation of privileged interest groups as being neocorporatist would mean that each consideration of interests that is based on dependency could be called corporatism. The differentiation between pluralism and corporatism would disappear (Czada 1994:53).

[9] The only meaningful example that could be classified as macro-corporatism at the EU level is the so-called *Social Dialogue* uniting selected *social partners* – mainly associations involved in labour issues; conditions in the Social Dialogue differ from mainstream lobbying, which is treated here. For reasons of clarity, this kind of state-interest relation is not addressed here.

to some loss of detail, although the general character may become clearer. The evidence offered for a pluralist conceptualization is the large number of lobbying actors and access points. Contrasting approaches point to the Commission's tendency to consult interest groups (or even create them), thereby rather supporting a neocorporatist perspective (Gorges 1996).

Agreement about how to interpret relations between interest groups and EU-bodies seems to exist only with regard to the failure of the macro-corporatist *Euro-corporatism* (Streeck 1992: 100; Streeck and Schmitter 1994: 185). Statements on mesocorporatist relations are less clear, as they are based on the observation of large sector-specific differences. Authors who lean rather towards a neocorporatist interpretation (see Gorges 1996: 10–26) point to the least formally institutionalized consultations of interest groups by the European Commission at the beginning of legis-lative processes. Furthermore, since European associations receive pre-ferential treatment as compared to other forms of representation, and diverse consultative bodies including interest group representatives exist, there seems to be further evidence of neocorporatism.

Those in favour of the pluralist interpretation remark that the lack of direct participation of interest groups in binding decisions is an essential part of the relations of EU institutions and associations. Consultative committees, round tables, public hearings and consultations exist, but their establishment is not consistently regulated. Only in a few cases is the European Commission obliged to follow the negotiated results (Eising and Kohler-Koch 1994; Traxler and Schmitter 1994: 53; Streeck 1991: 183; Pfeifer 1995: 31; see van Schendelen 1998; European Institute of Public Administration 2000).[10] The immense growth of lobby groups in Brussels accompanying the increase of power at the European level implies that at least individual groups cannot obtain a formal monopoly position.[11]Furthermore, the manifold access points to EU

---

[10] This refers to the comitology system: a number of formal committees, consisting of national civil servants, are formally involved in the development of implementing measures via a set of procedures. Non-governmental actors can be mandated experts of their governments, but in general, they can gain only an observer status in these committees and are thus not formally able to make binding decisions.

[11] This is backed by empirical studies observing a large increase of activities of associa-tions since the 1980s (Andersen/Eliassen 1991:173). In 1992 the Commission esti-mated there were approximately 3,000 interest groups and 10,000 lobbyists in Brussels (European Commission 1993). In a recent study Greenwood and Webster (2000) count 1,347 interest groups and 247 company-public affairs offices. Those numbers are difficult to verify, since a lot of the listed associations exist by name only and are represented by a political consultancy or a lawyer who represent more than one association but are listed for each one of them in directories. Actual numbers could thus be lower. On the other hand, no lobbyist is obliged to register in Brussels, which means that numbers could also be higher.

decision-makers in the member states render the establishment of a manifest monopoly position impossible (Mazey and Richardson 1997: 111; Gorges 1996: 28). This suggests that pluralism exists.

THE CORE PROBLEM OF DEBATE: COMPARING APPLES AND PEARS?

The debate about which structures to identify in the EU suffers from two problems. Firstly, different elements of the concepts, that do not correspond to their counterparts, are compared. Secondly, the debated concepts are not entirely compatible with the EU political system, since they have been developed for the nation-state system.

Focusing on the first problem, when pluralist authors argue that the neocorporatist interpretation is not appropriate because of a lack of direct and binding participation in decision-making processes, they address state-interest group relations but fail to respond to the neocorporatist core argument of the strong role of the institutions in shaping the interest group landscape. Neocorporatist authors, on the other hand, propose different interpretations for some of the empirical criticism put forward by pluralists. One of these reinterpretations concerns the observable existence of a diversity of non-hierarchical organizations without a monopolist position. Neocorporatist scholars argue that the weak preferential treatment given to certain interest groups by the Commission amounts to neocorporatism because such a preference can be seen as a certain form of monopoly (see Gorges 1996). This does not seem entirely correct, as certain pluralist ideas are being neglected, such as the general openness of most negotiation processes to all articulated interests, at least during their initial phase. Instead, the disagreement appears to be the manifestation of the problem of transferring a rather simplistic model from a less complex political nation-state system to a far more intricate supranational system where monopolies and neocorporatist relations are more difficult to characterize.

The problem is also reflected in some of the attempts to find a clear terminology for the character of relations whilst integrating both pluralist and neocorporatist arguments. Efforts aimed at assessing the weight of lobbying at the European level often assume that pluralist relations exist. This is based on the conviction that lobbying is an element of pluralist structures (Nollert 1997: 113). Relations between the European institutions and associations are partially, and very vaguely, described as quasi-corporatist or as pluralist with corporatist elements (Traxler and Schmitter 1994: 53), or the problem is avoided by stating differences from sector to sector and case to case, without being more specific. Greenwood *et al.* (1992: 239), for instance, simply state vaguely that some relations were rather pluralist, others are rather corporatist. None of these explanations helps to answer the question about how to define the structures of interest intermediation found empirically in the EU. However, they reveal that it may be time to cease looking for either pluralist or neocorporatist features and admit their co-existence.

With regard to the second problem identified above, the empirical evidence suggests that neither of the two concepts is completely compatible with the European structures. A basic condition, essential to both pluralism and neocorporatism, is the existence of a single point of reference: the 'state'. This point of reference may consist of several levels located in ministries or parliamentary committees, but since these levels are all expected to behave consistently within the coordinated state structures and processes, pluralist and neocorporatist elements are unlikely (and not expected) to co-exist. By contrast, at the European level several governmental structures possess equal weight and compete with a supranational umbrella organization, so that the involvement of non-governmental actors[12] is influenced by these structures at all levels of decision-making. Hence, it is possible for rather pluralist patterns to prevail at one level and neocorporatist ones at another.

Taking this as a starting point for further research, an alternative proposal for analysis is put forward in this chapter. Scholars should seek to scrutinize the individual stages of European decision-making processes rather than reach a more generalized conclusion, as has been done previously. Instead, research should focus on the factors that *cause* the interaction between the institutions and interest groups, rather than concentrate on the structures that result from them. This approach enables an analysis of the relationship between the decision-making stage, its characteristics and the type of participation that occurs (i.e. whether it is pluralist and/or corporatist). Depending on which decision-making stage is studied, different patterns of interaction might be discerned. Analysing the reasons for these patterns could help to explain *why* and *when* pluralism and/or neocorporatism occur. Having identified the character of each phase, it should be possible to derive explanations for the overall process.

It seems likely that the degree of involvement of non-governmental actors in EU decision-making depends on the incentives available to decision-makers. Pluralist and corporatist structures of interaction are, thus, likely to be a function of the needs of the individual institutions. For example, the amount and kind of information required by an EU

---

[12] I use the term *non-governmental actors* to mean all lobbyists from outside government/ EU institutions, hence including business as well as public interests, groups as well as individual lobbyists.

institution, in general and at a specific stage in the process, will probably determine whether pluralist or corporatist patterns prevail. The role of a particular institution in the decision-making process itself, and the decision-making procedure in operation, will also probably affect the type of interaction that occurs.

DIFFERENTIATING BY DECISION-MAKING STAGE: CASE-INHERENT CO-EXISTENCE OF PLURALISM AND CORPORATISM

In essence, the changing access opportunities open to non-state actors result from EU decision-making processes themselves (Hix 1999; Andersen and Eliassen 2000; Mazey and Richardson 1993; Wallace and Young 1998). Accordingly, the following patterns can be expected to manifest themselves.[13] As the initiator of legislation, firstly the Commission potentially affords access to a number of privileged groups. This stage is followed by a period of institutional passivity with regard to the involvement of interest groups, during which the groups compete freely. Opportunities to influence decision-making for interest groups diminish as the draft progresses up the bureaucratic hierarchy of the Commission. As soon as the Commission proposal reaches the Parliament the process becomes less calculable. General, institutionalized procedures for the involvement of non-governmental interests do not exist. Interest groups can, but do not have to, be consulted and heard. Access opportunities at Council level hardly exist.

This basic account of the interactions between EU institutions and interest groups becomes convincing when one considers that the fundamental relationship between them is one of *exchange*. EU institutions seek information. Non-governmental actors seek influence.[14] The openness of the Commission and the Parliament can, thus, partly[15] be attributed to the extent to which they need information. A lack of staff makes it difficult for these institutions to generate information by themselves. Given the

---

[13] This interpretation is backed by scholarly literature on lobbying, by the brief case study following in the latter part of the chapter, by continuous interviews across different sectors undertaken by the author and by participant observation. Nonetheless, this evidence can of course not account for each potential situation of European decision-making. The focus is, therefore, on the way interaction with interest groups is structured within the formal procedural rules of European decision-making processes.

[14] The concept of exchange can be traced in most approaches to EU-interest intermediation (see Schmitter 1979; Pappi and Henning 1999).

[15] Other reasons include the search and the need for political support – whereas the Parliament needs electoral support, the Commission seeks a quasi-legitimacy to counter the reproach of its lack of democratic legitimization via elections.

inter-institutional rivalries, as well as the need for checks and balances, the Commission and the Parliament prefer to rely on additional informational sources (other than the member-state governments themselves) (Pollack 1997; Kohler-Koch and Edler 1998). The need for information diminishes the further the process progresses. This leads to the gradual closure of the process to interest groups but, paradoxically, also to a larger degree of pluralism, because interest groups can engage in free competition to provide fresh additional information. Once the institutions have decided that they have obtained sufficient information to take a decision, interest groups can try to be more than 'mere information providers' and attempt to actively influence the process.

In order to explain more fully the stages-approach, it is necessary to review the legislative process and, especially, the role(s) played by the main institutions at the EU-level. Each institution has different ways of dealing with external input, which also means that lobbyists trying to influence these institutions need to adapt to the structures they find, which are sometimes pluralist and sometimes neocorporatist. The further along the decision-making process a decision progresses, the fewer the opportunities that are available to interest groups to influence it. In the following section this argument will be outlined in detail for the main decision-making institutions: the Commission, the Parliament and the Council.[16]

The European Commission

More than the other institutions, the Commission has a primary interest in obtaining information. This is because, as formal initiator of first pillar legislation, it has to draft the legislative text, whereas the tasks of the European Parliament and the Council are mainly to evaluate and to amend this text. Since information supplied by member-state governments to the Commission will already have been filtered and politically interpreted, the Commission actively supports the creation of European umbrella groups that consist of non-governmental actors that will (potentially) be affected by the decision.[17] For a period interaction was restricted to Euro-groups, but this could not be sustained because of problems of efficiency. Euro-groups were often unable to aggregate the

---

[16] Given the relatively limited powers of the two other involved institutions, the Economic and Social Council (ESC) and the Committee of the Regions (CoR), no further comment is made on these two institutions.

[17] A very recent example is the creation of a European Services Forum (ESF) in 1998/99 with the support of the then Commissioner, Sir Leon Brittan, who was looking for a service sector association to help him create the negotiation position of the European Commission in the negotiations on the General Agreement on Trade in Services (GATS).

individual member interests and present a homogeneous and yet sub-stantial opinion (see e.g. Pfeifer 1995: 85; Hey and Brendle 1994: 381).

As a result of its role as an initiator of legislation, its receptivity and its control and administrative functions, the Commission is often the first point of contact for organized interests. Within the Commission three levels can broadly be distinguished. The most senior level consists of the 20 Commissioners. Their cabinets are subordinate to them. Directorate-Generals (DGs) constitute the category of the bureaucracy. Whereas Commissioners and cabinets would describe themselves as 'political', DGs see their role as purely 'technical-administrative' in nature (Rometsch 1995: 160). Legislation is first drafted at the DG level and then passed through the entire hierarchy, until the 20 Commissioners have agreed upon an official proposal. The apparatus is open to interest group input at all levels, since the comparatively small bureaucracy relies on external sources for information (as discussed above). Nonetheless, the DG level is generally seen as being more receptive to lobbying by interest groups, since technical rather than political expertise is needed, which often goes beyond the skills of the civil servants in charge. For the interest groups the information that they possess (and which the Com-mission seeks) provides them with important leverage during negotia-tions. The input from organized interests also enables the Commission to bypass national governments and reach a consensus among those who are affected (Nollert 1997: 108).

Neocorporatist interpretations apply especially to consultations and hearings at the lowest Commission level, where they have been quasi-institutionalized. Before a proposed regulation is drafted, *certain* interest groups are usually contacted for their comments in order to try to make the regulation practicable and to ease implementation (see Aspinwall and Greenwood 1998: 4). But as soon as a draft has been finalized, the DG ceases actively to seek external input. Throughout the remainder of the process within the Commission, and until an official proposal is presented, interest groups must continue to present themselves in an interesting way. They will need to remain active if they want to keep in touch with what is happening. In this rather pluralist phase, non-privileged groups that have not been contacted previously have an equal chance of gaining entry to the process, provided that they can offer fresh information.

The section above reveals the extent to which the Commission and non-governmental actors are interdependent. Such is the nature of their relationship that the Commission is actively involved in the creation of interest groups. It also reveals the strenuous efforts made by the institu-tion to maintain control over the interaction and the degree of influence that is allowed to interest groups. The Commission can exercise control by closing the process to some extent after initial information has been obtained. Alternating between neocorporatist and pluralist ways of interacting with interest groups thus seems to be a product of the demand for information on the one hand and the need to control the input on the other hand.

The European Parliament

The European Parliament has become increasingly attractive to lobby-groups as a result of its increased legislative power, especially regarding the use of the Co-decision procedure. As with Commission proposals, parliamentary amendments do not originate in a vacuum. They are partially initiated in contacts with Commission officials, and partially by external pressure or in co-operation with interest groups (Corbett *et al.* 1995: 235). Interest groups constitute a source of information for the Parliament in the same way that they do for the Commission, enabling it to maintain a certain degree of independence from the other European institutions (Diekmann 1998: 290). Access points within the Parliament include the committees, the individual Members of Parliament (MEPs) and the entire plenary with its different political groups.

Amendments to Commission proposals are first formulated by the Parliamentary Committee Rapporteur. The entire Committee then votes on the amendments, which in turn are passed to the plenary (which then casts the final vote). Corporatist forms of participation are to be found in the first phase (if at all), i.e. at Committee/Rapporteur level. They depend largely on the personality and the political interests of the Rapporteur in charge. Thus, the Rapporteur decides whether to reject external input or to approach a selected number of interest groups or experts in a neocorporatist way or to open the discussion to all interested parties in a rather pluralist fashion. As soon as the report with the amendments is drafted and given to the rest of the Committee to vote on, corporatist structures can no longer be discerned. Even if interest groups were contacted actively beforehand, this activity will largely have ceased. During this rather pluralist phase, lobbying individual MEPs directly becomes more important, since the majority of the Parliamentarians, even those on the specialist committee, may not be in full possession of all of the details of the case which is due to be voted on. They are likely to be willing to receive (more) information.

The importance attached to lobbying the Parliament by interest groups tends to depend on the procedure under which the Parliament is parti-cipating, and that in turn affects whether there are pluralist or corporatist relationships. The Consultation procedure allows little influence via the Parliament, since the Council is not obliged to act on amendments put forward by Parliament. In some cases a Parliamentary committee can simply block decisions by delaying the formulation of amendments until the Commission and the Council agree on compromises, but this is the exception rather than the rule (see Westlake 1994: 34). The now rarely used Co-operation procedure makes it much harder for the Council to overrule the parliamentary amendments, because a unanimous decision is needed to pass legislation against its objections. Moreover, the Co-decision procedure, which is used in more than two-thirds of all proposals in the first pillar, provides the Parliament with a veto power and renders it very important for organized interests (see Earnshaw, Wood and Warleigh, this volume). Failure to influence decisions at the Commission level could be rectified at the Parliament level. Thus, again in the European Parliament whether the relations are pluralist or corporatist largely depends on the decision-making procedure. Assessing the nature of the relations between the European Parliament and interest groups is more complicated than for the Commission. On the one hand, its needs are similar to those of the Commission, although MEPs, even more than Commission staff, depend on expert information because they are elected generalists and politicians rather than technical specialists. On the other hand, MEPs are under more pressure from the electorate than any other EU institution and they are more heterogeneous (since party preferences are combined with cultural differences). As a result MEPs have less clearly determined preferences about whom to engage with. Since the Commission is generally more neocorporatist and the EP more pluralist, the extent to which the EP is involved in any given decision-making process is significant. Processes under the Consultation procedure are likely to be more neocorporatist, whereas Co-operation and especially Co-decision processes tend to be more pluralist.

The Council of the European Union

The last element in the EU's decision-making process is the *common position* of the Council. After the Commission and the Parliament have played their part, the Council begins to negotiate officially on the draft proposal. The intergovernmental body of national ministers is assisted by about 200 or more working groups of national civil servants (see European Institute of Public Administration 2000). Despite this large substructure, opportunities for influencing policy at the Council level are relatively poor for interest groups, since the preparatory Council committees have to work to a strict national mandate. Fresh negotiations may be necessary in the member states if the negotiating margin is exceeded at the EU level and that may offer new opportunities for interest groups to influence policy outcomes. When the Council meets at the EU level, it is more or less closed to external input. Should external interests hope to be considered by member state governments, they are likely to have to contact national-level officials and thus inform member state bargaining positions through domestic lobbying. Expertise sought during Council negotiations is very selective, whereas pluralist input is hardly possible any more. Contacts between diverse committees and interest groups do exist, but their impact can hardly be measured since political considerations play an even greater role at this level than in the other European institutions. Political horse-trading is dependent on interdependencies between states and is thus less subject to specific non-state lobbies. It is therefore even more difficult than in the other institutions to determine whether the input given by interest groups has actually had an impact on the final outcome. With regard to the Council, the decision-making procedure in operation also matters. Co-decision procedures make it difficult for the Council to override the Parliament's amendments, but this is not the case under the Consultation procedure. In co-decision, the involvement of the Parliament and its ability to demand amendments are likely to be very important. This gives more weight to the pluralist input of interest groups at the Parliamentary level.

A PRACTICAL EXAMPLE:
THE GMO DIRECTIVE 90/220 EEC

How can the above trends and patterns be traced in concrete cases? This section provides an empirical case study that serves to portray processes outlined above in operation. The case revolves around the revision[18] of Directive 90/220/EEC, which regulates the intentional release of genetically modified organisms (GMOs) into the environment and their offer for sale for experimental and commercial uses. The reformulation of the directive provoked heavy lobbying by consumers, environmentalists and the chemical as well as the biotechnology industries. Its progress up to and including the final decision provides a graphic illustration of the significance of the type of decision procedure in operation, the role played by the institutions and the sort of relations that prevail.

The process began in a neocorporatist fashion. In August 1997 the responsible DG (DG XI, now DG Environment—ENV) sent out for consultation to the member-state administrations, as well as to privileged interest groups, a list of potential revisions. On the basis of the feedback

---

[18] A more recent revision has been negotiatiated in 2001, but this case study concentrates on the 1999 process. The briefly outlined case study is based on 18 interviews conducted in Brussels in March 1999 with involved actors and has been explored in more detail in the unpublished master's thesis of the author.

desk officers at DG XI wrote a first draft, which was then subject to a hearing with interest groups. From this hearing an initial proposal was passed up the Directorate hierarchy, which evolved as it progressed. It was subsequently discussed in a general hearing with interest groups. Following this stage, DG XI started bilateral talks with individual interest groups and companies. With the information collected from these meetings, the officials in charge put an end to their corporatist interaction with associations and other interests.

From that point onwards the non-governmental actors were no longer included formally in the Commission's decision-making, but the next phase provided significant opportunities for pluralist interest intermediation. The positions of organized interests as well as those of the DG were now known and publicly available. Although no further public hearings were held, interest groups had good opportunities to remain involved by actively approaching the officials in charge and offering new and useful information. BEUC, for instance, followed a strategy of controlling the amount of information that it released to the Commission, supplying just enough to 'stay in the game' and be able to produce new knowledge as appropriate. Finally, an official Commission proposal was reached on 23 February 1998 (European Commission 1998) and passed on to the Parliament. This bore the hallmarks of interest group input.

In common with the early phases of negotiations in the Commission, the process at the Parliamentary level started with a rather corporatist involvement of interest groups. This was due to the personal preferences of the Rapporteur, who called for hearings and bilateral meetings with interest groups as well as with Council officials and Parliamentarians of all parties. Once a committee vote had been taken, no further formal meetings with non-governmental actors were held. Interest groups were then compelled to approach Committee members, informally and actively if they wanted to try to influence the voting.

After the Commission's response to the Parliamentary amendments (that were very much in line with Commission's initial ideas), the GMO revision formed part of the agenda of the Environmental Council on June 25, 1999. National standpoints, that were to the forefront of the meeting, had been developed in the national ministries; lobbying had been carried out by national interest groups in the member states. At the European level the influence opportunities for interest groups were largely exhausted. Non-governmental actors did try to contribute to the debate, but the access channels to the EU-bodies were now very largely closed. The General Secretariat of the Council harshly criticized the extensive lobbying efforts (mainly from business groups) and stressed that no additional positions would be debated. The *common position* that was finally reached proved to be highly controversial and mirrored the indecisiveness of the member-state governments and the very different national opinions.

In sum, the GMO case reveals rather neocorporatist structures in Commission and Council phases, with slightly more pluralist opportunities in the former than in the latter. The Parliamentary phases of the GMO decision-making process were characterized by more pluralist involvement than was apparent in the other two institutions. For all three institutions interaction with interest groups added value to their work, although the outcome was only a limited success from the point of view of interest groups. Deciding about *how* and *to what extent* to interact with organized interests was, therefore, linked to the individual needs of each institution, the phase of the decision-making process and the type of procedure in operation.

CONCLUSIONS

The preceding analysis of decision-making in terms of the type of procedure in operation, the role played by the various institutions at each stage in any given decision-making process and the institutions' needs (e.g. in terms of information) lead to the conclusion that a simple choice between pluralism and corporatism does not reflect the reality of the structures and processes at the EU level. A close look at the practical decision-making process implies that the structure of relations between the EU institutions and organized interests are, on the one hand, due to active shaping of the institutions themselves and, on the other hand, very largely dependent on the legislative conditions of the procedures. Based on the detailed analysis of the individual decision-making stages above, it can be discerned that generally the Commission tends towards corporatist behaviour whilst the Parliament tends to be pluralist. The Council can be characterized as closed or, as far as interaction with interest groups is concerned, rather corporatist. The net effect is that the less that the Parliament is involved in any given decision-making process,[19] the less pluralist the overall process is likely to be. On the other hand, the more involved the Parliament is, as with the Co-decision procedure, the more pluralist the overall process is likely to be. Crucially, therefore, in EU decision-making pluralism and corporatism can co-exist.

What conclusions can be drawn from these findings for the role of pluralism and neocorporatism as organizing paradigms in research on EU-interest intermediation? The initial conclusion is that *both* the pluralist and the neocorporatist concepts are, and remain, useful provided that the uniqueness of the European political system is taken into account

---

[19] This depends on the applicable parliamentary procedure.

by researchers. This means that notions of exclusion and inclusion that are helpful when analysing politics and policy-making at the national level (and lead to conclusions that relations are *either* pluralist *or* neocorporatist structures) are not so useful at the supranational level. Instead, given that pluralist and neocorporatist patterns of behaviour can be said to co-exist, this means that research on EU-interest intermediation may not demand new concepts, but rather an open-minded and adventurous combination of traditional concepts in novel ways. Such a combination of concepts may be inappropriate when studying the nation-state, but it can perform a useful function in relation to the EU because the latter consists of several individually structured layers that can each generate specific forms of interaction with non-governmental actors. Thus, new combinations of old concepts should be adjusted according to the nature of the EU system, to take into account the differences between it and the nation-state. Reformulated approaches that allow for the co-existence and complementarity of pluralism and neocorporatism can enable the detection of new forms or structures of interaction. This may also lead, in the longer term, to the elaboration of improved explanations of state and non-state interaction that can be applied to the EU.

REFERENCES

Andersen, S. and Eliassen, K. (1991): 'European Community Lobbying', *European Journal of Political Research*, 20:2, 173–187.

Andersen, S. and Eliassen, K. (eds) (2000): *Making Policy in Europe* (London: Sage).

Aspinwall, M. and Greenwood, J. (1998): 'Conceptualizing collective action in the European Union: an introduction', in J. Greenwood and M. Aspinwall (eds) *Collective Action in the European Union. Interests and the new politics of associability* (London: Routledge).

Bensch, O. (1996): *Multidisziplinäre Analyse des Problemfeldes Verbände unter besonderer Berücksichtigung der einfachen und komplexen Systemtheorie im Binnenbereich von Verbänden*, unpublished doctoral thesis, Munich.

Coen, D. (1997): 'The evolution of the large firm as a political actor in the European Union', *Journal of Public Policy*, 4:1, 91–108.

Corbett, R., Jacobs, F. and Shackleton, M. (1995): *The European Parliament,* 3rd ed (London: Cartermill).

Czada, Roland (1994): 'Konjunkturen des Korporatismus: Zur Geschichte eines Paradigmenwechsels in der Verbändeforschung', in W. Streeck (ed.) *Staat und Verbände*. Politische Vierteljahresschrift special ed. 25: 35 (Opladen: Westdeutscher Verlag).

Diekmann, K. (1998): 'Die europäischen Interessenverbände und -vertretungen', in W. Weidenfeld and W. Wessels (eds) *Jahrbuch der europäischen Integration 1997/98* (Bonn: Europa Union).

Eising, R. and Kohler-Koch, B. (1994): 'Inflation und Zerfaserung: Trends der Interessenvermittlung in der Europäischen Gemeinschaft', in W. Streeck (ed.)

Staat und Verbände, Politische Vierteljahresschrift special ed. 25:35 (Opladen: Westdeutscher Verlag).

European Institute of Public Administration (2000): *Governance by Committee: The Role of Committees in European Policy Making and Policy*, Research Paper 00/GHA (EIPA: Maastricht) http://eipa-nl.com/public/public_publications/default_working.htm.

European Commission (1993): *Ein offener und strukturierter Dialog zwischen der Kommission und den Interessengruppen*, Official Journal C 63/2. 5.3.1993.

European Commission (1998): *Vorschlag der Kommission für eine Richtlinie des Europäischen Parlaments und des Rates zur Änderung der Richtlinie 90/220 EWG über die absichtliche Freisetzung genetisch veränderter Organismen in die Umwelt*, KOM (98) 85 endg., 23.2.1998.

Greenwood, J., Grote, J. and Ronit, K. (eds) (1992): *Organized Interests in the European Community* (London: Sage).

Greenwood, J. and Ronit, K. (1994): 'Interest Groups in the European Community: Newly Emerging Dynamics and Forms', *West European Politics* 17:1, 31–55.

Greenwood, J. and Webster, R. (2000): 'Are EU Business Associations Governable?' *European Integration Online Papers* (EioP) 4:3. http://eiop.or.at/eiop/texte/2000–003a.htm.

Gorges, M. (1996): *Euro-corporatism? Interest intermediation in the European Community* (Lanham: University Press of America).

Hey, C. and Brendle, U. (1994): *Umweltverbände und EG: Strategien, politische Kulturen und Organisationsformen* (Opladen: Westdeutscher Verlag).

Hix, S. (1999): *The Political System of the European Union*, The European Union Series (Houndmills: Macmillan).

Jordan, G. (1990): 'The Pluralism of Pluralism. An Anti-Theory?', *Political Studies* 38, 286–301.

Kohler-Koch, B. (1992): *Interessen und Integration. Die Rolle organisierter Interessen im westeuropäischen Integrationsprozeß*, ABIII/No. 1, (Mannheim).

Kohler-Koch, B. and Edler, J. (1998): 'Ideendiskurs und Vergemeinschaftung: Erschließung transnationaler Räume durch europäisches Regieren', in B. Kohler-Koch (ed.) *Regieren in entgrenzten Räumen*. Politische Vierteljahresschrift special ed. 29:39 (Opladen: Westdeutscher Verlag).

Mazey, S. and Richardson, J. (eds) (1993): *Lobbying in the European Community* (Oxford: Oxford University Press).

Mazey, S. and Richardson, J. (1997): 'Policy Framing: Interest Groups and the lead up to 1996 Inter-Governmental Conference', *West European Politics* 20:3, 111–133.

Nollert, M. (1997): 'Verbändelobbying in der Europäischen Union – Europäische Dachverbände im Vergleich', in U. von Alemann and B. Weßels (eds) *Verbände in vergleichender Perspektive: Beiträge zu einem vernachlässigten Feld* (Berlin: Sigma).

Pappi F.U. and Henning, C.H.C.A. (1999): 'The organization of influence in the European agricultural policy: A network approach', *European Journal of Political Science Research* 36, 257–281.

Peterson, J. (1992): 'The European Technology Community: Policy Networks in a Supranational Setting', in D. Marsh and R. A. W. Rhodes (eds) *Policy Networks in British Government* (Oxford: Clarendon).

Peterson, J. and Bomberg, E. (1999): *Decision-Making in the European Union* (Palgrave: Houndmills).

Pfeifer, G. (1995): *Eurolobbyismus: organisierte Interessen in der Europäischen Union*, Europäische Hochschulschriften 31, Politikwissenschaft 271, (Peter Lang: Frankfurt a.M.).

Pollack, M. (1997): 'Representing diffuse interests in EC policy-making', *Journal of European Public Policy*, 4:4: 572–590.

Rometsch, D. (1995): 'Europäische Kommission', in W. Weidenfeld (ed.): *Europa von A bis Z*. (Bonn: Bundeszentrale für politische Bildung), pp 160–167.

Schendelen, M. (1998) (ed.): *EU Committees as Influential Policymakers* (Aldershot: Ashgate).

Schmitter, P. (1979): 'Still the Century of Corporatism?', in P. Schmitter (ed.) *Trends toward corporatist intermediation* (Beverly Hills: Sage).

Schubert, K. (1995): *Pluralismus, Korporatismus und politische Netzwerke*, Duisburger Materialien zur Politik- und Verwaltungswissenschaft 16 (Duisburg: Gerhard Mercator Universität).

Schumann, W. (1994): 'Das politische System der EU als Rahmen für Verbandsaktivitäten', in V. Eichener and H. Voelzkow (eds): *Europäische Integration und verbandliche Interessenvermittlung* (Marburg: Metropolis).

Schumann, W. (1996): *Neue Wege in der Integrationstheorie* (Opladen: Leske + Buderich).

Streeck, W. (1992): 'From National Corporatism to Transnational Pluralism: European Interest Politics and the Single Market', in T. Treu (ed.) *Participation in Public Policy Making. The Role of Trade Unions and Employers' Associations* (Berlin: de Gruyter).

Streeck, W. and Schmitter, .P (1994): 'From National Corporatism To Transnational Pluralism. Organized Interests In The Single Market', in V. Eichener and H. Voelzkow (eds) *Europäische Integration und verbandliche Interessenvermittlung* (Marburg: Metropolis).

Traxler, F. and Schmitter, P. (1994): 'Perspektiven europäischer Integration, verbandlicher Interessenvermittlung und Politikformulierung', in V. Eichener and H. Voelzkow (eds) *Europäische Integration und verbandliche Interessenvermittlung* (Marburg: Metropolis).

Wallace, H. and Young, A. (eds) (1998): *Participation and Policy-Making in the European Union* (Oxford: Oxford University Press).

Westlake, Martin (1994): *The Commission and the Parliament: partners and rivals in the European policy-making process* (London: Butterworth).

Part 2

European Union Actors and Interest Representation

Chapter 4

When the European Union is a Lobbyist: The European Commission and External Trade

Kerry Somerset

INTRODUCTION – PRINCIPALS, AGENTS AND EXTERNAL TRADE

How does the European Union (EU) engage with third countries in matters of trade negotiations? After all, the EU can usefully be understood as

> 'a compound polity whose distinct culturally defined and politically organized units are bound together in a consensually prearranged form of 'Union' for specific purposes without losing their national identity or resigning their individual sovereignty to a higher central authority.' (Chryssochoou *et al.* 1999: 49).

The member states remain, and attempt to consolidate their position as, the most important decision-makers in the EU in spite of the creation of a supranational Commission and a supranational and directly elected European Parliament. And yet, even outside issues of defence policy, if the EU is to be a useful means to 'seek ... solutions to problems which are less effectively resolved at the national level' (Armstrong and Bulmer 1998: 67), it often requires the ability to engage with powerful non-member states. In turn, this requires the EU to have, *inter alia*, a strong capacity as a negotiator and the ability to formulate and deliver a common EU position. The member states are thus faced with a conundrum: they remain keen to exploit the advantages of European integration (in this case, the ability to carry greater weight in international negotiations), but they also remain keen to limit the transfer of sovereignty to the EU level as far as possible. When the EU has to represent its interests externally, the member states thus have to find a way to maximize the gains of collective action whilst ceding as little autonomy to the EU level as possible.

Consequently, in EU external trade negotiations as in other areas of policy, the Council is generally seen to act as the principal and the Commission as (one of) its agent(s). In other words, the member states collectively decide the outcomes they would like the negotiations to produce, and simply entrust the Commission with the task of realizing these goals. In this line of thinking, the member states also surround the Commission with various control mechanisms (see below) in order both to ensure that the Commission does not depart from the line the member states have agreed and to restrict the Commission's capacity for independent action.

However, I argue that such is not an adequate reading of the complexities of the Council–Commission relationship in external trade policy. My aim is not to question the primacy of the role played by the member states, as the Council, in this or any other area of EU policy. However, in order to acquire a comprehensive understanding of exactly how the EU achieves its goals in external trade policy we must investigate exactly how the Commission is able to be a successful agent – that is, how it can achieve the goals set for it by the member states – by examining the dynamics of the external trade agreement negotiation process. In pursuit of its task the Commission must, in fact, exercise significant autonomy, given the need to perform three key functions: assembling complex coalitions both inside and outside the EU, developing detailed understandings of third countries' negotiating positions, and creating/delivering compromises which are equally acceptable to the member states and to the other parties within the negotiations.

Thus, in external trade negotiations the Commission can to some extent helpfully be understood as a 'purposeful opportunist' (Cram 1997: 156), which maximizes its strengths, particularly in the informal politics of negotiation. *At the operational level* there is a certain reworking of the principal/agent relationship between Council and Commission, because the latter must have some ability to innovate if the former are to meet as many of the goals as possible. In this chapter I therefore argue that the Commission's manner of fulfilling its role as the member states' agent in multilateral negotiations is inherently flexible and that it is this flexibility which allows the Commission to perform the negotiation task to the standard expected of it by its principals, the member states. As a result, external trade policy is perhaps one area in which the general decline of the Commission in recent years is likely to be avoided as a consequence of the logic of member state self-interest.

The chapter is structured as follows. First, I introduce the concept of the European Commission speaking with a 'single voice' (see Meunier and Nicolaides 1999) on behalf of all the member states in the external trade field.[1] I then give a brief overview of the methodologies and control mechanisms introduced in the Treaty of Rome in 1957,[2] which were put in place to ensure (or, at least, to try to ensure) the Commission's adherence to the member states' position, before I look at external trade negotiations themselves. The main part of the chapter will seek to identify the way in which the Commission operates, within the informal and formal domains, to lobby for specific outcomes to external trade negotiations and will then assess how successful it has been and what this may mean for the Commission in the future.

For a number of reasons I will use the example of the Uruguay Round of the General Agreement on Tariffs and Trade, or GATT, which took place between September 1986 and December 1993, to illustrate my argument. First, because the GATT predates the European Community (23 countries signed up to GATT in 1947), it was originally intended to be part of an International Trade Organization (ITO) which would cover 'not only trade liberalization but also the establishment of commodity agreements and the co-ordination of counter-cyclical policies' (Hine 1985: 38). But for many reasons the ITO negotiations failed and the GATT continued to be the most important regulator of world trade.[3] Because of GATT and its international standing, the EU's member states were not free to set 'whatever trade arrangements suited them best' (Hine 1985: 38) in the European Economic Community (EEC) Treaty and, subsequently, GATT has had a significant impact upon the making and substance of EU external trade policy. Second, the GATT agreement has been upheld in Community law (International Fruit case 21–24/72) and it has also been agreed that where GATT requirements overlap Community law, then the implementation of GATT is sufficient (from Vincenzi 1996: 60). This is particularly important when the Commission is negotiating trade agreements with third countries when, as I can testify from personal experience, one has to become an expert at deciphering which parts of the GATT have been codified in the third country's legislation and where the particular EU requirements, which are often much more specific, can be placed. Unfortunately there can be an uneasy fit between

---

[1] It should be noted that although the way the Commission handles external relations has changed significantly since the Rome Treaty (see Saurugger and Nugent 2002 for an excellent account of these changes), the mechanisms used by the Council and the responsibilities of the Commission in external trade, have changed little. Therefore I will not discuss successive Treaty changes here.

[2] Nugent (1999: 42) defines this as the EEC Treaty, to distinguish it from the other Treaty of Rome signed at the same time–the Euratom Treaty–and I shall use that terminology throughout.

[3] Until the establishment of the World Trade Organization (WTO) following the end of the Uruguay Round.

the two. Third, the GATT is interesting because although the Commission has held the role of negotiating trade agreements on behalf of the member states since 1957, it is not a Contracting Party to the GATT. In fact, 'the Community member states maintain individual membership even while the Commission speaks and negotiates for them' (Smith 1994: 259). This means that an EU country could, in principle, 'be outvoted in the Council of Ministers only to be able individually to withhold its signature from the new agreement within the GATT' (Teasdale 1993: 577) if it did not agree with the way the European Commission had conducted itself on its behalf. This is particularly important since the European Court of Justice (ECJ) Opinion 1/94 after Uruguay which

'explicitly stated that the Community had not yet acquired the competence necessary to conclude significant parts of the GATS (services) and TRIPS (intellectual property) agreements although it did have full competence in trade in goods' (Demaret 2000: 446–447).

Therefore, not only are the member states present, but they also have competence in specific areas of GATT business, which the Commission does not. Finally, examining the last completed GATT round is particularly timely because the subsequent round of trade negotiations, this time under the auspices of the WTO, began in Doha, Qatar, in November 2001 and is still continuing at the time of writing.

'SPEAKING FOR EUROPE': THE AGENT AS NEGOTIATOR

That the European Commission was given any responsibilities in the field of external trade was undoubtedly due to some tough bargaining amongst the founder members of the European Community at the Messina Conference in 1955, where further integration was discussed, and again at the Spaak Committee table later that year (with the eponymous Report issued in April 1956 and used as the basis for negotiations leading to the EEC Treaty). It is no coincidence that the Treaty of Paris of 1951, which founded the European Coal and Steel Community, envisaged no role in external trade for the forerunner of the European Commission, the High Authority. The French government, for example, was 'almost uniformly hostile' (Dinan 1999: 31) to any concept of a common market and common trade rules. Indeed, it was only when the Treaty of Rome was initialled, giving the Commission the 'pivotal function' (Smith 1994: 249) of 'proposing legislative measures ... overseeing the implementation of EEC policies and laws and representing the Community in trade negotiations with third parties' (Nugent 2001: 26) that all the member states appeared to have accepted the arguments for a strong Commission role in this area.

So why did the founders of the European Community consent to take this path? The initial suggestion came from the Dutch, who are usually considered advocates of a strongly supranational component to the EU. However, the Dutch were able to persuade all the member states, not just their usual 'small state' allies in Belgium and Luxembourg, that the Commission should be so empowered. Given that this was, for at least some of the EU's founders, the first stage in the building of a European federation, it is perhaps unsurprising that a separate agency was not established to address external trade issues, and that one of the existing institutions was preferred on the ground that this would help reinforce the coherence of the new structures. However, even this does not explain why the member states chose to give the negotiation role to the Commission rather than the Council – an interesting choice seeing that in the transition from the Paris Treaty to the Rome Treaty there was a marked tendency to increase the power of the Council as part of the price paid to reinforce the integration process.

Stirk and Weigall (1999: 278) suggest that there was a cynical reason for enabling the Commission to speak for Europe – namely that national administrations could then use this to their own advantage by 'attacking the EU in their domestic conflicts' – blaming the Commission rather than themselves for agreeing unpopular measures which they nevertheless believed they had no alternative but to accept. Moreover, as Hine suggests, trade policy was always 'to be the central element in the Community's relationship with non-member states' (Hine 1985: 74). Having the Commission speak for them could make the member states appear stronger and more united, allowing them to exert substantial pressure on countries which considered Europe a major market[4] whilst, at the same time, keeping their disagreements away from the negotiating table in a back room.

The activities of the EEC are set out in Article 3 of the EEC Treaty. This includes an introduction to, amongst other policy areas, the Customs Union, common commercial policy (CCP), freedom of movement of persons, goods, services and capital and common policies in agriculture and transport. The EEC Treaty, then, had been carefully written in order that it would be of benefit to all the member states, maybe particularly the recalcitrant ones – the Netherlands hoped for a larger market for its transport industry, France wanted to support its extensive agricultural sector through increased exports and through the promise of

---

[4] For more information on the EU as hegemon in the trade field see Pelkmans and Brenton (1999: 12–14)

a common agricultural policy, whilst Germany would benefit from the customs union (Hine 1985: 74). In addition, the smaller member states would have 'increased national leverage' (Meunier 2000: 103) through their association with the larger industrial players as well as assurance that, through the Customs Union, 'all firms would be on the same footing' (Dobbin 1993: 87) when it came to exporting their goods and identifying new markets. At the same time, there was a further level of issue linkage through the formation of EURATOM, created in another Treaty of Rome, which was concerned with the advancement of nuclear power for civilian use. This was particularly attractive to the French who were able to deflect public attention away from the unpopular single market to this development, which enjoyed much stronger public support (Ludlow 1997:20–21). Although Taylor (1983: 121) suggests that the outcome of having the European Commission act as a 'single voice' was simply pragmatism, the discussions and issue linkage, which had been carefully maximized to achieve this, would indicate that it was actually a radical move for an embryonic European Community with potential for cleavages between the member states if and when conflicts arose.[5]

Of course the key EEC Treaty article is, for the purposes of this chapter, Article 133 (ex 113) which states that there will be a common commercial policy 'based on uniform principles particularly in regard to changes in tariff rates, the conclusion of tariff and trade agreements, the achievement of uniformity in measures of liberalization, export policy and measures to protect trade'. The article goes on to elaborate how the Council would control this process specifically through its formal agreement to allow the Commission to negotiate and the 'special committee' to oversee the negotiations (set out in Nugent 2001: 305–6).

Having a single voice for 'Europe' could thus be economically and politically advantageous for the member states, but this does not mean that they ever intended to give the Commission free rein in negotiations. Politically, trade had always been highly sensitive – the European Coal and Steel Community had, after all, been set up in part to help post-war France's industrial reconstruction in which the steel trade played a huge part (Ludlow 1997: 13). There was always the suspicion that the Commission, with its 'pro-integration mission' (Armstrong and Bulmer 1998: 67) would make too many concessions at the negotiating table, ignite discord in a member state, which would then refuse to sign an accord at the outcome of any negotiations (as, for example, France later threatened

---

[5] It is worth remembering here that, as Meunier (2000: 107) points out, unanimity was not abandoned as the voting rule on external trade policy in 1966 even though the Treaty provided for this. This implies that the Commission's role was not simply a result of pragmatism but rather a bargain whose impact was closely monitored.

with the Final Accord of the Uruguay Round of GATT) and that this could ultimately jeopardize the entire European project. Therefore, the control mechanisms in Article 133 were particularly important in enabling Council to shape the negotiating mandate, the subject to which I now turn.

PRINCIPALS EXERTING CONTROL? NEGOTIATING THE COMMISSION'S MANDATE

As laid down in the Treaty, the Commission carries out multilateral negotiations on the basis of a mandate. This mandate has to be generated by the Commission in the first instance before submission to the Article 133 Committee, COREPER and the Council.

Once the Council formally agrees that the Commission can start negotiations, a general memo is circulated to Heads of Units in each Directorate-General (DG) with an interest, a briefing meeting is held at administrative level and then the representative of the DG gets together with all the other representatives of appropriate DGs in order to develop this draft for Commissioner approval. This is made complex because there are many Units, not to mention DGs, in the Commission with an interest in trade rounds (Bretherton and Vogler 2000). In the Uruguay Round, for example, although DGs I (External Relations) and VI (Agriculture) had the co-ordinating and negotiating roles, DG III (Industry) would also have had an interest and technical expertise in certain of the issues covered, as would DG VIII (Development), at least as far as relations between the EC and the developing countries were concerned. To arrive at the final version of a draft mandate there are, therefore, a number of often difficult internal meetings, from Commissioner to general administrative level,[6] to define a Commission position (Nugent 2001: 310–311, Cram 1997: 157) for submission to the Article 113 Committee.

The Article 113 Committee embodies 'the watchdog role of the member states' (Smith 1994: 256) but it also ensures that the Commission is 'kept fully abreast of positions in the Council' (Houben 1999: 300). Although the 113 Committee itself is a fairly recent construct, being established only in 1970, Lewis (2000: 277) notes that 'earlier Council groupings designed to deal with external trade date back to 1959'. Thus, the Council has always sought a role in mandate formation through a mechanism of this type. The 113 Committee consists of senior civil servants from each member state with a particular responsibility for trade. The Commission is also represented, as it has to present, and often argue, its case.

---

[6] I am speaking here from personal experience, having worked as a national expert in the European Commission (1996–99) specializing in technical barriers to trade.

The Article 113 Committee must be periodically consulted 'throughout the period of the negotiations' (Nugent 1999: 444), and is, in effect, a briefing and debriefing mechanism throughout the negotiation process. Although certain authors (e.g. Peterson and Bomberg 1999) have suggested that the Committee is confrontational, it is more the case that because its members tend to know each other, it 'work(s) with rather than against the Commission indicating to the latter what is and what is not likely to be accepted by Ministers' (Nugent 2001: 308). The 'continuity of membership' (Hayes 1993: 131) of the civil servants there means that they all meet each other at different times around other tables and tend to get to know each other, and most importantly, each other's priorities, quite well.

Once the Article 113 Committee has agreed the draft position, it is submitted to the next stage: scrutiny by COREPER. COREPER, an acronym for the Committee of Permanent Representatives (i.e. the representations of the member states in Brussels), is very important in the EU structure. It has a 'bottlenecking-effect' (Lewis 2000: 283) for the Council of Ministers in that items for the Council agenda first have to be passed through either COREPER II (the Committee of the Permanent Representatives) or COREPER I (the Committee of the Deputy Permanent Representatives). Bostock (2002: 232) notes that it is COREPER II which plays 'an essential role' in GATT/WTO negotiations. Although there is, officially, no hierarchy between the two COREPER groupings, it is nevertheless interesting that this function is taken by the Permanent Representatives themselves. This could provide further proof of the seriousness of the political agenda surrounding external trade.

Lewis (2000: 269–271) goes into great detail about the 'performance norms' of COREPER which he categorizes as 'thick trust, mutual responsiveness, the consensus-reflex and the culture of compromise', constituting a mutually supportive working environment. Rometsch and Wessels (1994: 205), however, suggest that this sometimes works against the Commission, whose officials have tended to see COREPER as their 'bureaucratic rivals', since COREPER officials 'not only knew Community procedures but were also a powerful body of experts'. However, Bostock (2002: 232) suggests that 'only in exceptional circumstances are COREPER discussions likely to call into question policy choices which have already been made', which I interpret as COREPER being unlikely to revisit (at least political) decisions taken at 133 Committee level.

Hine (1985: 94) reiterates that the ultimate power finally to approve the mandate before negotiations begin rests with the Council. In trade negotiations it is usually the General Affairs Council (GAC), consisting of foreign affairs ministers from the member states, which has this responsibility. However, Lewis (2000: 283) points out that nowadays the GAC is 'in decline ... described by many insiders as "laughable" or "clearly at the end of its capacity"'.[7] Nonetheless, because the agenda is so wide, it seems unlikely that discussion at this stage is substantive; instead it would probably focus on those issues highlighted by COREPER as having particular political significance where a steer from GAC would be necessary (Westlake 1999: 176). For example, in the Uruguay Round, France agreed to have agriculture on the agenda only 'in exchange for the inclusion ... of its most important concerns ... liberalization of investment and services, the issue of exchange rate fluctuations and the rebalancing of former privileges' (Meunier 1998: 198), whilst, at the same time, refusing to discuss audio-visual trade, which had been a particular request from the USA.

In any case, once the GAC approves the mandate, it is returned to the Commission, allowing it to begin the negotiating process. *Prima facie*, because of the processes that the mandate has to go through before the final version is sent to the Commission, perhaps one could assume that the document would be comprehensive in the extreme. Perhaps it should have considered all the sensitivities of each member state, perhaps it should leave nothing to doubt or interpretation. It should make targets clear and the means to reach them achievable, and it should consider the potential fall-back positions. Of course, this is impossible. To have a document which could mention all possible outcomes for all items would be impossible to negotiate with – better give the opponents a copy and wait for them to read it! Not only would the briefs be huge, having to discuss the ins and outs of every possible position but, more importantly, the mandate itself could not adequately reflect the national differences that are intrinsic to its interpretation. This aspect is particularly important, first, because the member states are also sitting around the GATT table, listening to the Commission all the while, as signatories to the Agreement. Second, as a result of the presence of different national agendas the Portuguese, for example, might think it most important to get an agreement with Countries X and Y on textile manufacture, the United Kingdom (UK) might believe that copyright agreements should be given first priority, and these positions would have to be carefully considered by the negotiators. This is summed up by Chryssochoou (1998: 193), who suggests that the Commission, when negotiating, has to 'strike a balance between the two contradictory but by no means mutually exclusive principles: national autonomy and transnational unity'. Thus, it is important that the Commission represents the Council

---

[7] This is echoed in the European Commission's White Paper on Governance 2001 which says that GAC 'is no longer capable of exerting the necessary leadership' (p. 29).

to the latter's satisfaction but, at the same time, the Commission has a duty (also set out in the EEC Treaty) to foster harmonious trading relationships between the EU and the rest of the world.

The member states, then, are able to exert a strong degree of control over how the Commission's mandate is developed (through the Committee structure from the EEC Treaty). This does not mean, however, that the Commission has no influence. In fact, there are four ways in which the Commission can exert influence in the process of developing the mandate.

First, as Schmidt (2000: 41) suggests, the Commission can take advantage of the member states' 'differences in interests' in order to escape direct Council control. Because of the negotiator's need to have the flexibility to adopt a compromise position, it would be difficult to exert pressure for specific results (this is explored further below). Second, the EU perspective is only one of the many that need to be considered at the table. Although the member states may have an idea of the main wishes of the other parties, the Commission may, through its Representations and network of informal contacts outside the EU, have a more thorough understanding of the positions to be taken by opponents at an early stage in the development of the mandate, which it can use to exhort the Council to be more flexible on particular issues. Third, the Commission tries to make sure that there is a strong possibility that its view will prevail with the member states when the mandate is being developed Therefore, its officials attempt to 'legitimize their own position through the setting up of a number of committees' (Cini 1996: 132), taking advantage of the close contacts between Commission officials and their national counterparts in the trade ministries (or, indeed, agricultural, transport, development ministries, etc.) of the member states. Through this mechanism, which can be formal or informal, the Commission can use senior national officials (perhaps even those who sit at the Article 133 Committee table) as a sounding board before submitting their proposals officially. In this way, member states feel that they are being given an insight into the policy generation processes of the Commission, while the Commission uses committees to refine their proposals and build up allies around the table.[8] Finally, the Commission knows that the mandate itself is not set in stone. The Commission is able to return to the Article 133 Committee for an amended mandate if it needs more flexibility or if the negotiations have stalled for any reason (Nugent 1999). Woolcock (1993: 556) points out that although in the original mandate for Uruguay the European Commission was instructed to oppose the setting up of a dispute resolution mechanism with more teeth, by 1991 the European

---

[8] This section is informed by my experience with informal committees of senior civil servants.

Commission had endorsed Section 5 of the draft final act of the Uruguay Round which contains just that. Therefore although the mandate is important in defining, in general terms, what Ministers will accept, it does not mean that it cannot, ultimately, be changed.

I now turn to the negotiations themselves and how the Commission can again use its expertise in the informal politics of negotiation to influence them.

AGENTS EXERCIZING AUTONOMY? THE NEGOTIATION PROCESS

The Formal Role: the Flexible Mandate

Formally, as has been noted above, the Commission's role in trade negotiations is shaped by the negotiating mandate issued by the Council. Certainly in the Uruguay Round the Commission was concerned that it would be unable to operate effectively if this mandate proved too narrow. Meunier (2000: 105) suggests that a loose mandate is important because otherwise the EU does not have 'a lot to offer its negotiating opponent in order to extract concessions' and, furthermore, 'the EU cannot hide its bottom line' because this is included in its mandate. She suggests, then, that for the Commission to negotiate successfully it needs to have significant flexibility at the negotiating table.

Jupille and Caporaso (1998: 214–9) believe that the EU structure actually gives the Commission that flexibility. They suggest four criteria of 'actorness' (recognition, authority, autonomy and cohesion), which, if applied to the Commission's role in external trade policy negotiations, lend support to such a claim. For Jupille and Caporaso the first criterion cannot be applied successfully here, because the EU, with the Commission as its mouthpiece, is not a contracting party to the GATT. However, the EU (and the Commission in particular) does meet the second criterion because the 'legal competence to act' is given to the Commission by the member states through the Council's negotiating mandate. Jupille and Caporaso classify autonomy as 'institutional distinctiveness and independence from other actors', meaning specifically state actors. The Commission would seem to have this through its 'distinctive institutional apparatus' and by its ability to 'go(ing) outside standard operating procedures'. Finally, Jupille and Caporaso argue that the Commission can, at least to some extent, create and elaborate its own preferred policy outcomes which are internally coherent.

Schmidt (2000: 41) takes this notion of flexibility even further, as I hinted earlier in the text. He argues that the principal/agent relationship between the Council and the Commission actually allows the Commission to evade control. He gives three reasons why this is so:

1) the Commission can 'profit from information asymmetries'
2) the Commission can take advantage of the 'different capacities for long-term planning' between themselves and the member states, and,
3) the Commission can 'exploit differences in interests among multiple principals'

He infers, then, that the Commission can use the benefit of its wide institutional knowledge and experience, that is, it can factor in extra time for negotiations and it can push its view forward as a compromise position. This puts the Commission in a strong position when it is negotiating. There is some evidence to support this assertion in the Uruguay Round where, especially towards the end with the Blair House Agreement, a vital compromise package was negotiated between the USA and the European Commission on aspects of agricultural policy despite serious gaps between the positions of the member states.

Devuyst (1995: 455) goes into these areas of dissent in some detail. It is enough here, however, to see what they were and how they were resolved. First, France, Ireland and Belgium thought that the Agreement went further than the proposed changes to the Common Agricultural Policy as set out in the MacSharry Plan;[9] second, France was concerned that the Blair House Agreement would 'exclude the Community from participation in the foreseeable expansion of world agricultural markets'; third, France, Ireland, Belgium, Germany, Italy and Luxembourg were concerned that the measures in place which complied with GATT rules should be untouchable for longer than the six years of the implementation period for the tariff cuts and export subsidies reductions; finally, the UK was determined not to reopen the negotiations while the French were, conversely, determined to renegotiate.

Ultimately, the Commission was able not only to defuse a potentially catastrophic (for the EU and the other GATT members) situation whereby one member could have vetoed the entire Agreement, by agreeing to revisit some of the decisions made at Blair House, but they also managed to persuade the Americans to agree to meet again after the USA had said that the issues were effectively resolved (see Meunier 2000: 126). Ultimately, then, '(Commissioner) Brittan managed to defuse French requests for a reopening of the package' agreeing instead to seek 'clarification of a number of aspects' (Swinbank and Tanner 1996: 109), while, at the same time, the Commission was successful in 'getting even

---

[9] The MacSharry Plan was put forward by the Agricultural Commissioner, Ray MacSharry, with proposed changes to the Common Agricultural Policy.

more concessions from the USA' (Reiger 2000: 198) on behalf of the member states.

The Commission, then, does have a limited flexibility in the formal side of the negotiations. However, the informal mechanisms that have arisen from them allow the Commission to take initiatives and to propose individual solutions to particular problems. I will show the importance of the informal processes around the negotiations below. Most of my evidence is participant observation: it is taken from personal experience of representing the Commission at the negotiating table and illustrates the importance of knowing how the game of negotiation is played. This is where the Commission has a huge institutional advantage.

The Informal Role: Playing the Game

In reality, negotiating trade agreements begins well before one sits at a table in Washington, Geneva or Brussels. The EU must ensure that the agenda for the negotiations reflects its chief concerns, as elaborated in the mandate. Although as a major player the EU can expect to get most of the items it wants on the agenda and keep off those items it wishes to exclude, there are still informal discussions to be had with the other parties in order to define the order and content of the agenda. After that stage, the agenda is circulated before the formal talks begin to allow the participants to start to gather their briefs.

As a negotiator sitting at the table with any organization, one studies the agenda and tries to second-guess what the opponents are going to say for each point and how they will react to the issues that are raised. How can one make one's proposals more palatable? What can be given in return? Perhaps there is a small budget line in an assistance programme, which can be used as a 'sweetener' – perhaps for the most recalcitrant country, or perhaps for a group of them. Perhaps by making a concession at the table, one can get an armful of more important concessions, which are of much more value to the EU.

All participants are likely to know quite a lot about the other people representing key countries and the sectors within them. If they are negotiating on the Commission side, they will have intelligence about the participants, and their likely stance, from the Commission Representation in the country concerned. Perhaps one of the other delegation leaders said something unguarded in a conversation, which can be used to Commission advantage. Perhaps one country is likely to be difficult on Item 1 but will thaw later if it achieves a favourable outcome on Item 4. Perhaps someone has spoken to them in a previous forum, and a little bilateral meeting beforehand 'with more than a glass of water' (Hayes 1993: 131) will iron out any difficulties. Perhaps they share educational backgrounds with key people around the table. They may share political affiliations or perhaps one of the negotiators knows that they like coming to one of the EU countries on holiday, giving a negotiator a useful excuse to talk to them outside the meeting and bring up, by chance of course, certain questions that he or she may have on their stance. The importance of negotiating skill, personality, shared experience and mutual interest should not be underrated (see Taylor's [1983] analysis of the Commission's role in the GATT Tokyo Round).

In the case of the Uruguay Round, the Commission was able to marshal all these resources, ultimately negotiating a successful agreement. Indeed, the Commission played the lead role in information gathering (Coleman and Tangermann 1999) and coalition formation (Smith 1999). It was also able to bridge significant divisions both externally (the USA saw the EU as a rival, standing in the way of a level playing field in agriculture [Hocking and Smith 1997]), and internally (both between its then President, Jacques Delors, and the then Commissioner for Agriculture, Ray MacSharry, as well as between the member states, most notably between France and Germany [Cini 1996]).

Thus the Uruguay outcome indicates the Commission's skill in meeting the goals of the member states by using its expertise in negotiation practice, lobbying and the inbuilt flexibility of the mandate. However, given both the growing contentiousness of the global trade agenda and the current context of institutional reform in the EU, which builds on the Commission's own White Paper on European Governance, I close the chapter by asking whether the process of re-thinking the EU is likely to undermine the Commission's role in external trade policy.

CONCLUSIONS: NEW CHALLENGES TO THE COMMISSION?

As international trade negotiations have progressed, they have become more rather than less controversial and complex: for example, the Uruguay Round suffered from the fact that most of the more straightforward issues had already been addressed (Moon 1996). As a parallel phenomenon, the growing strength of the EU as an economic bloc has led to increased tension with the USA over matters of trade regulation. Given this increasing complexity and controversy, it is plausible that the member states may seek to reduce the flexibility which is the secret of the Commission's success in representing their collective interests externally.

Brulhart and McAleese (2001: 525) point out that the Commission's negotiating role may become more difficult in the future as a result of another issue, 'the growing heterogeneity among EU members (which) is likely to increase the difficulty of reaching consensus on trade policy' (see also Neunreither 2000: 194). This is going to be made more complicated after enlargement where there will be additional countries to consider, each with its own views on trade priorities and sensitivities.

However, there is as yet no convincing proposal for a different way of carrying out external trade negotiations. As discussed at the beginning of this chapter, when the EEC Treaty was being developed there were three choices of negotiator: the Commission, the Council or an independent agency. Although in theory the Council could take over the role of negotiator, this is unlikely because it would require significant and extensive reform to the basic institutional structure and balance of the EU. It would also require a change to the EEC Treaty, which would be subject to unanimity in Council. Such unanimity is unlikely. As Devuyst says (1995: 463), the conflict between the interventionists and free traders could be felt in any debate. Moreover, such a change would run counter to the main reason behind the creation of the present *modus operandi*, namely the ability of the member states to shift blame for unpopular decisions to the Commission, a cynical logic which the Fifteen appear to like quite as much as the Six. The other alternative would be to establish an independent, specialist agency. Such agencies have proliferated since the 1950s and are now an established feature of EU governance in many policy areas. However, in external trade policy the cross-sectoral linkages are so extensive that any such agency would face significant organizational problems. Moreover, it would in all likelihood fail to bring to the negotiating table the knowledge, breadth and depth of experience and political acumen that the Commission has acquired.

In sum, then, it is likely that the Commission will continue to act as the agent of the member states in international trade negotiations, using its skills in both formal and informal practices to lobby for outcomes which suit the purposes of the member states. In the current climate, and given the general logic of European integration, the Commission is perhaps unlikely to be the recipient of further authority in this area. By the same token, however, the Commission's ability to 'speak for Europe' on issues of external trade policy appears likely to remain: despite its increasingly atypical relative autonomy in this area, the Commission is not only a useful servant of the member states but able to use its own means to achieve their aims. For these reasons, the member states are likely to conclude that it is 'better the agent they know' than the agency they don't.

REFERENCES

Andersen, S. and Eliassen, K. (eds) (1993): *Making Policy in Europe* (London: Sage).

Armstrong, K. and Bulmer, S. (1998): *The Governance of the Single European Market* (Manchester: Manchester University Press).

Bretherton, C. and Vogler, J. (2000): 'The EU as Trade Actor and Environmental Activist: Contradictory Roles?' *Journal of Economic Integration* 15:2, 163–194.

Bostock, D. (2002): 'Coreper Revisited', *Journal of Common Market Studies* 40:2, 215–34.

Brülhart, M. and McAleese, D. (2001): 'External Trade Policy', in A. El-Agraa (ed.) *The European Union Economics and Policies* (Harlow: Pearson), 498–526.

Chryssochoou, D., Tsinisizelis, M., Stavridis, S. and Infantis, K. (1999): *Theory and Reform in the EU* (Manchester and New York: Manchester University Press).

Chryssochoou, D. (1998): *Democracy in the European Union* (London: Tauris Academic Studies).

Cini, M. (1996): *The European Commission* (Manchester: Manchester University Press).

Coleman, W. and Tangermann, S. (1999): 'The 1992 CAP Reform, the Uruguay Round and the Commission: Conceptualizing Linked Policy Games', *Journal of Common Market Studies* 37:3, 385–405.

Commission of the European Communities – European Governance: A White Paper COM(2001)428 final, 25.7.2001, Brussels.

Cram, L. (1997): *Policy Making in the EU. Conceptual Lenses and the integration process* (London: Routledge).

Demaret, P. (2000): 'The Respective Powers of the European Community and Member States in Transatlantic Regulatory Co-operation', in G. A. Bermann, M. Herdegen and P. Lindseth (eds) *Transatlantic Regulatory Co-operation* (Oxford: Oxford University Press), 431–449.

Devuyst, Y. (1995): 'The European Community and the Conclusion of the Uruguay Round', in C. Rhodes and S. Mazey (eds) *The State of the Union Volume 3 – Building a European Polity?* (Boulder, Colorado: Lynne Reiner), 449–467.

Dinan, D. (1999): *Ever Closer Union – An introduction to European integration* (Basingstoke: Macmillan).

Dobbin, F. (1993): 'What Do Markets Have In Common? Towards A Fast Train Policy for the EC', in S. Andersen and K. Eliassen (eds) *Making Policy in Europe* (London: Sage), 71–114.

Hayes, J. P. (1993): *Making Trade Policy in the European Community* (Basingstoke: Macmillan).

Hine, R. C. (1985): *The Political Economy of Foreign Trade: An introduction to the trade policies of the EEC* (Brighton: Harvester-Wheatsheaf).

Hocking, B. and Smith, M. (1997): *Beyond Foreign Economic Policy: The United States, the Single European Market and the Changing World Economy* (London: Pinter).

Houben, H. (1999): 'The 113 Committee' in M. Westlake *The Council of the European Union* (London: John Harper), 299–302.

Jupille, J. and Caporaso, J. (1998): 'States, Agency and Rules: The EU in Global Environmental Politics', in C. Rhodes (ed.) *The European Union in the World Community* (London: Lynne Riener), 213–229.

Lewis, J. (2000): 'The Methods of Community in EU Decision-Making and Administrative Rivalry in the Council's Infrastructure', *Journal of European Public Policy* 7:2, 261–289.

Ludlow, N. P. (1997): *Dealing with Britain – The Six and the First UK Application to the EEC* (Cambridge: Cambridge University Press).

Memedovic, O., Kuyvenhoven, A. and Molle, W. (1999): *Multilateralism and Regionalism in the post-Uruguay Round Era. What Role for the EU?* (Dordrecht: Kluwer Academic Press).

Meunier, S. (1998): 'Divided but United: European Trade Policy Integration and EU-US Agricultural Negotiations in the Uruguay Round', in C. Rhodes (ed.) *The European Union in the World Community* (London: Lynne Riener), 193–211.

Meunier, S. (2000): 'What Single Voice? European Institutions and EU-US Trade Negotiations', *International Organization* 54:1, 103–135.

Meunier, S. and Nicolaides, K. (1999): 'Who Speaks for Europe? The Delegation of Trade Authority in the EU', *Journal of Common Market Studies* 37:3, 477–501.

Moon, B. (1996): *Dilemmas of International Trade* (Colorado, Oxford: Westview).

Murphy, A. (1996): *The European Community and the International Trading System Vol 2* (Brussels: CEPS).

Neunreither, K. (2001): 'The European Union in Nice: A Minimalist Approach', *Government and Opposition* 36:2, 184–208.

Nugent, N. (1999): *The Government and Politics of the European Union* (Basingstoke: Palgrave).

Nugent, N. (2001): *The European Commission* (Basingstoke: Palgrave).

Nugent, N. and Saurugger, S. (2002): 'Organizational Structuring: The Case of the European Commission and its External Policy', *Journal of European Public Policy* 9:3, 345–64.

Peterson, J. and Bomberg, E. (1999): *Decision Making in the European Union* (Basingstoke: Macmillan).

Pollack, M. A. (2000): 'The End of Creeping Competence? EU Policy Making Since Maastricht', *Journal of Common Market Studies* 38:3, 519–538.

Rieger, E. (2000): 'The Common Agricultural Policy', in H. Wallace and W. Wallace (eds) *Policy Making in the European Union* (Oxford: Oxford University Press), 373–399.

Rometsch, D. and Wessels, W. (1994): 'The Commission and the Council of Ministers', in G. Edwards and D. Spence *The European Commission* (Harlow: Longman), 202–224.

Rosamond, B. (2000): *Theories of European Integration* (Basingstoke: Macmillan).

Schmidt, S. K. (2000): 'Only An Agenda Setter? The European Commission's Power Over the Council of Ministers' *European Union Politics* 1:1, 37–61.

Smith, M. (1994): 'The Commission and External Relations', in G. Edwards and D. Spence (eds) *The European Commission* (Harlow: Longman), 249–273.

Smith, M. (1999): 'Regions in World Trade – the EU', in B. Hocking and S. McGuire (eds) *Trade Politics – International, Domestic and Regional Perspectives* (London and New York: Routledge), 275–289.

Stirk, P. and Weigall, D. (1999): *The Origins and Development of European Integration – A Reader and Commentary* (London: Pinter).

Swinbank, A. and Tanner, C. (1996): *Farm Policy and Trade Conflict* (Ann Arbor: University of Michigan Press).

Taylor, P. (1983): *The Limits of European Integration* (New York: Columbia University Press).

Teasdale, A. L. (1999): 'The Life and Death of the Luxembourg Compromise', *Journal of Common Market Studies* 31:4, 567–579.

Warleigh, A. (1998): 'Better the Devil You Know? Synthetic and Confederal Understandings of European Unification', *West European Politics*, 21:3, 1–18.

Westlake, M. (1999): *The Council of the European Union* (London: John Harper).

Woolcock, S. (1993): 'The European Acquis and Multilateral Trade Rules: Are They Compatible?', *Journal of Common Market Studies*, 31:4, 539–558.

Chapter 5

The European Parliament as Entrepreneur: New Trends, New Challenges

David Earnshaw, Josephine Wood and Alex Warleigh

INTRODUCTION

The European Parliament (EP; Parliament) is now an important and influential European Union (EU) institution with the power to amend legislation, act as joint budgetary authority with the Council of Ministers, grant discharge of the budget, appoint EU actors (including Commissioners and the Ombudsman) and dismiss the Commission (Burns 2001). Successive Treaty changes in recent years have granted the EP increasing formal significance: indeed, Parliament is now empowered by the Co-decision procedure to act as co-legislator with the Council of Ministers in most areas of legislation adopted under the first pillar. However, the EP still does not appear to be recognized by member-state citizens and publics as an instrument with which to make EU decision making more democratic. The newly empowered Parliament has so far appeared to be less than worthwhile to EU citizens, at least if turn-out rates at EP elections, which are actually declining, are a valid indicator. Crucially, instead of claiming authority by being the 'voice of the people(s)', in fact, much of Parliament's influence to date has depended upon its ability to act entrepreneurially in pursuit of its own interests. These cannot automatically be assumed to be the same as those of EU citizens. As one of us argues elsewhere (Warleigh 2001), in EU politics, as in other systems, institutions are often far from neutral. They seek not only to promote their own interests and condition the world-views of actors within them, but also to impede outsiders' ability to contribute to policy making. Thus, as the EP's powers and influence have grown, it is not entirely surprising that this has failed to translate into greater legitimacy.

The EP's lack of legitimacy may be because it has only recently emerged as an institution with a clear and powerful role in the EU's decision-making process. Parliament has long been required to represent its interests – that is, to act to protect its formal powers when the member states appeared to wish to disregard them – and has sometimes been able to do so only by enlisting the support of the European Court of Justice (ECJ) (Bradley 1987). Thus, Parliament's recognition as a powerful body by the public is questionable. Indeed, even expert scholars debate whether the creation of co-decision in the Maastricht Treaty (Treaty on European Union, 1992), or its revision by the Amsterdam Treaty (1997), marks the point at which the step-change in the EP's formal status occurred (see below). However, in any case the EP has had, at the time of writing, at most ten years as an officially recognized and powerful legislator. In a transnational polity such as the EU, where decision making appears distant and unfamiliar to most citizens, this is not a long time in which to permeate or change popular perception. According to Blondel, Svensson and Smith (1998), in fact, the EU institution most commonly perceived to act in the citizens' interest is the European Court of Justice (ECJ), not the EP.

Nonetheless, the EP's importance as a legislative actor has certainly grown over time. Parliament has been adept at using its rules of procedure to develop influence over the legislative process in anticipation of formal powers to do so (Burns 2001). In addition, the EP has often been able to secure its goals through active membership of EU policy networks and skilful use of the relatively small powers it enjoys (Elles 1984; Corbett 1989). Thus, it has been able to develop significant expertise in informal as well as formal politics. There is no doubt that the EP has a strong track record as what Laura Cram (1997) calls a 'purposeful opportunist', that is, as an institution (or at least a set of actors) which is capable of identifying, pursuing and securing its aims by means of a range of strategies that exploit accidental or fortuitous events as they arise. However, an issue which is far less clear is the extent to which Parliament's various powers will allow it to adapt to the challenges of post-Nice politics in the EU.

This is for one principal reason: the fact that the formal empowerment of the Parliament through co-decision serves to reinforce rather than remove its need for mastery of informal politics. Co-decision is a complex procedure, requiring intricate inter- and intra-institutional negotiation in Brussels and Strasbourg (and even Luxembourg – it was not entirely insignificant for its future that the final conciliation meeting on a recently negotiated Directive, for example, took place in Luxembourg), as well as interaction with extra-institutional actors and those at the member state level if it is to work. This is because both Council and Parliament can veto any proposed legislation under the Co-decision procedure, should they be unable to reach a mutually acceptable agreement. Thus, neither of them can afford to seek to impose their preferences on a proposal which the other considers important, especially when the two institutions differ in their view of the substantive content of the proposal. Moreover, in a legislative process which requires input from at least three internally pluralistic, and often divided, supranational institutions, not to mention attention to, and participation by, actors powerful in the domestic politics of the member states, the potential for what Crombez (1996; 2001) calls 'indecision' – the failure to agree policy – is high in the absence of such iterated networking and negotiation. Thus, the EP's ability to influence legislative outcomes depends upon two key factors: first, Parliament's ability to preserve its internal unity, second, its capacity at least to co-construct a winning coalition of actors in an alliance which reaches horizontally into both Commission and Council and vertically into the member states. That Parliament is capable of this appears beyond doubt (Garman and Hilditch 1998; Warleigh 2000). However, what is also clear is that under such complex and intricate legislative procedures as those of the EU, formal empowerment (that is, the right to participate in the process) is only the first step. Developing and using the skills of informal politics are the keys to translating formal power into real-world influence and, as a consequence, the EP must continue to behave as a 'purposeful opportunist' if it is to have legislative weight.

In this chapter we seek to establish the extent to which Parliament is capable of exploiting the opportunity granted to it by co-decision to be a real legislative force in the EU system. We first set out briefly what we consider to be some of the key variables in the changing policy-making context of the Union. Subsequently we investigate the EP's history as an entrepreneur, which we characterize as an actor which can 'mobilize and manipulate policy-building resources in order to sustain policy change and policy replacement' (Wallace 1996: 28), and analyse the impact of co-decision on this history. We then proceed to examine new challenges to Parliament's ability to continue this success (such as the apparent decline of the 'Grand Coalition' in the EP, and the advent of new, or at least newly significant, cleavages in the Parliament). Our argument is that Parliament appears to be capable of meeting many of these new challenges, but also that the complexity of the inter-institutional politics of co-decision and the secrecy of its endgame – 'conciliation' between EP and Council – may make it difficult for Parliament to use its legislative powers as a means to improve its perceived legitimacy with the public. The EP has had to learn to use informal politics to develop its powers, and even after co-decision it is principally through informal politics that Parliament matters as a legislative force. Consequently, it may be that the biggest challenge for Parliament will actually be to translate its often considerable powers into a higher public standing.

SOME NEW TRENDS IN EU DECISION MAKING[1]

Over the last few years certain important trends in EU policy making have emerged, or at least become more apparent. Many of the traditional features of EU politics are changing, or even disappearing, as a result of the post-Maastricht process of slowly deepening European integration. For example, the Commission has clearly become less central to the policy-making process than in the past (in particular under co-decision) if, indeed, it remains important. Thus, relations between the EU institutions are in an ongoing process of evolution and change, meaning that whilst the EU is a dynamic and evolving system it is also one with significant instability (Richardson 1996). To some extent there is nothing new about the EU being in a state of permanent change in the period post-Maastricht, for change and evolution have always been important characteristics of the EU's constitutional make-up. On the other hand, the 1990s and the beginning of the 21st century have witnessed a speed of change and a growth of its significance out of all proportion to the change that occurred in earlier periods of EU history.

The executive and legislative functions of 'government' at EU level continue to be shared by the EP, Commission and Council, albeit according to a formula which is itself subject to continual review and revision. Thus, the institutions – or at least, key actors from each of them – must operate in partnership to make the policy-making process work. Moreover, the EU now makes meaningful policy in a far greater number and range of issue areas than previously, and these areas now include some of those which would be classified as core components of national sovereignty, such as the Rapid Reaction Force and the single currency. Political integration is catching up with economic integration, even if the latter remains more advanced. Hence, EU politics today is becoming more about the political choices that are more normally associated with the national polity in Europe. However, by the same token the EU is a more flexible and variegated system than before: it is also increasingly being 'hollowed out', in that many of its new competences rely upon benchmarking, regulation and new forms of intergovernmental co-operation and 'soft policy' rather than strong central authority (Wallace 2000).

In terms of the mechanics of day-to-day decision making, significant changes are also evident. Policy-making has become a more politicized and less predictable process as the issue areas addressed have proliferated. Globalization, new modes of political activism and the speed of

---

[1] An obvious change here is the growth in influence of the EP itself. However, as we discuss this below in some detail, we do not focus on it here.

change in contemporary technology are exerting new pressures on the EU system, opening up Easton's 'black box' to a greater extent than previously.[2] The increased competences of the EU have resulted in its becoming a vital reference point for ever greater numbers of interest groups (Marks and McAdam 1996), and even, to some extent, individual citizens (Wiener 1998). The increased range of EU competence has also raised the stakes involved for all those seeking to affect EU decisions. Put simply, more actors now seek to shape what the EU does and, as a result of the EU's increasing powers, what it does matters more. This has made EU decision making a more unpredictable process, because the number of actors involved has grown significantly at the same time as the 'Community Method' of decision making (in which, typically, the policy-making process was a Commission–Council dialogue that generated a uniform polity based on 'hard' policy) has been increasingly abandoned, or at least supplemented.

Thus, there is something of an irony to be noted in that the EU's shift towards 'soft policy' has been accompanied by an increase in the competitiveness of the EU arena: national governments, EU institutional actors and diverse kinds of organized interest groups must compete and ally with one another in order to secure their objectives. Private interest groups now often appear to lobby through '*ad hoc* coalitions' made with actors other than those in their own trade federation, because this *modus operandi* allows clarity of focus, flexibility, greater retention of independence and reduced potential for free-riding (Pijnenburg 1998). One of us (Warleigh 2000) has argued that a similar approach can also be seen on the part of other actors, including the EU institutions, member governments and public interest groups. Indeed, making an impact on EU policy outcomes now regularly requires actors to 'hustle', i.e. to create issue-specific alliances based on symmetrical concerns and the pursuit of marginal advantage rather than shared values. Thus, EU decision making has become a highly complicated process of alliance construction in which entrepreneurship is vital for non-accidental success. Another factor leading to the relevance of the 'hustle' model to describe EU decision making is the secular decline of ideological politics in Europe. Whereas previously ideology defined and structured politics in Europe, this is being replaced across the EU countries (albeit in varying degrees in different countries) with a political style founded less in ideology and more in electoral calculation. In such a political style the 'hustle' is obviously a more appropriate strategy for actors seeking to influence political outcomes.

---

[2] David Easton's ground-breaking work on political systems and how they function can be read in Easton 1965a, Easton 1965b.

THE EP AS ENTREPRENEUR

Before Co-decision

For the EP as a legislative actor the changes described above have offered significant new opportunities. The relative decline of the Commission has allowed Parliament to fill something of the gap thereby created, as the member states may even have intended when creating co-decision (Moravcsik 1999). The part played by the EP in the demise of the Santer Commission, for example, was unprecedented, giving Parliament at least temporarily a greater prominence with the public. Furthermore, its increase in formal powers has lent it both credibility in Brussels circles and greater attractiveness as a venue for lobbying, with the result that its ability to play the network system has increased impressively (because Parliament has both the formal right to be present and the consequent ability to make alliances with greater numbers of actors). In seeking to capitalize on these opportunities Parliament has drawn on its entrepreneurial expertise, which we mentioned above but discuss more fully here.

The EP has long been able to use its limited formal powers to good effect by the adoption of strategic behaviour. This is not to say that Parliament has always been at the heart of EU legislation. However, the EP has been able to use various devices to advance its interests more successfully than might be imagined from a *prima facie* examination of the Treaty. For instance, Own Initiative Reports have been adopted by the Parliament as a means of moving issues up the Commission agenda and thus making a legislative proposal more likely (Judge and Earnshaw 1994). When the EP has been able to raise public support for its stance, such reports have even influenced decisions made by the Council (Elles 1984) – although such cases are perhaps not statistically significant. Individual members of the EP (MEPs), their staff and EP officials, particularly those working for the party groups, have been able to act as innovators. In an evolving system such as the EU the potential for creativity is great and EP actors have occasionally been able to shape the system by simply taking the initiative and proposing action to member states and the Commission, often successfully (see for example Judge and Earnshaw 1994 on the role of the EP Environment Committee and its then Chairman, Ken Collins, in the creation of the European Environment Agency). Moreover, EP actors have tended to concentrate their legislative activities in areas which maximize their formal power: research by Earnshaw and Judge (1995) indicated that most MEPs sought to focus on proposals which carried the co-operation procedure, which gave the EP its maximum legislative importance in the pre-Maastricht period.

However, it is the perception of the need to develop interinstitutional dialogue which has been the key to Parliament's influence. As Hubschmid and Moser (1997) show, even under the Co-operation Procedure (which gave the EP the ability to propose amendments to a given piece of legislation and a second reading of Council's position on it, but no power ultimately to insist upon its own view) Parliament was regularly able to shape legislative outcomes by acting to ensure support for its position in the Commission and Council. In essence, the EP made good its lack of a veto power by constructing alliances with actors who did have it, enlisting the support of key Commission actors and exploiting differences of opinion between the member states. Of course, this gave the EP influence at one remove and required it to be a very skilful negotiator, not least because without Commission support for amendments by Parliament it could have no influence whatsoever in the post-proposal stage of the policy process (Earnshaw and Judge 1996). By developing these entre-preneurial skills, Parliament nonetheless managed to acquire at least some legislative power before the Maastricht Treaty.

After Co-decision[3]

In its Maastricht Treaty form co-decision gave both EP and Council two readings of the Commission's proposal but now provided for a process known as conciliation if the two institutions were unable to agree on the content of legislation. The goal of the conciliation process (held with only Parliament and Council as formal participants) was to produce a 'joint text', which would then be approved by both institutions. If conciliation failed, the Council could seek to impose its own view (the 'Common Position' of the member states), unless the EP rejected it by an absolute majority, in which case there would be no legislation.

As revised at Amsterdam, co-decision is a somewhat more streamlined process, with the emphasis still on conciliation but with the ability of the Council to impose its Common Position formally removed. Thus, if conciliation fails, there is no legislation and both institutions are hence under greater pressure to reach an agreement. The Amsterdam Treaty also enabled this agreement to be made after both institutions have had their first reading of the proposal. If Council and EP can agree at that stage, there is now no need to undertake the second readings and conciliation. Fundamentally, co-decision created a political context in which the wishes of 15 national governments alone could no longer determine EU outcomes. The EP henceforth had veto power by wielding an absolute majority at second reading, or even by simple majority at third reading (as in the case of biotechnology patenting in 1995, and the takeover directive in 2001).

---

[3] The following paragraphs draw on Warleigh 2003 (forthcoming), chapter 4.

Amongst scholars co-decision has been controversial on three main counts. First, it has been questioned whether the procedure really empowers the Parliament or whether it is an elaborate mechanism by which the member states retain all meaningful power whilst weakening the Commission (Moravcsik 1999; Garrett and Tsebelis 1996). Second, it has been contended that a meaningful transfer of power to the EP did occur, but at Amsterdam rather than at Maastricht (Tsebelis and Garrett 2001). Third, it has been suggested that the empowerment of the EP, at least regarding the post-Amsterdam variant of co-decision, is a risk for the EU system because it makes 'indecision' (the failure to agree legislation) more likely (Crombez 2001).

Andrew Moravcsik's (1999) account of co-decision is a useful illustration of the first school of thought. In this view co-decision is a deliberate tactic to dissolve the traditional, if by no means always reliable, alliance between the EP and the Commission by a strategy of divide-and-rule. For Moravcsik, co-decision represents not so much a transfer of sovereignty from national to EU level, but rather a redistribution of the powers already delegated to the Union by the member states in favour of the EP and to the detriment of the Commission. This was done by reducing the power of the Commission to reject amendments proposed by the EP, and by making it far easier for Parliament to negotiate directly with Council. Moravcsik argues that it is important to remember the limited scope of co-decision. Even after the Nice Treaty it still does not apply across the board, and it does nothing to reduce the Commission's formal near-monopoly on the right of legislative initiative in the first pillar.

Moravcsik's arguments hold at least some water. Westlake (1994) points out that MEPs were initially wary of co-decision, some of them considering that the Maastricht variant left Council in the dominant position. Dankert (1997) argues that the main policy areas to which the procedure initially applied – those relating to the single market – reduced the importance of co-decision, not because this policy area is unimportant but because the bulk of the relevant legislation was already in place. Moreover, as pointed out by Dinan (1997), co-decision did nothing to reduce the use of comitology, meaning that EP influence over the general content of legislation might be outweighed by the influence wielded by national experts sitting on the relevant technical committees.[4]

Other commentators (Garrett and Tsebelis 1996; Tsebelis *et al.* 2001) have argued that at least the initial variant of co-decision in fact

---

[4] However, as pointed out by Garman and Hilditch (1998), the EP has in fact used conciliation negotiations to raise the issue of comitology and secure certain changes. Burns (2001) points out that since 1999 the EP and Council have agreed a *modus operandi* on comitology.

undermined both the Commission and the EP. According to Garrett and Tsebelis the EP's supposed veto power was actually very unlikely to be used, because a majority of MEPs would prefer almost any legislation to a legislative vacuum, in order to boost the *acquis communautaire*. Thus, those actors likely to be truly advantaged by co-decision were those national governments whose preferences were close to those of the EP, and who could use the threat of an EP veto as a device to generate a Council position which reflected their own position. However, it is unclear why some governments would perceive the fallacious nature of the EP's veto threat and others would not, particularly as the governments whose preferences are close to those of Parliament are likely to change according to the issue at hand. Tsebelis *et al.* argue that (at least under the Maastricht regime) the EP did less well in terms of proposing amendments which actually reached the statute book under co-decision than it had under the co-operation procedure, because it was obliged under co-operation to make effective interinstitutional partnerships. These partnerships represented a joint position of many stakeholders from different institutions rather than a unilateral stance adopted by the Parliament as a sole actor, meaning that the EP was more likely to be part of the winning coalition of actors, even if by the same token that influence was likely to be limited by the constraints of the partnership. Co-decision could thus be dangerous for the Parliament if it was thereby tempted to forget the need to make interinstitutional alliances and rely on its ability to veto.

However, this danger appears to have been something of a 'phantom menace'. Garman and Hilditch (1998) demonstrate that Parliament, Commission and Council all learned to make the conciliation process function successfully with remarkable speed, laying particular emphasis on the 'trialogues': informal meetings between key actors from each institution, which enable negotiations to progress 'behind the scenes' and then receive formal approval. Scully (1997) has argued that conciliation often works to the advantage of the EP, since its delegation is far more flexible than that of the Council, whose members must refer back to their national capitals for guidance during negotiations. Thus, it can be easier for the EP than the Council to be entrepreneurial during conciliation. And the Parliament may therefore be more likely than Council to generate an interinstitutional compromise in its favour. Indeed, one of us (Earnshaw and Judge [1996]) found that even in the early days of co-decision the EP was able to help produce legislation which was significantly different from both the Commission's proposal and the Council's Common Position. Most significantly, it appears that the member states acknowledge this new balance of power (Shackleton 2000), facilitating an interinstitutional 'joint legislator' culture of sorts. The two institutions try to identify likely problems before conciliation begins in order to solve them speedily. Institutional trust has developed, in that actors from both institutions expect their counterparts to be prepared to negotiate and to deliver ratification of the compromise text.

The second school of thought – that co-decision has empowered the EP, but only as a result of the Amsterdam Treaty – is advanced by Tsebelis and Garrett (2001). Their concern that the EP would in fact lose influence under co-decision (by being lured into the abandonment of the pursuit of interinstitutional partnerships in favour of an unusable veto, which Council could trump) was mitigated by the Amsterdam Treaty provision for conciliation to be the absolute end of the decision-making process. In this reading the EP's loss of its veto is relatively unimportant compared with Council's loss of the ability to impose its Common Position, thereby forcing the EP to try to oppose it by absolute majority, because Council unanimity is considered more likely than the generation of an absolute majority in the EP. Consequently, both institutions have an incentive to enter into conciliation negotiations with a constructive purpose and the likelihood of the EP being constantly unable to secure its objectives is reduced.

The third line of argument is put forward by Christophe Crombez (2001), who maintains that although the Amsterdam Treaty clearly raises Parliament to a position of joint legislator with Council in most legislation of the first pillar, this ascent has been mismanaged. Crombez argues along almost diametrically opposed lines to Garrett and Tsebelis. He submits that Amsterdam actually makes it more difficult for Parliament to secure its objectives because the Commission rather than the Council is weakened considerably, and conciliation has become an all-or-nothing process: if it fails, there is no legislation. Given that there is no fall-back position and that the Commission's ability to broker agreement between the negotiators is much reduced (because EP and Council negotiate directly), Crombez fears Parliament may find itself in difficulties. If the EP cannot reach a suitable compromise with the Council, it will have to choose between two unpalatable options: either agreeing to legislation it does not really want or accepting a legislative vacuum. Either way, the outcome would be unsatisfactory. However, it is not clear why Parliament should be more vulnerable in this way than Council. Moreover, it is by no means certain, given experience of co-decision to date, that the threat of an expanding legislative vacuum is real. In fact, in the light of Shackleton's findings mentioned above, it appears that such an eventuality is unlikely.

Thus, it seems clear that Parliament's legislative strength now relies on a new kind of fusion between formal and informal politics: the Treaty gives Parliament significant legislative power, but the EP is dependent upon the adroit use of informal mechanisms to translate this *de jure* power into *de facto* influence. Co-decision has not replaced Parliament's dependency on entrepreneurship. Instead, it has acknowledged it and mutated it through entrenchment in Treaty prescription. In the next section of the chapter we examine how this revised entrepreneurialism sits alongside other challenges to the Parliament.

NEW CHALLENGES TO THE EP: DEVELOPMENTS AFTER NICE

The future development of the EP will in all likelihood depend on how it responds to three sets of challenges (in addition to member state agreement to expand its formal powers). These can be understood as follows: first, the still limited extent of EP competence; second, an apparent increasing tendency towards internal division; and third, the tension between legislative effectiveness and legitimacy.

The Nice Treaty (still to be ratified at the time of writing) makes it clear that significant future development of the Parliament's legislative powers cannot be taken for granted. Although this Treaty does make small extensions to the use of co-decision and gives Parliament greater *locus standi* before the ECJ (Burns 2001), it appears to end the EP's rapid development of the 1990s. Thus, Parliament's first challenge may be to improve upon its limited competence. Significantly empowered in pillar one, it is almost entirely powerless in matters of pillars two and three, and is thus at a disadvantage in many of the most dynamic policy areas of the Union – especially when its limited capacity to scrutinize the European Central Bank is recalled. This challenge is likely to be compounded by the 'post-Nice' Convention and the next round of Treaty reform (scheduled for 2004), in which national Parliaments rather than the EP are expected to be moved closer to the heart of EU decision making (the Convention's mandate has the role of national parliaments in EU policy making as one of only four items on its obligatory agenda, the others being subsidiarity, the simplification of the Treaties and the status of the Charter of Fundamental Rights).

A further challenge is the need to retain internal unity in the face of what appear to be significant new divisions. The traditional 'grand coalition' between the Socialist Group and the Christian Democrat group in the EP now appears to be breaking down. After the 1999 EP elections the Christian Democrats became the biggest party group and chose the Liberal Democratic and Reform Group as their coalition partners instead of the Socialists. This appears to have set the tone for the current Parliament, where party political differences seem to be increasingly conspicuous (Hix 2001). Indeed, the battle for the EP Presidency in 2002 was fought in a manner without precedent, culminating in a contest between the Socialist, David Martin, and the Liberal, Pat Cox, with the latter emerging victorious largely thanks to Christian Democrat support. This new emergence of partisan politics poses a problem for the EP because co-decision obliges it to adopt a single position as an institution in order to negotiate successfully with Council. If party politics makes such unity difficult to achieve, the EP's effectiveness as a legislator may well suffer.

Other differences, themselves in part the product of the EP's greater formal influence, may also threaten Parliament's ability to be a successful policy entrepreneur. For example, there is often leadership tension between the EP's committee structure and its political-party groupings. In constituting conciliation delegations, for example, the post-Maastricht formula under the EP's rules was that it would be party groups which would select members of the delegation, which would 'normally' comprise the chair and rapporteur from the relevant committee. Occasionally, tension also becomes visible in disagreements between committee chairs and party leaders. Party Group leaders can claim legitimacy from ideology. Committee Presidents can claim it from expertise and transnational compromise forged in committee deliberations. National parties can seek to exert influence over 'their' MEPs and ensure that they follow domestically decided political lines rather than those agreed upon at EU level, especially in cases such as the United Kingdom (UK) where political parties have ultimate control of who is granted a place on the electoral list, and can therefore both award and remove patronage.

There are also tensions between committees and plenary. Here, the issue is a straightforward one of control: a committee which has debated an issue and reached an informed judgement on it is unlikely to enjoy seeing this judgement unpicked during a plenary vote for reasons of national (party) interest. The post-Amsterdam process of co-decision allows EP and Council to agree after first reading, thereby to some extent privileging the relevant EP committee over plenary. Maastricht also established a *de facto* general reliance of Parliament on the members of its relevant committee to negotiate for it with the Council during conciliation. Given the shift towards partisan politics alongside increased 'national' involvement in the EP, it is probably not surprising that there is an emerging tension within Parliament between those members who emphasize the possibility of reaching early agreement with Council during first reading, and those who continue to focus on the first reading under co-decision as the opportunity for Parliament to set its political negotiating agenda in readiness for later stages of co-decision.

Perhaps the most significant challenge before the Parliament, however, is to generate for itself a greater public sense of its legitimacy. The EP's growth in legislative influence has not won it the support of most EU citizens, who still appear to consider it an institution of secondary importance. This is partly because there is no substantive European *'demos'*. Although all enfranchised member state nationals comprise a single electorate for EP elections, there is still no real sense of shared 'European' political identity which could be harnessed by EU institutions (Chryssochoou 1998; Warleigh 2003). Instead, EU citizens continue to see themselves primarily as member state nationals focused on national institutions, even if this stance is less monopolistic than in the past (Wiener 1998). However, beyond this 'no demos' argument lies another issue: the fact that co-decision has removed any doubt about Parliament's effectiveness as a player in EU policy networks rather than made it the visible locus of political debate or a body able to exert independent influence (Lambert and Hoskyns 2000). EP elections, for example, remain unique in Europe in having no executive outcome. Meanwhile, the conciliation process obliges Parliament to become *in camera* co-legislator with Council, and thereby restricts rather than increases its ability to reach out to (or represent) civil society, just as qualified majority voting makes it impossible for any citizen to rely upon her/his national government to defend her/his interests.

This is the paradox of the EP: legislative influence is more obvious than ever, but citizens' ability to use Parliament as their voice remains open to question, albeit in a reconfigured manner. Thus, citizens no longer need to consider Parliament an ineffective institution worthy of their interest, but they do need to consider whether they can actually influence what the EP does. It may be that, instead of considering Parliament to be their natural representative in Brussels, citizens seeking to influence EU outcomes will consider it one potential source of support among many, to be lobbied as any other. If so, the EP will be obliged to reconsider its developmental trajectory, or at least squarely to address the issue of its public standing. It is to be hoped that the telegenic and affable Pat Cox will be able to address this issue during his term as EP President.

CONCLUSIONS

In this chapter we have argued that the EP has a long and proud history as a policy entrepreneur, seeking and able to defend its interests and maximize its influence through a variety of semi-formal and informal means. We have argued that co-decision is the continuation – and so far, the apex – of this tradition, rather than its replacement, and that as a result Parliament's new legislative powers are best viewed as part of a developmental continuum. The changing context of EU policy making, however, appears to offer the Parliament new challenges rather than security. Parliament's very influence has increased both its attractiveness to member governments as a possible arena for the defence of the 'national interest' and its worth as a venue for 'para' but partisan (and hence potentially divisive) politics. Parliament must decide how to manage these challenges and, in particular, it must address the issue of what balance it should strike between effectiveness as a legislator (which requires adroit use of informal, and hence not public, politics) and legitimacy/representativity (which requires greater resonance with, and participation by, civil society). There may be room for manoeuvre here: for example, the increase in partisan politics discussed above might lead to greater public visibility and recognition as a place of meaningful debate (Lambert and Hoskyns 2000). However, there is no doubt that the EP must reconfigure its ability to be entrepreneurial and find a way to balance legislative influence with greater legitimacy. At the turn of the millennium, we submit, this is now the most appropriate way for the EP to represent its interests and secure a sustainable future.

REFERENCES

Blondel, J., Sinnott, R. and Svensson, P. (1998): *People and Parliament in the European Union: Participation, Democracy and Legitimacy* (Oxford: Clarendon).

Bradley, K. St C. (1987): 'Maintaining the Balance: The Role of the Court of Justice in Defining the Institutional Position of the European Parliament', *Common Market Law Review* 24, 41–64.

Burns, C. (2001): 'The European Parliament', in A. Warleigh (ed.) *Understanding European Union Institutions* (London: Routledge).

Corbett, R. (1989): 'Testing the New Procedures: The EP's First Experiences with its New 'Single Act' Powers', *Journal of Common Market Studies* 27:4, 359–72.

Cram. L. (1997): *Policy Making in the EU: Conceptual Lenses and the Integration Process* (London: Routledge).

Crombez, C. (1996): 'Legislative Procedures in the European Community', *British Journal of Political Studies* 26, 199–228.

Crombez, C. (2001): 'The Treaty of Amsterdam and the Co-decision Procedure', in G. Schneider and M. Aspinwall (eds) *The Rules of Integration: Institutionalist Approaches to the Study of Europe* (Manchester: Manchester University Press).

Chryssochoou, D. (1998): *Democracy in the European Union* (London: Tauris).

Dankert, P. (1997): 'Pressure from the European Parliament', in G. Edwards and A. Pijpers (eds) *The Politics of European Treaty Reform* (London: Pinter).

Dinan, D. (1997): 'The Commission and the Reform Process', in G. Edwards and A. Pijpers (eds) *The Politics of European Treaty Reform* (London: Pinter).

Earnshaw, D. and Judge, D. (1995): *Prelude to Co-decision: A Qualitative Assessment of the Co-operation Procedure in the 1989–94* European Parliament Luxembourg: European Parliament Directorate General for Research Project IV/93/54.

Earnshaw, D. and Judge, D. (1996): 'From Co-operation to Co-decision: The European Parliament's Path to Legislative Power', in J. Richardson (ed.) *European Union: Power and Policy Making* (London: Routledge).

Easton, D. (1965a): *A Systems Analysis of Political Life* (New York: Wiley).

Easton, D. (1965b): *A Framework for Political Analysis* (Englewood Cliffs, NJ: Prentice-Hall).

Elles, Baroness (1984): 'Perspectives of the European Parliament', *International Relations*, November, 157–75.

Garman, J. and Hilditch, L. (1998): 'Behind the Scenes: An Examination of the Informal Processes at Work in Conciliation', *Journal of European Public Policy* 5:2, 271–84.

Garrett, G. and Tsebelis, G. (1996): 'An Institutional Critique of Intergovernmentalism', *International Organization* 50:2, 269–99.

Hix, S. (2001): 'Legislative Behaviour and Party Competition in the European Parliament: An Application of *Nominate* to The EU', *Journal of Common Market Studies* 39:4, 663–88.

Hubschmid, C. and Moser, P. (1997): 'The Co-operation Procedure in the EU: Why Was the EP Influential in the Decision on Car Emission Standards?', *Journal of Common Market Studies* 35:2, 225–42.

Judge, D. and Earnshaw, D. (1994): 'Weak European Parliament Influence? A Study of the Environment Committee of the European Parliament', *Government and Opposition* 29:2, 262–76.

Lambert, J. and Hoskyns, C. (2000): 'How Democratic is the European Parliament?', in C. Hoskyns and M. Newman (eds) *Democratizing the European Union: Issues for the Twenty-First Century* (Manchester: Manchester University Press).

Marks, G. and McAdam, D. (1996): 'Social Movements and the Changing Structure of Political Opportunity in the European Union', *West European Politics* 19:2, 249–78.

Moravcsik, A. (1999): *The Choice for Europe: Social Purpose and State Power from Messina to Maastricht* (London: UCL Press).

Pijnenburg, B. (1998): 'EU Lobbying by Ad Hoc Coalitions: An Exploratory Case Study', *Journal of European Public Policy* 5:2, 303–21.

Richardson, J. (1996): 'Policy-making in the EU: Interests, Ideas and Garbage Cans of Primeval Soup', in J. Richardson (ed.) *European Union – Power and Policy Making* (London: Routledge).

Scully, R. (1997): 'The European Parliament and the Co-decision Procedure: A Reassessment', *Journal of Legislative Studies* 3:3, 139–68.

Shackleton, M. (2000): 'The Politics of Co-decision', *Journal of Common Market Studies* 38:2, 325–42.

Tsebelis, G. and Garrett, G. (2001): 'The Institutional Foundations of Intergovernmentalism and Supranationalism in the European Union', *International Organization* 55:2, 357–90.

Tsebelis, G., Jensen, C., Kalandrakis, A., and Kreppel, A. (2001): 'Legislative Procedures in the European Union: An Empirical Analysis', *British Journal of Political Science* 31, 573–99.

Wallace, H. (1996): 'Politics and Policy in the EU: The Challenge of Governance', in H. Wallace and W. Wallace (eds) *Policy Making in the European Union* (3rd ed) (Oxford: Oxford University Press).

Wallace, H. (2000): 'The Institutional Setting: Five Variations on a Theme', in H. Wallace and W. Wallace (eds) *Policy Making in the European Union* (4th ed) (Oxford: Oxford University Press).

Warleigh, A. (2000): 'The Hustle: Citizenship Practice, NGOs and "Policy Coalitions" in the European Union – The Cases of Auto Oil, Drinking Water and Unit Pricing', *Journal of European Public Policy* 7:2, 229–43.

Warleigh, A. (2001): 'Introduction: Institutions, Institutionalism and Decision-making in the European Union', in A Warleigh (ed.) *Understanding European Union Institutions* (London: Routledge).

Warleigh, A. (2003, forthcoming): *Democracy and Reform in the European Union: From Theory to Practice?* (London: Sage).

Westlake, M. (1994): *A Modern Guide to the European Parliament* (London: Routledge).

Wiener, A. (1998): *'European' Citizenship Practice: Building Institutions of a Non-state* (Boulder, Colorado: Westview Press).

Part 3

New Issues in European Union Interest Representation

Chapter 6

'Frame Bridging' and the New Politics of Persuasion, Advocacy and Influence

Carlo Ruzza

INTRODUCTION

How influential are public interest organizations in Brussels? How do they exert their influence? To answer these questions one can begin by noting that in recent decades European Union (EU)-level policies have emerged in some policy fields where there have been significant media concern, social and political controversies and prominent social movement involvement. I refer to environmental policy, certain aspects of regional policy in countries where there have been prominent ethno-nationalist movements and some aspects of social policy, such as those affecting gender issues, racial equality and a few other areas of social inclusion. Within these policy areas have emerged strong public-interest groups which are often connected to social movements.

The relationship between movements' advocacy and EU-level policy can be usefully categorized in terms of three levels of analysis corresponding to three types of arena and institutional actor. The first level comprises state actors in relation to national electoral arenas and national cultures; the second, top EU decision-makers and policy-debating elites; and the third, sets of policy communities with civil servants working on specific policy initiatives. Some policy fields and related policy communities are particularly relevant to social movements and related public interest associations. These three levels relate to movements in distinctive ways, which this chapter will examine.

I shall first identify movements' advocacy coalitions, locating their social relevance and the extent of their influence on the policy process among a set of debating arenas, including the following three: policy communities, EU elite debates and national publics. At the member-state level I stress the relevance of the general media, which mediate the electoral considerations of state actors. At Brussels level I stress a discursive arena of conferences and public debates where a paramount role is played by the legitimacy considerations of EU elites. Thirdly, in relation to specific policy events, I emphasize deliberating forums and policy networks where detailed policies are discussed. My thesis is that *new spaces of influence are opening up for advocacy coalitions and social movements as a result of recent changes in EU governance, which is increasingly deliberative and inclusive as a means to address the 'democratic deficit'.* As one result, the overpowering influence of private lobbies helps them win the argument at the level of detailed policy making, but neglect of the relevance of public discourse at international and EU level can subsequently constrain the choices of private interests.

Within each arena the priorities of movements, the way in which they frame policy problems and possible solutions clash with consolidated institutional approaches, engendering policy controversies. For media-tions to emerge, movements and their advocates can be incorporated into the policy process and their goals made compatible with dominant institutional goals and approaches. Such mediations entail compro-mises on how problems are framed, and on how solutions are envisaged and pursued. Because they refer to alternative ways of framing pro-blems and solutions, I will call these mediations 'frame bridges' and argue that factors such as the characteristics of the actors involved in the policy process determine which frame bridges are possible and therefore which social movements are more likely to have a policy impact.

As this chapter is specifically concerned with the EU level my discus-sion will concentrate on the levels of the first and second arenas: policy communities and the broad discursive arena of policy elites in Brussels. However, some consideration of the impact of the broader political arenas of member states will also be necessary, particularly with refer-ence to the impact of state actors on EU-level dynamics. Before discuss-ing these three arenas, I shall contextualize the operations of public interest groups and show how they undertake the activity of 'frame bridging'.

This chapter is based on a set of in-depth interviews and documentary analysis conducted in the fields of environmental, anti-racist and (aspects of) regional policy at EU level over the last eight years. This inquiry has shown that in areas where social movements are prominent, they reach the EU policy machinery both through their impact on public discourse, as reflected in the electoral considerations of policy makers, and through their participation in advocacy coalitions operating within EU institutions. This marks out an important role for the variety of organizations and individuals that support social movements. This chapter will first briefly describe social movement groups in relation to EU institutions and show that understanding their impact requires a broader perspective than a purely Brussels-centred focus. It will then investigate the dynamics that connect movement-related activism to policy outcomes.

PUBLIC INTEREST REPRESENTATION IN BRUSSELS

In the constantly changing political and economic structures of the EU governance system, both public and private actors must frequently redefine their conception of interest which, given substantial political and technological uncertainty, is far from being self-evident and stable. The EU policy-making milieu tends to produce relatively unstable aggregations of interests, with alliances that form, solidify, but often collapse and reorganize according to contingent political and technological developments. Awareness of perceptions of interests and control over their formation is crucial to policy makers. Particularly at EU level – where decision making is of necessity largely based on consensus – the involvement of representatives of important social sectors in a dialogic process (Majone 1989; Majone 1993) underlies public policy and fosters a process by which associations communicate with their memberships, influencing their behaviour to some extent and thereby improving interest aggregation and chances of compliance.

In addition to general features applying to all interest organizations, there are specific characteristics pertinent to diffused interests, such as public interest groups, which can be categorized as facilitating or hindering aspects of the EU policy process. Several scholars have noted the weakness of public interests and the obstacles they encounter in Brussels, where a dominant neo-liberal ethos conflicts with the values and approaches of public groups. Lacking technical competence, resources, negotiating skills and sometimes the ideological willingness to mediate on principles, they are generally unprepared for the EU system. These features may reduce their relevance in the policy process (Mazey and Richardson 1994: 213) and undermine their ability to remain involved throughout the process (Paterson 1991), so that they lose out in the competition with private interests (Greenwood 1997: 178).

However, in recent years scholars have noted the onset of a positive climate in favour of representatives of diffused interests and they have pointed out that public interest associations are still better represented at EU level than they are in member states, owing to the supporting role of the Commission and a certain activism of the Court in social and environmental fields, and helped by the freedom of the Commission arising from its relative insulation from the political process (Majone 1996: 78). Similarly noted have been the advantages that diffused interests derive from the availability of multiple access points (Pollack

1997). Moreover, a major recent source of strength is the EU perception of a crisis of legitimacy. To overcome these perceptions EU institutions have attempted to facilitate access to public interest organizations, explicitly addressing the issue of legitimacy as part of the search for 'good governance' at EU level (Greenwood 1997; Della Sala 2001; Warleigh 2001; Goehring, this volume).

Thus one may conclude that *diffused interests, including public interests, are stronger at EU level than in several member states, and yet they are weaker in 'Brussels' than private interests.* To sum up, their relative strength is in part connected with the structure of the EU process and in part with recent developments, particularly the debate over the 'democratic deficit'–the widespread perception that EU politics is distant, unaccountable, clientelistic and skewed in favour of private lobbies.

Nonetheless, the infuence of public interest group organizations is not automatic. Firstly, their relative power varies according to whether there is political support from elected officials who reflect opinion climates in member states. Secondly, their influence varies according to whether there is a legal basis in their policy area of reference: associations able to address existing common policies are clearly in a different situation from those that cannot. Social policy – one of the main areas of interest for public pressure groups – has always been modest. But even in this case, important legal developments, such as approval of article 13 of the Amsterdam Treaty on anti-discrimination, have empowered anti-racist organizations (Ruzza 2000a), which are among the most prominent social policy advocates. Thirdly, in recent years the emphasis on a 'hollowed out' state has allocated a stronger role to non-governmental organizations (NGOs), churches, co-operatives and other non-profit organizations, which are increasingly put in charge of administering welfare programmes. The inclusion of these actors in the decision making attendant on service delivery helps institutionalize the sector, which receives increasing funding and responsibility. But this benefits some sectors, those where non-state service delivery is needed, more than it does those others where it is not. Fourthly, the involvement of the non-profit sector allows the testing of social policies, but again this is not true across the board. For instance, at Community level several pilot schemes in various aspects of social policy are in progress, but they are unevenly distributed across policy fields. The presence of social movement-related advocates increases the chances that initiatives will be undertaken in specific sectors. In this respect, one could for instance consider awareness campaigns on ethnic prejudice or gender issues or peace – fields in which there are reservoirs of social activism in most member states. Finally, the type of institutional set up given to the policy sectors that public interest groups address plays an important role. Considerations of bureaucratic politics differ in relation to the mechanisms (i.e. bureau shaping and budget maximizing[1]) that prevail in different sectors (Dunleavy 1991). Thus, environmental policy has major institutional relevance in Brussels, with a dedicated DG as its institutional basis and an unusual set of relationships with industry (which can be generalized as contentious with traditional actors and more cordial with those seeking to utilize environmental regulations to obtain first-mover advantages or product standardizations).

Thus, public interest associations derive their influence from a variety of factors which include structural factors of institutional design and factors relating to different political cultures, considerations of legitimacy in Brussels and public opinion dynamics in member states. Ways must be identified to subsume, or at least to order, the main factors that affect NGOs in relation to policy making. One approach is to focus on the factors in public discourse that enable or undermine public interest associations. While debate of policy ideas is integral to all forms of policy making, it is particularly so for European policy making, which is forced by the relative institutional weakness and non-hierarchical nature of EU-level politics to rely on consensus to a greater extent than national decision making (Majone 1989; Majone 1993). The policy deliberation that takes place in different sectors and in public discourse at large is an important precondition for institutional changes. I will consider three levels at which it is possible to identify factors that play a dominant role in influencing the chances of public pressure groups.

The views of national policy makers are influenced by public opinion dynamics in member states. The impact of state actors constitutes the first level of analysis. Considerations of legitimacy are important at the level of EU elites, which constitute the second level. Budget maximizing, bureau shaping and moral support from sectors of the bureaucracy are important at the level of detailed policy making, which is the third one. At each of these three levels the world of public interest associations is highly differentiated in terms of relations between associations and political and social institutions, in terms of relevance in public opinion and in terms of reservoirs of activism.

I will concentrate in particular on a class of public interest associations of great relevance: public interest organizations directly connected to social movements. Movements have a public importance that derives from the social controversies that they reflect and help magnify. Associations related to movements are distinctly connected to the dynamics of

---

[1] 'Bureau shaping' is the practice by which certain officials seek to entrench and expand their role and powers; 'budget maximizing' is the practice by which officials seek to gain the greatest possible funding for their part of the bureaucracy.

the public sphere, so that they are paradigmatic of the connection between diffused interest organizations and the issues of legitimacy, democracy and fairness in representation that have so preoccupied the European Union in recent years.

MACS,[2] PUBLIC DISCOURSE AND BUREAUCRATIC POLITICS

The impact of social movements and related organizations can be understood by considering the factors that give them distinctive power and resources. Whilst the resources of private interest organizations come from the economic sector and are generally justified by the profit motive, those of public interest associations, including social movements, consist largely in the free or nearly free donation of time and energy by volunteers, and the reasons for these donations need to be explained with reference to social norms, broader cultural dynamics and the functioning of the public sphere. Thus, the power of private interest organizations derives from various mechanisms, such as their possession of information needed by policy makers, their political control over their members and their influence on elected and bureaucratic officials by means of a variety of economic levers relatively independent from public discourse.

The power of public interest organizations, however, is more directly connected to the public sphere. They address ideal causes that, to the extent that they are popular with European publics, grant them a measure of legitimacy that policy makers must bear in mind. The role of the two kinds of organization is therefore somewhat different at all levels and in the policy machinery of EU institutions.[3] Typically, public interest organizations receive EU funds to counterbalance what many perceive to be the problematic absence of a level playing field in the competition for influence over EU policy. But this support needs to be justified before public opinion to an extent that private organizations do not have to consider, and the problem of the representativeness of public interest organizations recurs in official documents, as the influential White Paper on Governance, for instance, emphasizes (Commission 2001). Salience is the paramount criterion for acquisition of public resources for movement organizations.

---

[2] Social movements are mostly influential in policy making when they are able to mobilize broader advocacy coalitions. Movement Advocacy Coalitions (MACs henceforth) are coalitions of movement actors, their allies and sympathizers whose action is coordinated across different institutional realms.

[3] The literature of social movements has traditionally stressed the difference between movements and interest groups.

Thus, when examining public interest organizations at EU level, one must ask how they relate to the public sphere and how they relate to the values and operating modalities prevalent in the EU institutional framework which they address. They must bridge the space between public discourse and institutions. In the rest of this chapter I will examine how they do so.

Public opinion is notoriously unstable and the salience of issues changes quickly, but there are recurrent controversies in Europe that have acquired relevance and relative stability, have polarized political views and have stimulated the emergence of NGOs, social movements and broad movement-inspired advocacy coalitions. These movement-related advocacy coalitions may well include organizations that have previously been or are currently engaged in protest events, such as social movement organizations, yet they are broader than movements in composition, objectives, and methods. Their 'movement character' survives as a voice of organized civil society, but it is complemented by other organizations and undergoes a process of re-elaboration that differentiates broad-based advocacy coalitions from short-term social activism. In particular, MACs are able to rely on institutional allies and institutional bases in bureaucratic and political formations, on the resources of sectors of the state and on the support of sections of the mainstream press and television media.[4] Such factors as the reflected impact of their public opinion relevance through the advocacy of elected officials, the influence of sympathetic bureaucratic actors and the legitimacy considerations of institutional architects support and enhance the position that movements have acquired. However, the transition from a movement to a broad advocacy coalition requires political relevance and a resonance with a variety of institutions that is not available to all movements.

Moreover, if broader social relevance and discursive prominence are conditions of the impact of movements, how does a social movement acquire legitimacy in broader socio-institutional contexts? As a set of innovative and contested opinions, the argument of effective movements must resonate with existing social institutions. They must enter a public discursive sphere and propose convincing approaches to existing problems. Totally innovative approaches are unlikely to be successful because they run counter to the 'taken for granted' assumptions of social and political life and the stable norms that characterize institutional behaviour. Relatively successful social movements must find stable niches in dominant social and political institutions by combining and

---

[4] For the concept of institutional activist see for instance W. A. Santoro and G. M. McGuire (1997). 'Social movement insiders: The impact of institutional activists on affirmative action and comparable worth policies.' *Social Problems*, 44(4): 503–519.

merging their norms and agendas with institutional ones. This process of merging takes place in a set of different arenas: in the media arena, which relates to a general public sphere, and within specific institutional settings like political institutions, churches and work organizations. It also takes place in the policy deliberation that emerges within EU policy communities. Even though incorporated into decision-making processes, MACs retain their relevance in a set of debating arenas, including the social controversies on contested movement views debated in the general media.

Social movements manifest a public visibility, a politicization of issues and a publicly emphasized donation of time and energy for protesting and advocacy purposes that is unlikely to be possessed by other associations. From this point of view, I believe it useful to distinguish movement-related organizations from associations orientated to other social issues, such as church-related groups or associations focused on assisting disadvantaged groups because of their relevance in engendering social controversies and maintaining a high profile in public discourse.[5]

FRAME BRIDGING

Useful insights into this emerging centrality of public discourse in the EU are provided by the social movements literature. The diffusion of movement ideas has been examined by the 'framing' tradition,[6] some of whose key concepts can usefully be employed to shed light on the relationship between EU institutions and movements.

The concept of frame and frame alignment proposed by Snow and colleagues (1986), and the notion of consensus put forward by Klandermans (Klandermans 1988), facilitate description of the nature of the alliance that develops among advocacy groups in specific policy areas and comes to constitute a MAC. Snow points out that a movement needs a 'master frame' that condenses the grievances of its members into a single concept. By means of a 'master frame' certain aspects of reality are identified and given prominence while others are omitted. Certain connections between elements are highlighted and others are ignored. For a social movement to achieve wider support, its master frame must resonate with the priorities of sectors of the general public. Movements attempt to enhance this resonance by means of 'frame alignment' strategies whereby their frames become aligned with dominant cultural frames.

---

[5] However, in some cases the two will coincide, for instance when assistance to certain social groups is also the focus of a social movement and advocacy goes hand in hand with forms of political protest, political advocacy and other forms of activism.

[6] For a summary of this tradition, which emphasizes socially constructed ideas in collective action see D. McAdam, J. McCarthy and M. Zald (eds) (1996): *Comparative Perspectives on Social Movements.* (Cambridge: Cambridge University Press).

Working within this perspective, Klandermans distinguishes between consensus mobilization and consensus formation:

> 'Consensus mobilization is a deliberate attempt by a social actor to create consensus among a subset of the population ... Consensus formation is the unplanned convergence of meaning in social networks and subcultures.'

The two processes are interrelated in that actors attempting to mobilize consensus take the existing consensus as their initial reference. In unplanned consensus formation dominant social institutions and the media play a fundamental role related to their social visibility and their influence on society and institutions. In order to mobilize consensus movement organizations must refer to the existing discourse. One strategy is to attempt to subvert it with an alternative discourse. This approach implies a conception of social movement groups as strategically focused organizations. It also implies that they have and pursue clear, independent goals.

However, a different and perhaps more viable strategy is to borrow the discourse of powerful institutions and attempt (strategically or because of a cognitive merging of taken-for-granted frames) to modify it in order to legitimate activism or other forms of support for a social movement. This modification can take different forms. The linkages among the discourses of different organizations are of especial interest. Snow and Benford (Snow 1986: 467) and the tradition of social movements research that developed from their work calls these linkages, which are a particular type of frame alignment mechanism, *frame bridging* and defines them in the following terms:

> 'By frame bridging we refer to the linkage of two or more ideologically congruent but structurally unconnected frames regarding a particular issue or problem.'

The concepts of frame bridging, consensus formation and mobilization are important tools with which to determine how positions emerge, change and are modified for strategic and identity reasons by social movements and their allies. These frame bridgings can express instances of *consensus mobilization* when they are intentionally pursued as a strategy, but they can also reflect *consensus formation* when they are of the unaware, taken-for-granted kind.

Processes of consensus formation occur in institutions as emerging frames are reinterpreted in terms of the main institutional ethos. For the neo-institutionalist Krasner (Krasner 1988: 51), these reinterpretations are instances of institutionalization where a newly emerging institution such as a social movement acquires links with specific institutional environments. It becomes deeply embedded in the identity of institutional actors and structurally connected with other institutions. The breadth and depth of connection is Krasner's measure of institutionalization (1988: 76–77).

For analytical purposes it is helpful to separate linkages that occur at the level of public discourse and linkages that occur within institutional realms. The two types of linkages have been studied by different bodies of literature but they are in fact interconnected. The linkages at the level of public discourse examined by the framing tradition (Snow 1986; Gamson 1992; Zuo and Benford 1995) and the linkages that connect public discourse and policy areas (Rein and Schon 1977; Rein and Schon 1994; Radaelli 1995; Ruzza 2000b) are only separable for analytical purposes, given that even very insulated institutions are immersed in broader inter-institutional culture. Differentiating between these different kinds of linkages are the mechanisms and the agencies that promote them. Thus the media are of central importance at the inter-institutional level. Institutional actors with multiple memberships and institutional gatekeepers (Bleich 1998) are important in mediating the relationship between public discourse and institutions and, additionally, internal networks are important in activating internal linkages.

Since the concept of 'frame bridges' refers to mechanisms of negotiation and formation of policy ideas, it is important to connect these mechanisms to actual influence, which is a crucial concern of all negotiations. Policies have what one can call 'a software' – the ideational part – and a hardware, the structures in which they operate (Alink, Boin *et al.* 2001). In our context influence refers to how certain organizations impose their objectives on other organizations – that is, how organized interests change public decision-making processes. Influence is a process that includes a variety of factors – both 'soft' and 'hard' – of which the framing of claims by interests and the response by decision makers is only one. The framing of claims and counterclaims shapes a policy area and orientates the perception of appropriateness of existing structures, and it is therefore an important aspect of influence. However, there are structures and other processes that affect the ability to exert influence. At the discursive level several competing framings, including conflicting attempts at frame bridging, can coexist at any point in time, reflecting a plurality of sponsors of policy ideas. As a frame bridge is often a compromise between competing institutional discourses, we can argue that the price of influence is often 'dilution'. However, no amount of dilution ensures success, as other structural factors and processes come into play and different approaches to 'diluting' might be competing. On the one hand, when frame bridges emerge spontaneously in society or in specific institutions as instances of consensus formation we cannot properly speak of 'influence', which presupposes intention. On the other hand, bridging processes within specific institutions articulate general linkages in terms of the priorities of different institutional settings and often have strategic 'importers' of general frames, who may do this for normative reasons, bureaucratic politics, etc. This process by which general frame bridges are produced, and its articulation in specific institutional settings, can now be examined with reference to specific MACs and their relation to EU institutions.

THREE MACS

As previously mentioned, in-depth interviews were conducted in the fields of environmental, anti-racist and regional policy at EU level, the aim being to examine the interaction between MACs and EU institutions. For each of these three fields, I considered various actors involved in interaction and concentrated on their framings of issues. Each of the MACs had wide resonance in European societies and comprised a set of social movements known for their main claims–masterframes in the language of frame analysts–which articulate the following concepts: that the environment is neglected in modern society and 'environmental sustainability' is essential; that racial prejudice is rampant and damaging to minorities; and that regional cultures are marginalized by nation states. The processes by which these claims were made relevant in specific institutional settings (frame alignments for frame analysts) were examined in order to determine how emerging framings of movements had helped or hindered their institutionalization and their impact. In particular, I considered the master frame of each movement, how this frame was incorporated by state actors (and therefore how it played a role in their electoral calculations), EU elites and Brussels-based policy communities. I paid particular attention to which specific institutional domains can utilize dominant frame bridges and whether new emphases and reinterpretations of existing frames emerged.

Environmentalism

It is difficult to ignore the salience of environmental policy in relation to other aspects of European policy making. Environmental policy is one of the newest and fastest-growing policy areas in the West. Emerging in the seventies as a result of pressure from public opinion and environmental movements, it has grown into a comprehensive set of concerns and has been diffused across a variety of other policy areas (Ruzza 2000b). European institutions are crucial in environmental regulation both because of the integrated character of European economies and because of the cross-border nature of many environmental threats. For these reasons institutions such as the European Commission and the European Parliament have aroused a great deal of interest among industrial lobbies and public interest groups. Environmental themes are also crucial in the considerations of state political actors who reflect a public opinion generally favourable to higher environmental standards and are more supportive than on other issues promoted by social movements.

This movement had many key objectives and approaches, ranging from anti-modernist ethos to environmental aspects in relation to social justice, to a focus on environmental lifestyle witnessing. All these components were subsumed by the keyword 'environmental sustainability' – a goal pursued by a variety of small-movement parties, epistemic communities and NGOs. The components most easily institutionalized in the politics of member states were those whose objectives were well encapsulated by the key term 'sustainable development.' This term is a condensing metaphor, a social utopia of a society that, while continuing to progress economically, prevents fundamental damage to the environment.

In part, because of its very ambiguity,[7] the concept of sustainable development has for the first time freed industry from its earlier uncompromisingly negative role, and allowed it to recast itself as a potential partner with governments in the development of technologies to solve environmental problems. I thus consider the idea of sustainable development to be an instance of frame bridging in which the concept of environmental protection supported by the environmental movement has merged with the concept of development crucial in the policy language of European states. 'Sustainable development' also resonates well within EU institutions. This bridging was crucial in creating the cultural and structural conditions necessary for a set of accommodations resulting in a powerful environmental MAC at Community level (Ruzza 1996).

For state actors environmentalism was an important electoral issue. For EU elites it was a way to carve out a special role for European-level policy making that took account of the need for legitimate areas of intervention. The EU has stressed the pan-European dimension of environmental threats, the fact that much environmental regulation emerged from European institutions in a situation of virtual absence of environmental policy in several southern member states, and therefore the fact that the EU was able to produce something that the citizens wanted and needed and that states were not providing to a sufficient extent–in other words, the framing of environmental regulation gave rise to a discursive attempt to achieve a measure of output legitimacy (Scharpf 1999). Furthermore, the legitimating role of environmental

---

[7] See for instance: M. Redclift, *Sustainable Development: Exploring the Contradictions.* (London. Routledge 1992.)

policy has continued over the years, remaining a popular and valid area for EU intervention (Flynn 2000).

At the level of policy communities, particularly for business actors, environmental regulation constitutes both an opportunity and a threat. Environmental regulation may provide industry with an opportunity to expand its market share through product standardization and an opportunity for competitive advantages against competitors unable to fulfil the requirements of timing, costs, or technology necessary for regulatory compliance. It may provide bureaucrats with an opportunity for budget maximization. For instance a civil servant noted:

> 'my friends should be called the envirocrats because although they can claim they want to protect the environment, they are interested in their own survival and importance, and they emphasize the importance of their regulation' (Commission official, 1996).

Thus, in terms of frame bridges, merging *sustainability* and economic *development* was one possible frame bridge that made a social movement discourse appealing to a new range of actors and in fresh institutional contexts. These included EU policy makers with a pro-industry ethos and business actors who could accept a type of environmentalism compatible with economic and technological development, whilst rejecting 'back to nature' and 'small is beautiful' approaches. This does not mean that there is no resistance to environmentalism. Because of cost considerations some sectors of industry may counteract the environmentalist frame by means of frames that attempt to depict environmentalism as utopian, anti-modern or exaggerated in its perceptions of danger. But the movement has sufficient allies to play a significant role in member states and in Brussels. Over time the concept of environmental sustainability has acquired a taken-for-granted character that precludes much open questioning of its now self-evident value. However, resistance can still take place, especially when rhetoric about sustainability has to be translated into specific, detailed policy – as several interviewees noted.

Several processes and structures facilitated the emergence of frame bridges at all levels. Environmentalists, together with actors from industry, were included in a number of forums at local, subnational and national level, particularly in northern countries that both led on environmental issues and had a tradition of the involvement of civil society in decision making. At the EU elite level the abundance of environmental discussion groups and workshops provided opportunities to develop new environmental frames. In consultative committees the voice of organized civil society was influential in policy debates and in policy communities the presence of committed institutional activists brought movements' views within the realm of comitology. An important role in developing frame bridges is also played by expert committees where different national policy ideas – which experts are expected to represent fairly faithfully – are debated in a deliberative atmosphere more than in the light of scientific rationality (Flynn 2000: 87–88). To be stressed here is the fact that the heyday of environmentalism has long passed, but basic policy structures are now in place and, to understand these, one should refer to the initial stages of development of environmental policy. Whilst the activism of movements and its impact on Brussels policy making has now considerably diminished, and Commission officials report the greater impact of industrial lobbies and government hostile to environmentalism, the frame-bridging influence of movement is by now institutionalized and pro-active environmental policy ideas remain available as tools in policy deliberation.

Regionalism

The EU has played an important role in the promotion of regions as relevant policy actors in the EU polity since the 1980s. There are several reasons why the EU has encouraged regionalization and a redistributive regional policy. For instance, regional policy has been conceptualized as a pay-off for poor regions forced to compete in an integrated market against stronger industrial regions. It is part of a more redistributively orientated European social model. Regional autonomy enables regions to develop technological niches, which improves systemic competitiveness. Regional decentralization helps policy delivery, which is crucial for overburdened states.

However, demands for more regional autonomy predate EU regional policy. They are a constitutive element of a family of regionalist movements to be found in most EU member states, including the Basque, Catalan, Breton and Welsh movements. This is a long-established family of social movements, which are particularly strong in regions with minority languages and cultures. Their master frame involves contesting the equivalence of nation and state which is ideologically inscribed in the political culture of European nation-states. For minority nationalists their regions are nations and should be recognized as such; they should be granted the necessary political authority and their culture should be protected.

These movements are represented in EU institutions in several ways. There are umbrella parties and inter-groups in the European Parliaments which support regionalist parties and minority languages. There are Commission programmes that finance the protection of minority languages. And there are NGOs and regional offices of minority regions that promote regional cultural initiatives. At member state level throughout

Europe a process of regionalization corresponding to the devolution of political authority has been in progress since the 1970s. One outcome of this process is a network of regional offices in Brussels and relatively powerful political institutions in some member states, such as regional parliaments and assemblies, which are often supportive of the goals of these movements. Member states have accepted but redefined the movements' claims by opposing all aspirations to statehood though supporting claims for autonomy. The strong version of regionalism espoused by movements of minority nationalists has been redefined in terms of the emphasis by states on the emerging values of responsiveness to local specificity.

Thus redefined, regionalism has become broadly appealing. As the literature on strategic essentialism shows,[8] strong regional identities can be claimed for opportunistic reasons even when their historical bases are weak or non-existent (Achleitner 1997). Demands for fiscal and administrative autonomy have permeated all regions, which have increasingly come to utilize the language of minority rights regardless of the historical foundations of their alleged distinctiveness. This is a political discourse that not infrequently joins an economic and a cultural claim to distinctive identity in order to legitimize claims for increased political influence. These developments are seen as positive by EU elites, which can use regional demands and EU-mediated regional financial empowerment to erode state power from below. The bridging metaphor of 'Europe of the regions' has acquired wide currency in EU circles but it is mainly limited to regions conceptualized as actors like any other interest group, not to regions *qua* nations as advocated by 'strong regionalists.' Strong regionalism, with its cultural claims, remains marginalized. For instance, there is only a limited budget for the protection of minority languages and specific demands for the introduction of legislation on linguistic diversity, and demands for Article 13 to be extended to language discrimination have so far been unheeded. At the level of policy communities the strong version of regionalism is marginalized, whilst weaker regionalism – a regionalism compatible with the current institutional structure – has spurred the attention of a variety of policy networks whose interests are connected to the utilization of regional funds. There is thus an objective dilution of the demands put forward by these movements, but in this context there has been a limited institutionalization. Regionalism has been redefined from separatist self-determination and an emphasis on conflict with nation-states into a frequently proclaimed model of nested territorial identities able to coexist harmoniously.

---

[8] It refers to the instrumental use of identity concerns in a number of policy areas, including regional policy.

Anti-racism

Anti-racism is a policy area with repercussions across a broad range of sectors. Problems of social exclusion grow increasingly important as several member states experience greater ethnic diversity following a period of sustained inward migrations. Racist attitudes are combated at the EU level both by the investment of resources in the cultural and educational sector and by legislation addressed to areas in which racism is most detrimental. Support for anti-racist initiatives is promoted throughout Europe by a set of advocacy coalitions which espouse the ideas of anti-racist movements. In the more economically orientated area of legislation pertaining to labour markets, anti-racism is also connected to a somewhat different constituency involving the trade unions, parties of the left and subnational levels of governance.

'Anti-racism' refers to a loose cluster of ideas and organizations; it does not have a strong all-encompassing discursive frame. Racism is a problem that anti-racist movements have tackled with different approaches reflecting differences in national political cultures. These range from assimilationist approaches in which racial differences are subordinated to unifying concepts (such as the concept of 'citizen') to multicultural approaches, in which a cultural understanding of 'race' is inscribed as a component of a rich cluster of attributes that each culture possesses and whose respect is normatively stressed. In member states reaction to attacks against immigrants has promoted an institutionalization of anti-racism within the electoral left. Various areas have been singled out for attention. Particular focus has directed on education, labour markets, trade union participation, social security, health and access to goods and services. The framing of the issue in member states tends to exclude militant forms of anti-racism and to define it as an unjust distribution of opportunities that penalizes racial minorities.

Anti-racism also plays a role at EU level. In a recent communication (COM 2001 [387]) the Commission stressed that 'failure to develop an inclusive and tolerant society which enables different ethnic minorities to live in harmony with the local population of which they form part leads to discrimination, social exclusion and the rise of racism and xenophobia.' Race-based social exclusion is experienced in education, housing, labour markets, health, justice, etc. At the EU level the concept of 'mainstreaming of anti-racism' acts as the dominant condensing metaphor that guides regulatory discourse. The concept of 'mainstreaming of anti-racism' implies the normalization of anti-racism and its inscription in a broad set of policies as a necessary if not taken-for-granted element – a horizontal policy to be entrenched in all common policies. The concept of mainstreaming is similarly applied in order to combat other forms of discrimination, such as discrimination against homosexuals and gender discrimination (Mazey 2001). One of the main areas in which the EU has concentrated its efforts is the labour market. Its recognized ability to improve the functioning of labour markets is therefore applied to something different – the fight against discrimination. In this sense, 'mainstreaming of anti-racism' constitutes a frame bridge in which the EU applies its consolidated skills in the diffusion of horizontal principles across policy areas to the field of anti-racism – a field relatively new to Community action. By stressing the similarity of this area to other policy areas, the European nature of the threat and the need to intervene so that racism does not hinder the freedom of movement of individuals in labour markets, the EU espouses a framing of anti-racism that is institutionally appealing and congruent with efforts to enhance European integration.

In specific policy communities, definitions of the nature, causes and ideal solutions of racism co-exist and are debated with the NGO community. Taken together, these conceptions give identity and professionalism to the relevant policy network, but in a fragmented and contested fashion (Ruzza 2000a). Thus a civil servant summarized the concerns of her unit in charge of anti-racist policy as:

> 'something which is creative thinking, something that has been done all those years by the NGOs, what can we at the European level add to that which is appealing to the NGOs but which is also appealing to the general public? Because if you think about it our biggest challenge is to reach the general public. Because we reach the converted, people who are even more convinced than we are, but we have to reach your neighbour' (Commission official, 1998).

This preoccupation with popular acceptance has on occasion been criticized by NGOs in the field. For instance, an EU-level cadre of a Commission-sponsored network dealing with issues of discrimination noted that the Commission tends to encourage the participation of the representatives of 'respectable' citizens in consultations to the exclusion of more radical ones. This has for instance resulted in the perception of an excessive inclusion of non-white affluent businessmen who are not representative of poor and discontented members of minority communities. Episodes like this explain some of the processes that underlie the formation of frame bridges.

The credibility of frame bridges depends on their political viability. Anti-racist frames remain difficult to bridge in a period of widespread preoccupation with the impact of migrations. Yet, the recent successes of the extreme right constitute a political opportunity for the anti-racist MAC, as some of the core values of Europe are called in question and political responses become necessary. Anti-racism is somewhat less usable and less institutionalized both in member states and at Community level, but its importance is growing. At member state level it directly affects smaller constituencies, but it is entrenched in the values of the electoral left. It is discursively connected to the category of 'human rights' increasingly used by member states for self-definition, which gives it growing relevance. The concept of mainstreaming has resonated with the EU focus on freedom of movement, which is necessary for an effective integrated market. But, when connected to migration, it refers to an area still largely under state control. As Geddes notes in the case of migration policy, the consequence of 'lowest common denominator' decision making is that a preoccupation with control overwhelms a concern with the integration of migrants (Geddes 1999: 181). This indicates another type of structure that orientates the direction in which frame bridges tend to develop. The power of anti-racism as a mobilizing metaphor at policy community level is restricted by the limitations of EU social policy.

DISCUSSION

There are several types of process and structure by which frame bridges occur within policy environments and between policy environments and general culture. Here I can only indicate some of those most frequently apparent in the cases examined. In addition to low-intensity modifications and redefinitions of policy discourses in which cross-fertilization occurs between political institutions (and this is typically the case of consensus formation), frame bridges can arise as responses to crises, as a consequence of the multiple roles that institutional actors may come to play and as a consequence of the role of movement sympathizers working in institutional environments.

Policy crises are thoroughly discussed in the literature and often related to social controversies in which a nexus of interactions emerges between the media, social movements and policy-making institutions. Public debates on social issues tend to focus on a limited number of issues at any one point in time. Few remain central for several years and result in articulated political and social controversies. Themes such as the environment, regional devolution and racism have attracted sustained attention and controversies, giving rise to social movements which in turn have contributed to magnifying them. In normatively charged issue areas such as these, specific events such as environmental crises or asylum crises may give rise to the perception of a policy crisis – the widespread idea that a policy sector has gone adrift and that a turn is necessary. Crises compel interested actors to propose new policy ideas and structures and force a debate. Thus policy crises are a general stimulus to construct frame bridges. The range of potential solutions varies, but the extent of the involvement of social movements and of the media are key variables in the diffusion of this debate and its articulation into distinctive and recognized positions.

The impact of crises varies according to the sector. One can distinguish between highly institutionalized sectors with long-standing policies and comparatively new ones which are relatively non-institutionalized and characterized by a wide-ranging debate. Processes of administrative and political personnel selection and the differential attrition of policy units shape frame bridges in these sectors. When a new policy area emerges – that is, when a previously under-thematized issue becomes politically salient, like the environment in the 1970s, policy-making institutions select new personnel. In some circumstances, such as a scarcity of qualified staff and pre-existing epistemic communities, the available personnel tend to share a common ideational framework. Secondly, there are processes of selective attrition. Participants in emergent and contested policy communities tend to remain involved to the extent that they have a normative commitment or an interest. This reduces the number of frames available as at any point in time and promotes stable fields with similar negotiations over policy ideas (Ruzza 2000).

More established sectors face a dilemma between the preservation of existing practices and responsiveness to political challenges. The outcome may be institutional rigidity or negotiation over policy ideas and structures, trial and error approaches and purely reactive policy-making (Alink, Boin *et al.* 2001). All these mechanisms constitute structures for frame bridging. Policy frames emerge from negotiation with stakeholders, including MACs, from the subsequent justification of emerging practices in garbage can[9] processes where problems and solutions are tossed in and taken out by different institutions, and from path-dependent approaches (see several contributions in Steinmo, Thelen *et al.* 1992). *In both old and new sectors, by straddling the tension between preservation and responsiveness, policy makers select and import from society those ideas that are most compatible with existing approaches.* Institutionalized social movements and MACs are in this sense in a strong position to offer viable policy discourses.

All sectors face special challenges when regulated at the EU level, where the value pluralism of national government has to be reconciled. This is achieved not only through specific policy decisions but also through agreements on common framings – often appropriately encapsulated in 'framework' programmes – which may still be internally ambiguous and contested but nonetheless constitute a reference point in which dominant national and partisan frames are bridged through key

---

[9] For the concept of Garbage Can in Organizational Behaviour see J. March (1988): *Decisions and Organizations.* (Oxford: Oxford University Press).

ideas such as 'mainstreaming' or 'sustainable development'. On the one hand, the bridges possible at EU level are those that prevail in member states at decision-making time, as governments want to minimize the cost of adopting new policies. Also, because of the EU's stringent decision-making rules, only policy ideas compatible with all members tend to be supported. This orientates frame-bridging activity towards a minimum common denominator. On the other hand, there also emerges a specific character of EU crisis management that has been characterized as reformist (and therefore proactive in promoting frame bridges) but of low effectiveness (Alink, Boin *et al.* 2001).

A second structure that, particularly at EU level, facilitates frame bridging is the multiplicity of institutional roles that actors come to play. I refer to the case of civil servants who take early retirement and work for lobbies, or scientific experts selected to represent their governments and the multiple roles that straddle the divide between member state and EU functions. I have called these people boundary personnel, pointing to the fact that personal and institutional needs for coherence stimulate frame bridging (Ruzza 1996). A related category, which is pertinent to MACs, is the role of institutional activists – institutional personnel whose first normative commitment is to a social movement (Ruzza 2000b).

To summarize, the processes by which frame bridges occur are processes of *institutionalization* and of *selection*. Once publicly affirmed, dominant frame-bridges underlie the creation of new institutions, and this has happened is my case studies, where a new set of institutions has been created even in recent years with a mandate to actualize the policy ideas of dominant frame bridges. One might consider for instance the European Monitoring Centre in the case of anti-racism or the Committee of the Regions. In a period of multi-level governance successful frame bridges are unlikely to remain confined to one policy environment. They will diffuse throughout the integrated policy system. However, there could well be competition for framing issues between policy actor and levels of governance. Intentional frame bridging takes place at all the three levels considered. Heads of state represent activists' demands that are not strongly opposed by other interests. European elites favour proposals that imply more power for Europe. EU institutional actors operating on the basis of bureaucratic politics and normative concerns favour compatible policies. Unintentionally, frame bridging processes emerge in the three sectors as taken-for-granted approaches connected to path dependency and garbage can processes which become 'naturalized' in specific policy communities or in culture at large.

Frame bridges can then be seen as a 'dilution' of social movements' ideas which make them acceptable to key social institutions, but the extent to which they succeed, and the reaction of political institutions, are highly variable. Several other variables come into play in the exercise of actual influence and outcomes may range widely: from full response to rejection and from pre-emption to ritualized acceptance (Gamson 1975). Nonetheless, the acceptability of social movements' ideas to broad social sectors plays a key role in the causation of outcomes. Redefined environmentalist ideas such as sustainable development are more acceptable to one of the main actors of environmental policy: industry. Redefined regionalist ideas appeal to regional authorities, and redefined anti-racist ideas appeal to welfare state regulators in a way that the original social movement ideas did not.

At the EU level the institutional locations where processes of frame bridging resulting from consensus formation can occur are the consultative forums whose abundance characterizes the EU system of governance. All the three policy areas examined are likely to produce an interaction of EU and movement actors, and a merging of frames which can empower these movements as well as a set of actors which are connected to these movements for normative or purely instrumental reasons. However, this influence can be mitigated by the absence of clear rules for inclusion in the policy process, and the weakness of some MACs at member state level. Movement-related groups are, however, good test cases for studying the impact of the transition from 'government' to 'governance' on organized civil society. If the challenge of governance consists in a new and broader battle to accommodate conflicting interests and discover ways to take co-operative action, then social movements, and particularly institutionalized social movements, are at the forefront of this battle. Their hopes for policy relevance rest on their ability to stimulate the formation of effective advocacy coalitions and to provide innovative ideas to the policy process that can enable co-operation between diverse actors.

By studying MACs in relation to their ideational impact on policy processes we can identify the emerging traits of a system that is in many respects new and contrast two models: a traditional model which is essentially state-centred, in which public discourse has limited impact on decision making and is different in different countries; and an emerging model, which is already manifesting itself at the EU level and displays new features and new challenges. In this system new political entities have developed which interact with the institutionalized political system in ways different from those exhibited by old parties and social movements, which are historical formations that the development of the process of EU integration and governance as a consequence of globalization may well throw into crisis (Marks and McAdam 1996). In such a system institutionalized social movements and advocacy coalitions, interacting directly with transnational/supranational institutions and international business, may become the accepted norm. 'Soft power', self-regulation and concepts of corporate citizenship may come to characterize the environment to which social movements will need to react, employing on the one hand the boycotting power of consumers and on the other a much more engaged and scientifically grounded approach, as several NGOs representatives are gradually coming to advocate (Edwards 2000).

However, the transition to a territorially broad governance system implies additional costs and difficulties for public interest groups seeking to influence EU policy outcomes. The criteria for selecting NGOs as EU interlocutors will in all likelihood become increasingly contested, and the growing accusations that NGOs lack transparency, accountability and internal democracy may force a general restructuring of the sector (see Commission 2001, Warleigh 2001). Here, the issue is that good ideas are not necessarily the prerogative of the large and powerful public interest groups which are more likely to be able to meet such criteria: smaller groups might become increasingly marginalized. In addition, MACS may find it more difficult to aggregate members' interests to the advantage of policy makers, as their organizing criteria and constituencies proliferate in an ever more complex and enlarging system where conflicting logics of nationality, sector, political positioning and size interact. This might undermine the striving for solidarity which characterizes the sector, and make it more competitive. We could therefore see the emergence of a larger and more internally fragmented sector, despite (or even as a result of) its becoming increasingly institutionalized and influential.

CONCLUSIONS

This chapter has examined those elements of the EU socio-political and institutional context which facilitate or hinder the work of social-movement-related public-interest associations. It has described three families of social movements in Brussels: environmental, anti-racist and regionalist, and has analysed the related process of institutional incorporation in EU institutions.

In the course of the chapter I have considered how social movement ideas are included in public-interest associations and in EU institutional realms, how their priorities are adopted or reinterpreted, and their activists incorporated. To this end I stressed the processes that shape their ideological mix and examined the ideal and instrumental reasons that induce institutions to pay attention to movement-related organizations.

A key concept employed has been that of 'frame bridging'. This is a cultural mechanism by which a synthesis between the dominant ideas of social movements and institutions emerges. I have argued that the presence and increasing popularity of collegial forms in politics, and the EU's concern for transparency and the participation of civil society, foster frame-bridging processes. Consensus formation processes arise whereby existing political ideologies and the emerging ones in social movements are merged. Social movement ideas are thus incorporated through movement lobbying and their impact upon policy-making and movement resource-acquisition strategies. In relation to framing processes, I highlighted the importance of debating arenas in which consensus on preferred policy approaches develops and then trickles down to specific policy events, although at times there is a distance between the principles that emerge in policy-debating arenas and those utilized in concrete policy making. This contributes to the new politics of persuasion and advocacy by bringing together under one frame actors who used to oppose each other, thereby shaping both the ideational context and the content of EU policy.

REFERENCES

Achleitner, F. (1997): 'Region, ein Konstruct? Regionalismus eine Erfindung?', in F. Achleitner *Region, ein Konstruct? Regionalismus eine Pleite?* (Basel: Birkhäuser).

Alink, F., Boin, A., *et al.* (2001): 'Institutional Crises and Reforms in Policy Sectors: The Case of Asylum Policy in Europe', *Journal of European Public Policy,* 8:2, 286–306.

Bleich, E. (1998): 'From International Ideas to Domestic Politics:Gatekeepers, Priors and Educational Multilateralism in England and France', *Comparative Politics* October: 81–100.

Commission (2001): 'European Governance: a White Paper', COM(2001)428.

Commission Official (1996): Personal Communication.

Commission Official (1998): Personal Communication.

DellaSala, V. (2001): 'Constitutionalizing Governance: Democratic Dead End or Dead On Democracy?' *Constitutionalism Web-Papers, ConWEB* (http://les1.man.ac.uk/conweb/).

Dunleavy, P. (1991): *Democracy Bureaucracy Public Choice* (New York: Harvester).

Edwards, M. (2000): *NGO Rights and Responsibilities: a New Deal for Global Governance* (London: The Foreign Policy Centre).

Flynn, B. (2000): 'Postcards from the edge of integration? The role of committees in EU environment policy-making', in T. Christiansen and E. Kirchner *Committee Governance in the European Union* (Manchester: Manchester University Press).

Gamson, W. A. (1992): *Talking Politics* (Cambridge: Cambridge University Press).

Gamson, W. A. (1975): *The Strategy of Social Protest* (Homewood, Ill: The Dorsey Press).

Geddes, A. (1999): 'The development of EU immigration policy: supranationalism and the politics of belonging', in A. Geddes and A. Favell *The Politics of Belonging: Migrants and Minorities in Contemporary Europe* (Aldershot: Ashgate).

Greenwood, J. (1997): *Representing Interests in the European Union* (London: Macmillan).

Jachtenfuchs, M. (1996): *International Policy-Making as a Learning Process? The European Union and the Greenhouse Effect* (Aldershot: Avebury).

Klandermans, B. (1988): 'The Formation and Mobilization of Consensus', in B. Klandermans, H. Kriesi and S. Tarrow *From Structure to Action: Comparing Social Movement Research Across Cultures* (Greenwich, CT: JAI Press).

Krasner, S. (1988): 'Sovereignty: an Institutional Perspective', 21:1, 66–94.

Majone, G. (1993): 'When Does Policy Deliberation Matter?' in *Politische Vierteljahresschrift* (Herbst).

Majone, G. (ed.) (1996): *Regulating Europe* (London: Routledge).

Majone, G. (1989): *Evidence, Argument, Persuasion in the Policy Process* (New Haven: Yale University Press).

March, J. (1988): *Decisions and Organizations* (Oxford: Oxford University Press).

Marks, G. and McAdam, D. (1996): 'Social Movements and the Changing Structure of Political Opportunity in the European Union', in G. Marks, F. W. Scharpf, P. C. Schmitter and W. Streeck *Governance in the European Union* (London: Sage).

Mazey, S. (2001): *Gender Mainstreaming in the EU* (London: Kogan Page).

Mazey, S. and Richardson, J. (1994): 'Interest Groups in the European Community', in S. Mazey and J Richardson *Pressure Groups* (Oxford: Oxford University Press).

Paterson, W. (1991): 'Regulatory Change and Environmental Protection in the British and German Chemical Industries', *European Journal of Political Research* 19, 307–26.

Pollack, M. A. (1997): 'Representing diffuse interests in EC policy-making', *Journal of European Public Policy* 4:4, 572–590.

Rein, M. and Schon, D. A. (1994): *Frame Reflections* (New York: Basic Books).

Rein, M. and Schon, D. A. (1977): 'Problem Setting in Policy Research', in C. H. Weiss *Using Social Research in Public Policy-Making* (Lexington, MA: D.C. Heath).

Ruzza, C. (1996): 'Inter-Organizational Negotiation in Political Decision-Making: EC Bureaucrats and the Environment', in N. South and C. Samson *Policy Processes and Outcomes* (London: Macmillan).

Ruzza, C. (2000a): 'Anti-Racism and EU institutions', *Journal of European Integration* 22:1.

Ruzza, C. (2000b): 'Sustainability and Tourism: EU Environmental Policy in Northern and Southern Europe', in K. Eder and M. Kousis *The Europeanization of Environmental Politics: Sustainable Development in Southern Europe* (Kluwer Press).

Scharpf, F. W. (1999): *Governing in Europe: effective and democratic?* (Oxford; New York: Oxford University Press).

Snow, D., Rochford, A., Burke, E., Worden, Steven K. and Benford, Robert D. (1986): 'Frame alignment processes, micromobilization and movements participation', *American Sociological Review* 51: 464–481.

Steinmo, S., Thelen, K., *et al.*, eds. (1992). *Structuring Politics* (Cambridge: Cambridge University Press).

Warleigh, A. (2001): 'Europeanizing Civil Society: NGOs as Agents of Political Socialization', *Journal of Common Market Studies* 39:4, 619–39.

Zuo, J. and R. D. Benford (1995): 'Mobilization Processes and the 1989 Chinese Democracy Movement', *The Sociological Quarterly* 36:1, 131–155.

Chapter 7

Interest Representation and Legitimacy in the European Union: The New Quest for Civil Society Formation

Rebekka Goehring

CIVIL SOCIETY AND EUROPEAN POLITICS

The notion of 'civil society' has gained unprecedented popularity in European Union (EU) politics. The term features prominently in the general reform discourse of the 1990s, from which some concrete proposals have emerged at the EU level. Responding to the crisis of 1999, which saw the departure of the Commission, a historically low voter turnout in the European Parliament (EP) elections and an increase of Euroscepticism throughout the member states, the Commission has devoted itself to promoting 'genuine reform to usher in a new era' (European Commission 1999). The EU's 'new governance' is supposed to make European politics more legitimate by strengthening its democratic structures and processes. In these efforts, citizens, civil society and non-governmental organizations (NGOs) are expected to play a prominent role, since their active engagement is considered to be necessary to remedy various (perceived or actual) defects and deficiencies. Two of the EU's institutions have taken on a leading role in the drive for improved legitimacy: the Commission and the Economic and Social Committee (ESC).

Using the three-way classification developed by Schimmelfennig (1996) that analyses legitimacy in terms of outputs, inputs and the social dimension, this chapter will examine the issue of legitimacy in relation to the EU's recent attempts to engage civil society in its policy-making processes. Output legitimacy, which is efficiency-orientated and has a functional basis, is particularly important as, ever since its inception, the EU has focused on providing efficient solutions that cannot be constructed at national level alone. Input legitimacy constitutes the second category, and can be characterized as being 'substantial' in character. It has been argued that the EU requires somewhat broader foundations in order to achieve properly legitimate institutions and decision making. This would demand a common identity or a consciousness of belonging. Schimmelfennig labels this type of legitimacy as social legitimacy according to which the

'... legitimacy of a political order depends on the degree of social homogeneity, the strength of civil society institutions, and the existence of a collective identity among citizens' (Schimmelfennig 1996: 5).

The remainder of the chapter unfolds as follows. Firstly, there is an examination of the definitional problem surrounding the term 'civil society'. In the second section, the issue of the representativeness of civil society organizations is tackled. The chapter then proceeds by reviewing a number of case studies that reveal a variety of approaches used at the EU level to involve civil society in EU decision making, focusing on the work of the Commission and the Economic and Social Committee (ESC). This will be, of course, by no means an exhaustive study of all the proposals and opinions that have been tabled so far. However, the chosen examples should suffice to illustrate the main issues and to permit some reflection on the primary goal of the reforms: making EU politics and processes (more) legitimate. The case studies include the Commission's and the Council's efforts under the auspices of the 'Dialogue on Europe' and the debate on the 'Future of the European Union'. In addition, the chapter will contain a review of the Commission's 2001 White Paper on Governance and consider what kind of framework it proposes for engaging civil society organizations with European institutions. The discussion of the White Paper will be followed by an analysis of the 'civil dialogue' in the field of World Trade Organization (WTO) negotiations, which is issue-specific, aims at involving organizations which are concerned with WTO-related matters, and is entirely organized by the Commission. Finally, the ESC proposal to set up an internal, institutionalized group of civil society will be explored.

PROBLEMS OF DEFINTION

The notion of civil society was first employed by Aristotle in order to demarcate the borderline between the public and the private sphere. The Greek *polis* was seen as identical with civil society, in contrast to the life of the private households. This ancient identification of civil society with the commonwealth prevailed until the early modern era: the Aristotelian notion of civil society was used by political thinkers such as Hobbes and Kant. At the beginning of the modern era, however, the political and economic spheres grew gradually apart. This was reflected in a new conception of civil society, which viewed it as being separated from the 'body politic'. Montesquieu was the first to make a distinction between the political and the civil 'state' (*l'état politique, l'état civil*). In the twentieth century, the Italian communist Gramsci established a further distinction with regard to civil society. He understood it to be different from the political as well as the economic sphere (that was dominated by *bourgeois* interests). Hence, civil society was seen to be different from and opposed to *bourgeois* society. However, today the term civil society may point to one of the two more recent conceptions: the first being *dual* in character, conceiving of civil society in contrast to the state; the second being *tripartite* distinguishing between the state, the economy and civil society. Thus, depending on the approach chosen, civil society may be defined as a network of associations either located between the state and the private sphere, or between the state, the economy and the private sphere (Ehrenberg 1999: 208 and 233; Reese-Schäfer 2000: 76).

Crucially, as soon as the notion of civil society is no longer used as a broad and sometimes rather fashionable concept, but serves as the basis for institutionalized representation, the problem of definition becomes much more significant. At a fundamental level, how the term is defined determines who is 'in' and who is 'out'. In other words, the manner in which the term is used signals who has the right to participate and exert influence in policy making (and who has not). However, defining the term is not straightforward. Indeed, we get a very diffuse picture of civil society and its organizations if we compare four definitions that appear to have currency in the EU at the present time among a range of organizations. The first definition of the term is apparent in the Commission's proposal for a reformulation of Article 257 of the Treaty Establishing the European Community (ECT), which would replace a list ranging from farmers, workers and craftsmen to representatives of the general public with the term 'civil society'. According to such a definition all members of the ESC, including the employers' and workers' groups, would be defined as representatives of civil society. This definition matches the broad one contained in the Commission's 2001 White Paper on Governance. Similarly, for the purposes of a recent ESC conference, civil society organizations have been identified as those

'... organizational structures whose members serve the public interest through discussion and function as mediators between the public authorities and the citizen' (Economic and Social Committee 2000a: 107).

In concrete terms, this includes employers' associations and trade unions, all other representative social and economic organizations,

NGOs, community-based organizations and religious associations. Whilst the ESC definition is more encompassing and precise than the Commission's, in both cases the term civil society could be replaced by 'intermediary organizations'. By contrast a much more restricted definition is evident in one NGO perspective. For example, the Permanent Forum of Civil Society, which is an active organization that promotes civic issues in the European arena, excludes economic organizations (even co-operatives) from its membership. Charities, socio-cultural and sports organizations are similarly excluded. Instead, the European Confederation of Trade Unions is a member and so too are organizations representing the 'New Social Movements', such as associations promoting de-colonization, consumer protection and public health as well as the anti-nuclear, the students' and the women's movements (Dastoli 1999: 149). Finally, the least compelling version of the term can be inferred from DG Trade's Civil Dialogue where civil society is simply equated with public and private interest groups.

In sum, 'civil society' and 'civil society organizations' are not clearly defined terms. Sometimes they are even used in a mutually exclusive way, which can be seen if one compares the first two definitions with that given by the Permanent Forum of Civil Society. The first included all socio-economic organizations, whereas the latter excludes all economic ones categorically. Moreover, the definition of civil society used by the Permanent Forum of Civil Society may seem contradictory insofar as it excludes economic organizations but, at the same time, accepts trade unions. Finally, the confusion gets even worse when, as is often the case, civil society is equated with 'citizen' and 'consumer', and thereby any particular meaning of civil society is ignored. However, these definitional problems are not due to the complexity or newness of European politics. At least partly, they stem from a general theoretical vagueness of the term:

> '[p]art of the problem is that civil society is an unavoidably nebulous and elastic conception that does not easily lend itself to a great deal of precision' (Ehrenberg 1999: 234).

Against the background set out above, the basis on which the Permanent Forum of Civil Society rejects economic organizations, except for trade unions, should become clear. What seems to be at first sight a contradiction inherent to the definition is rooted in Gramsci's distinction between civil and *bourgeois* society. To Gramsci, civil society should function as the motor for overcoming capitalism that was represented by state authority and *bourgeois* society. According to this perspective, trade unions no longer appear as economic organizations but rather as 'the essence of civil society' (Boual 1999: 45) which is opposed to *bourgeois* capitalist society. Moreover, this example demonstrates the difficulties of finding an encompassing authoritative definition of civil society. Since civil society is always situated in relation to the state (and economy), that is exogenous factors, its definition hinges on the actual structures of civil society organizations on one hand, and on the political and economic environment on the other. Civil society cannot adequately be described in and of itself (Ehrenberg 1999: 235).

REPRESENTATIVENESS OF CIVIL SOCIETY ORGANIZATIONS

The problems that surround the task of defining civil society are apparent in the EU institutions' groping attempts to decide who should be included in policy making and how they should be included. Problems of definition with regard to the institutionalization of civil society, however, could be solved. At least theoretically, we could conceive of a binding definition of civil society, either following the dual or the tripartite conceptions outlined above, from which it could be inferred precisely which organizations would fit the criteria (and which would not). Yet, probably more important is a caveat that originates from the changing structure of civil society organizations themselves. What makes them valuable contributors to politics is their capacity to feed civic perspectives into the policy process. They, therefore, need to be close to the people they represent. This makes long-term institutionalization problematic (Warleigh 2001). In some cases the organizations least connected with European institutions are closest to their 'clientele'. As the former President of the Commission (Jacques Delors) suggested in a speech given to the ESC conference:

> 'Civil society organizations must not give in to the temptation of saying they represent the general interest. They may identify the general interest in their discussions. But that is quite a different thing. As for the associative interests that flourish around the European Commission, *it would be dangerous for those involved to become too much a part of the system*; to believe they alone have the right to represent society. Associative interests move just as society moves, and *care must therefore be taken not to ensconce privileged lobby groups while ignoring everything that emerges from society* as it evolves. But I think that more than ever we are counting on the representatives of civil society organizations to have their finger on the pulse of society' (Economic and Social Committee 2000a: 79, emphasis added).

Even though civil society organizations might have their finger on the pulse of society, they are not 'representative' *strictu sensu*. A consumer organization speaks for consumer interests, but it does not represent consumers in the same way as a European employers' umbrella organization represents its national members. Nevertheless, European institutions would like civil society organizations to be representative. In most cases this is impossible because of the great variety of organizations in one field which all have different approaches to a given issue. Moreover, representativeness of NGOs may be undesirable. What makes these organizations so rich in variety and scope, vivid and important is that they are not representative, but factional, and that they are not entirely formalized but have a more or less flexible organizational structure. Even so, there are some highly organized groups such as the Young European Federalists (JEF) that can claim an impressive membership all over Europe. However, this is an exception to the rule.

The ESC discusses these problems at some length in an Opinion on the Commission's discussion paper concerning the relationship between NGOs and the Commission. It states that representativeness can by no means be measured exclusively on the basis of membership, but must also take into account the organizations' capacity to generate expertise (Economic and Social Committee 2000a: 4). Yet, is the expert ever representative? Expertise might render European politics more efficient but this might have little to do with the input and social dimensions of legitimacy. The more the European institutions count on civil society organizations to provide links to the citizenry and, therefore, help to bolster the legitimacy of EU rule, the more they will demand that they are representative of interests which are, in turn, defined by the institutions. The relationship between 'state' and civic organizations is a very difficult and fragile one, especially if the latter become more and more dependent on funding and power resources provided by the former. Almost since the inception of the then European Economic Community, the Commission has created or helped to build up a raft of civil society organizations, some of which receive important funding resources from the Commission (if they are not financed entirely by it). The attempts to involve NGOs in an institutionalized context have therefore been criticized by several authors working in this field (Warleigh 2001; Boual 1999: 44). They warn against the danger that such efforts might lead to the creation of a false civil society by European institutions. In addition, the loss of independence due to the inclusion of NGOs might make an open debate about the content of European integration impossible. Such a debate is vital to the transformation of the former European Economic Community into a political project, with which Europe's citizens would be willing to identify (Hermann 1998: 144). Therefore, the strength of an institution like the ESC may not lie in the rigid institutionalization of representative civil society organizations but in its capacity to generate expertise, to issue opinions, to assemble groups and individuals and to provide a forum for discussion (Smismans 2000).

The 2001 White Paper on Governance (European Commission 2001a) also acknowledges that the relationship between NGOs and the Commission might be deemed to be 'too close'. Hence, the on-line database of civil society organizations is aimed at functioning 'as a catalyst to improve their internal organization' (European Commission 2001a: 15). Moreover, the Commission wants the proposed code of conduct to increase the representativeness of the consulted organizations. Finally, the new partnership arrangements can be entered into only if the organization concerned also takes over some duties, such as building up a working internal structure, providing expertise and leading debates in the member states (*ibid*: 17). It is no surprise, then, that the Commission conceives of participation as 'institutionalizing protest' in order to shape more effective policy (*ibid*: 15).

THE DIALOGUE ON EUROPE

Today much of the EU's engagement with civil society and the official rhetoric that accompanies it is concerned with output legitimacy and forms part of the elitist approach traditionally found among European policy makers towards integration: that is they have a 'pedagogic duty' towards citizens. As Leo Tindemans puts it:

'. . . we cannot blithely assume that the citizens will acquiesce in the cavalier adoption of integrationist strategies by our governments and parliaments. We must spell out what we are doing and why. [...] It is imperative that the European Union should better inform its people about its decisions and activities and about the reasons behind them' (Tindemans 1998: 140).

The 'Dialogue on Europe', an initiative launched by the Commission to accompany the last Intergovernmental Conference in Nice in 2000, fits into this 'pedagogic' logic. In concrete terms, the 'Dialogue' was supposed to raise awareness of European issues and to dispel the perception that the operation of the institutions suffers from a lack of democracy (European Commission 2000a). A dialogue that was intended to dispel allegedly 'wrong' perceptions by explaining the 'correct' ones would appear to be rather paternalistic. It hardly amounts to the sort of open dialogue that could channel societal demands and perceptions to the European institutions.

The 'Dialogue' and the way in which it has been managed demonstrate some of the difficulties faced by the Commission in trying to overcome its remoteness from the peoples of Europe. Although the 'Dialogue' was primarily targeted at 'ordinary people' (especially the young) and was designed to answer their questions and listen to their views (European Commission 2000b), critics would no doubt point out that it could be perceived as little more than a public relations exercise. This is one possible interpretation of the inauguration meeting of the 'Dialogue'. This was held in Brussels and took the form of a meeting between Commissioners, the President of the European Parliament and 700 recently arrived *stagiaires*, newly graduated students who had secured one of the most sought after internships in Europe. These individuals could hardly be regarded as typical of the 'average European citizen', being probably at least better informed about the EU than most people (and possibly more committed to it).

Arguably, input legitimacy, as well as any social dimension, were distinctly absent from the EU's 'Dialogue'. Its rather paternalistic, elitist, one-way approach still dominates the thinking of many European policy-makers. Where the term 'democracy' appears, its use suggests that it is merely equated with a larger degree of public debate and understanding, which can be measured by public opinion polls. Democracy is certainly not seen as a matter of substantial input, as some type of 'government *by* the people'. Thus, the following quote drawn from a speech given to the Parliament is characteristic of the Commission President's stance towards democracy. Prodi explains the advantages of the restructuring of the EU Treaties as follows:

'[i]t would concentrate the basic Treaty on essential matters, making it clearer and far more readable for the general public, *thus enhancing European democracy*' (European Commission 1999a, emphasis added).

Building on the experience of the 'Dialogue on Europe', the Commission, together with the Swedish and Belgian Council Presidencies and the European Parliament, launched a new debate on the 'Future of the European Union' on 7 March 2001. This amounted to a direct implementation of the Declaration on the Future of the Union (European Council 2001b) adopted by the Nice Intergovernmental Conference of 2000 and calling for a deeper and wider debate. To that end, the Declaration announced that the following should become involved:

'[A]ll those reflecting public opinion, namely political, economic and university circles, representatives of civil society . . . ' (*ibid.*: 12).

Given the persisting approach of 'debate and dialogue' as a means of generating support for the European project, it is not accidental that the Treaty of Nice Declaration does not mention individual citizens as parties to the debate, but only 'opinion multipliers'. Even the subsequent

Laeken Declaration, much hailed in the public arena because it finally speaks of broad participation in the shaping of the future Union, does not bring a change with regard to the (individual) citizen's role. Passages refer to the 'expectations of Europe's citizens' and how these could freely determine what citizens 'want', 'instinctively sense', or what they are 'calling for' (European Council 2001: 3–4) but the Declaration does not take into account the diversity of the attitudes found within modern societies. Rather, the quoted passage is reminiscent of some kind of Rousseau-like 'general will' that is supposed to emanate from a homogenous society and be defined by its elites. As was the case for the 'Dialogue on Europe', it remains doubtful whether such efforts are likely to reach the ever more alienated and sceptical European public.

However, learning seems to have taken place. A recent Commission document (European Commission 2001b) envisages open discussions with citizens regarding issues associated with European integration. At least in this document, elements central to the concept of debate can be found. It states that

'[i]f the debate is to lead to radical reform [...] [c]itizens must have the opportunity to express their specific expectations and concerns during this debate' (European Commission 2001b: 4).

It continues:

'[t]he issues of the European debate must be explained to as many people as possible so that, when the time comes, each person can express a view with a knowledge of the facts' (*ibid.*: 6).

Indeed, if the envisaged idea of a bottom-up, citizen-driven approach can be coupled with an efficient feedback mechanism (to those who are politically responsible) and this can be put into practice, this would mean a step towards a more democratic dialogue and debate.

THE COMMISSION'S PROJECT ON EUROPEAN GOVERNANCE

The Commission's efforts to usher in a new era, however, are not limited to initiatives such as the 'Dialogue on Europe' or the debate on the 'Future of the European Union'. Indeed, since the beginning of the 1990s the Commission's internal think-tank has been undertaking intensive research in the field of European governance with a view to modernizing the EU. Hence, in May 1999 the Forward Studies Unit presented its broad findings on improving the effectiveness and legitimacy of EU governance (European Commission 1999b). In October 2000 a comprehensive work programme was published (European Commission 2000c) as part of the preparations for the White Paper on European Govern-ance, which was eventually published in July 2001 (European Commis-sion 2001a). The White Paper proposes a range of governmental and legislative measures, such as a new open method of co-ordination, an intensified use of regulatory agencies, co-regulation, and defines the principles of good governance as being openness, participation, account-ability, effectiveness and coherence.[1]

The outcomes of these documents, however, are ambiguous. An analysis of the representational and legitimacy patterns shows that the Commission evidently has difficulty overcoming the barrier of 'techno-cratic administration'. The term legitimacy is, contrary to the research report's explicit intention (European Commission 1999b: 9), used as if it was just a public relations problem. This is reflected in passages of the White Paper that suggest that

'[t]he European agenda must come to be understood as more relevant by civil society' (*ibid.*: 15).

It is therefore no surprise that the background analysis sees a '*perceived* lack of [. . .] legitimacy' without being able to find any substantial and structural problems which might account for it (*ibid.*: 8, emphasis added).

The White Paper (European Commission 2001a) continues in a similar way. It starts out by stating that, despite its achievements, many Eur-opeans feel alienated from the Union's work, but that would be a problem common to all sorts of politics and political institutions around the globe (*ibid.*: 7). Hence, it seems to suggest that it would be superfluous to look for any systematic problems in the Union's own institutional setting and working approach. One might argue that this reflection does not constitute the ideal starting point for a democratic reform of the Union's institutions, a problem that is aggravated by a rather confusing use of the term 'democratic representation'. The White Paper defines the Community method of integration as mediating between different inter-ests with the help of two filters: firstly, the general interest represented by the Commission and secondly, democratic representation in the Council, the European and national Parliaments (*ibid*: 8). Unfortunately, the difference between this 'general interest' and the broad representativity of the Council and Parliament remains unclear. Whilst the White Paper comes close to the idea of input legitimacy, it does not go as far as seeing it as being of intrinsic value. Rather, policy makers are advised to stay in

---

[1] For a detailed discussion of the White Paper see C. Joerges, Y. Mény, J.H.H. Weiler (eds) *Responses to the European Commission's White Paper on Governance*, accessible via the Jean Monnet Program web site www.jeanmonnetprogram.org, and to be published as a book later.

touch with European public opinion to guide them in identifying European projects that mobilize public support. Openness is thought 'to improve the confidence in complex institutions' (European Commission 2001a: 12 and 10). Apparently, input legitimacy only serves to generate public support and transparency to generate trust. Of course, these are important elements of a political system's legitimacy, yet they are not the whole story.

Clearly, ideas of input and social legitimacy do not fit the logic of bureaucratic rule, nor does territorial representation. On the other hand, as for as the goal of enhancing output legitimacy is concerned, the Commission strives for new working methods that would turn its old approach upside-down. But this, it seems, is only possible in the field of collective representation (i.e. in co-operation with *organized* groups) not with regard to individual citizens. Territorial (and that means individualistic) representation is rejected as 'too broadly [...] based' (European Commission 1999b: 15). In concrete terms, the re-orientation of administrative working methods is supposed to transform the Commission from a bureaucracy that sets the general policy preferences and translates these into detailed programmes into an administration that prioritizes 'pluralistic scientific expertise' (*ibid*: 14), enables all groups affected by a policy to participate at every stage of the policy process and sets the general framework for their co-operation:

> "[t]he entire policy process from framing of problems, through the formulation of policy, its implementation, evaluation and revision needs to be opened up and liberated from the shadowy world it currently inhabits – *civil society needs to be engaged in and by European action*' (European Commission 1999b: 11, emphasis in original).

The White Paper provides us with detailed information about what the Commission understands by the term 'civil society'. In general, it is defined as giving a voice to the concerns of citizens, delivering services that meet people's needs, preparing the applicant countries for membership, acting as an early warning system in the field of development policy and as social partners, getting citizens more actively involved in achieving the Union's objectives as well as offering them a structured channel for feedback, criticism and protest (European Commission 2001a: 14–5). In a footnote (p. 14) the White Paper then enumerates the organizations which fit into these functional criteria. According to this document, civil society includes: trade unions and employers' associations ('social partners'), non-governmental organizations, professional associations, charities, grassroots organizations and organizations that involve citizens in local and municipal life (with a particular contribution from churches and religious communities). In its White Paper the Commission offers 'partnership arrangements' to this potential pool of organizations, which would function on the basis of a code of conduct and would, according to the Commission's calculation, be advantageous to both sides. In this context the Commission has already set up a consultation database, CONECCS, containing information about consultation procedures and providing for civil society organizations the possibility to register.

In the same vein the Commission strives for a newly defined partnership with NGOs. In its discussion paper on the relationship with NGOs the Commission tries to adopt a new stance towards the question about the role that civil society organizations should play in European politics (European Commission 2000e). The Commission identifies a range of questions that need to be answered with respect to NGOs. Should they only be consulted by the Commission? Should they be involved in the implementation process? Should the consultation procedure be formalized? Should NGOs have to register? The White Paper could be an important step in giving NGOs a more formalized place in European decision making. Yet it is too early to speculate on the final format of an NGO-Commission relationship, since the discussion on the White Paper is still being evaluated.

More importantly, against the backdrop of the overall reform of the EU's institutional structure, the questions above gain more relevance when considering the smooth functioning of the institutions. Defining civil society's place in European politics becomes even more complicated, if one takes all European institutions into account. If the third Group of the Economic and Social Committee (ESC) were to be transformed into a 'Civil Society Organizations Group', then the institutional role of the ESC would still need to be reviewed and clarified. Moreover, the European Parliament has to be taken into account, as it is not only the institution which represents individual citizens but it has also always played a very active role advocating the concerns of public interest groups.

The following two examples, however, of how civil society organizations have actually become engaged by European institutions might provide us with insights into the broader discussion of legitimacy and reform, as well as the relationship between the EU's institutions and civil society (organizations). The new governance approach of the Commission has been paralleled by the desire of some Directorates General (DGs) to organize their co-operation with NGOs within a more regularized framework which has come to be labelled 'Civil Dialogue'. As we will see from the example of DG Trade's dialogue in the field of WTO negotiations, this type of organizational-administrative relationship differs substantially from the envisaged institutionalized representation of civil society in the ESC (see below). In the first case, an approach which was originally meant to co-opt NGOs and to increase efficiency has developed the potential to alter the nature of EU politics and render it more legitimate and democratic. In the second case, however, there are important caveats with regard to the concepts of representation, and only if these are duly taken into account, might changing the composition of the ESC have a significant impact.

THE CIVIL DIALOGUE IN THE FIELD OF WTO NEGOTIATIONS

The Civil Dialogue in the field of WTO negotiations was initiated in 1998[2] by the then Commissioner Sir Leon Brittan. At its origin were the first demonstrations against issues of world trade. This development can partly be explained by the success of the General Agreement on Tariffs and Trade (GATT) itself. As the classical impediments to free trade have been dramatically reduced, state protectionism has expressed itself in other fields, such as environmental issues and services. Consequently, the international negotiations on free trade came to include questions of technical barriers and services as well as intellectual property (i.e. the General Agreement on Trade in Services (GATS) and the Trade-Related Aspects of Intellectual Property Rights (TRIPS)). This eventually led to a significant politicization of international trade agreements (see Somerset, this volume).

The Commission's approach, in this context, to dealing with the NGOs concerned was originally more of a public relations effort, the purpose of which was to allay public fears, than engagement in a dialogue in the proper sense of the word. Originally, the dialogue consisted of two meetings a year, during which more than 200 participants could listen to a 20-minute speech by the Commissioner. However, since its inception there has been internal debate in the Commission regarding how this could be changed. The format of today's Civil Dialogue looks quite different:

'[t]he objective of this dialogue is to develop a confident working relationship between all interested stakeholders in the trade policy field, to ensure that all contributions to EU trade policy can be heard [. . .] The process is designed to focus on issues where [. . .] we can get better mutual understanding of concerns and better contacts between the key players . . . ' (European Commission 2002).

Hence, in addition to general meetings, a contact group and a number of issue groups have been established. The contact group's task is to facilitate

[2] The following description is partly based on an interview with a high-ranking Commission official, currently member of Commissioner Lamy's cabinet, in September 2000.

DG Trade's work in the dialogue: to make sufficient information available to both sides and to the wider NGO 'constituency' and to co-ordinate the running of the issue groups. A restriction of the number of annual meetings is designed to ensure the latter's efficiency. The dialogue's participants, in co-operation with the contact group, as well as the ongoing WTO negotiations determine the agenda. Several mechanisms aim to make the work of the issue groups meet the requirement of transparency. The agendas are made available at least 20 working days before the meeting. The participating groups have the opportunity to make public their positions before the meeting, and the outcome, a *compte rendu,*[3] is published as well. In addition, the participants might give feedback after the meetings and contribute to DG Trade's review of the dialogue process. The general meetings have been maintained, but have also been transformed into occasions to discuss general topics of trade policy, to present the issue groups' work and to debate the dialogue's organization in general. As for representation, the 'constituencies' select their contact group members, not DG Trade. The participation in the issue groups is open to everybody who registers with DG Trade. The registration form is available on the Internet. It is a short document and places little administrative burden on the prospective participant. Hence, no formal accreditation of NGOs takes place. The only prerequisite for participation is making explicit the represented interest. This has gained some importance since, in some cases, private interest representatives had adopted the 'disguise' of an NGO to give their claims more weight. At the time of writing some 250 organizations feature in DG Trade's database, bringing together all sorts of public and private interest groups.

The Commission also undertakes some efforts to reach a broader public and has set up 'internet chats' as well as other forums. It is part of DG Trade's policy not to co-opt organized interests. Therefore, DG representatives also meet separately with those NGOs that refuse to participate in the dialogue for ideological reasons, such as Attac or l'Observatoire de la Mondialisation. In the initial stages of the dialogue, funding was not made available to enable interest groups to attend the issue group meetings because of the fear that the Commission might exert influence on NGOs (i.e. co-opt them by way of granting funds). As a consequence, participation became a problem for those NGOs that do not have sufficient financial resources at their disposal. Therefore, eventually, a pilot project for funding was set up.

In sum, a good deal of the international trade policy process has indeed been 'opened up and liberated from the shadowy world'. Civil society has

---

[3] The usual English term for the *compte-rendu* of a meeting is 'minutes'.

indeed become 'engaged in and by European action'. What at first had been dominated by an elitist-paternalistic approach very soon turned into a creative mechanism to engage civil society. Of course, it is in the Commission's interest to create such a dialogue in order to feed as much expertise as possible into the policy process and thereby to enhance efficiency. However, this kind of dialogue does not exclusively increase output legitimacy, as it has also significant ramifications on the input side. It is the Commission's intention to make conflict happen, but within the arena and among groups, not only between the DG and NGOs. This in turn helps to generate a genuine European public debate, even if it is confined and issue-restricted. As one high-ranking Commission official pointed out, the dialogue has not only helped the Commission to 'sell' its arguments to the NGO constituencies, but has meant that over time outside positions have come to influence, and partly even alter, the point of view of the Commission.[4]

ORGANIZED CIVIL SOCIETY AND THE ECONOMIC AND SOCIAL COMMITTEE

The visions of new European governance also affect the Economic and Social Committee, where they take quite a different shape. In October 1999 the ESC organized the 'First Convention on Civil Society Organized at European Level',[5] debating at length an ESC opinion issued on the contribution of civil society organizations to European integration (Economic and Social Committee 1999a). Since Europe's remoteness from its citizens has been identified as one of the main obstacles to overcoming legitimacy problems, it was seen as useful for the ESC to undertake efforts to become 'a bridge between Europe and civil society', as the institution's own description claims (Economic and Social Committee 2001). If these efforts were successful they might add political weight to an EU institution that has never played a central role in European politics and whose internal organization risked becoming outdated.

The relationship between civil society and the ESC has been developed in greater detail by Anne-Marie Sigmund, President of the Various Interests Group III (Economic and Social Committee 2000b). Drawing on a rich, though rather idiosyncratic, theoretical background, she has tried to demonstrate that civil society organizations can play a key role in European democracy. According to her approach, they represent indi-

---

[4] For a detailed analysis of how this kind of ideational merger happens, see the chapter by Ruzza in this volume.

[5] The English translation is partly misleading: this problem could have been avoided by translating the French terminology 'société civile organisée' as 'Civil Society Organizations'.

vidual citizens, stand for participation, public debate, openness and democracy, and function as mediators. Sigmund concludes that the link between European democracy, civil society organizations and the ESC is as follows:

> '[t]he citizens of Europe are in search of a new social contract which is based on the Rousseau concept of self-determination and does not look on the sovereignty of the people as transfer of power from top to bottom. It is obvious that civil society organizations have a key role in this 'Europe project'. The representatives of civil society organizations, and the Economic and Social Committee *as their legitimate representative*, have the opportunity but also the duty to influence this development' (Economic and Social Committee 2000b: 109, emphasis added).

What does that mean in concrete terms? Even though the ESC does not see itself as the exclusive voice of civil society, the Committee is nevertheless trying to become a central actor in this field and to function as the main intermediary between the other EU institutions and civil society organizations. For instance, in its opinion about the participation of NGOs in the WTO negotiations, the ESC proposes the creation of an internal WTO Committee that would serve as a hub between the WTO, the Commission's services and the European NGOs concerned (Economic and Social Committee 1999b: 6). It is remarkable that the document does not even mention DG Trade's civil dialogue and therefore does not deal with the question how the relationship between individual associations and the ESC as their self-appointed 'legitimate representative' should be conceived. In the same vein, the ESC aims at functioning as a facilitator for the debate between the ongoing European Convention and civil society organizations. It regularly organizes information meetings and dialogues on the European Convention in order to enable discussion between, among others, the Vice-President of the European Convention responsible for liaison with civil society (Jean-Luc Dehaene) and NGOs.[6]

More generally, recent plans to alter the composition of the ESC provide us with some insights into ESC's overall aspirations. The Commission had proposed a new formula for the last Intergovernmental Conference (IGC) which took place in 2000. This would have taken into account the changed institutional environment, namely the fact that the European Parliament has evolved into a co-legislator and that, as a corollary, the ESC's role should be mainly defined as a 'relay *vis-à-vis*

---

[6] The first two 'information meeting and dialogue on the European Convention' sessions were held on 18 April and 27 May 2002. For more information see www.esc.eu.int.

civil society', its legislative function being of minor importance (European Commission 2000d: 18). In concrete terms this would have implied a change in Articles 257 and 258 of the ECT. The Commission had suggested the replacement of the enumeration of professions in Art. 257 by the term 'civil society', so that the Treaty would simply stipulate that '[t]he Committee shall consist of representatives of the various categories of civil society'. Moreover, the distribution of seats by member state would have been abolished, so that the ESC would have become

> 'more representative of the various components of civil society of the European Union as a whole and of its different geographical aspects' (*ibid.*: 18).

These ideas were not adopted by the IGC 2000. Yet, it is conceivable that they will remain on the table for the IGCs to come. In this case, the implementation of the Commission's vision, even though it would mainly affect the Group III (Various Interests), leaving the other two Groups unaltered (Employers (I) and Workers (II)), could have far-reaching consequences. It could bestow upon the Committee a potentially powerful competence to be representative of *European* civil society as a whole. Indeed, an altered composition could enable the ESC to really function as some kind of transmission belt for civil society. However, the question remains whether this is desirable. The two caveats in the case of the ESC reform point to the overall problems faced by the EU in its attempts to engage civil society in policy making: the problems of definition and representativeness (as discussed above).

CONCLUSION

Representation is one of the central topics in the current debate on EU legitimacy. It is evident that different types of representation and participation have to be combined and reinforced in order to build a strong, enlarged, legitimate, and political Union. The Council must be efficient. The Commission must become more accountable and transparent. The European Parliament's institutional position needs to be strengthened. New channels of representation and participation have to be found and efficiently activated. In this context broadly organized debates between European policy makers and the citizenry may turn out to be useful once they are no longer conceived of merely as public relations exercises, but rather as genuine dialogues in which opinions and arguments are exchanged fully. Furthermore, the Commission's dialogue in the field of WTO negotiations clearly illustrates how new channels of representation and participation could operate in issue-specific areas. All types of dialogues, general and issue-specific, have the potential to bolster EU legitimacy (in terms of input, output and social inclusion). As long as they are well organized they could provide the EU with the required knowledge to improve its efficiency. This could, therefore, help to reinforce the output dimension of legitimacy. Dialogues may also have an impact on the overall orientation of European policies, thereby strengthening the input dimension of legitimacy. Finally, participation in dialogues may fortify a collective European identity and strengthen civil society organizations, therefore developing the social dimension of legitimacy.

It is, however, doubtful that any attempts to institutionalize civil society participation by forming a new group in the ESC or by restricting the access to the Commission to registered NGOs will help to make the EU more legitimate overall. To this end, the definition of civil society and its exact relation to the EU institutions would have to be determined. Efforts to make NGOs 'truly representative', as much as any form of institutionalized dialogue with restricted access, may weaken the vitality of civil society organizations rather than strengthen it.

Finally, there is a risk that *collective* types of representation become dominant overall, be they national-executive as in the form of the Council, or non-territorial-functional as in the case of the ESC debate. The significance of territorial representation for the *individual* within liberal Western democracies must not be forgotten entirely. It is probable that there will have to be more direct participation by Europe's citizens in EU affairs if it is to achieve (greater) legitimacy. Most importantly, there must be a switch from a Union in which the member states constitute the high contracting parties to a 'Europe of the peoples'. Proposals inspired to promote output legitimacy or based on collective representation are very important in bolstering EU legitimacy. However, they will not suffice if they are not complemented by components that emphasize individual representation. Unintentionally, Anne-Marie Sigmund has combined two concepts which have long been juxtaposed. In her first sentence she refers to Rousseau, who was fiercely hostile to any kind of intermediary institutions and then moves directly from his 'social contract' to the importance of civil society organizations. In this she expresses something which might be seen as a contradiction in terms, but should not be seen so in the context of future EU politics. Individual representation should still be at the centre of politics but can be usefully complemented by national, regional and functional representation.

REFERENCES

Boual, J.-C. (1999): 'Une Société Civile Européenne est possible', in J.-C. Boual (ed.) *Vers une Société Civile Européenne* (La Tour d'Aigues: Editions de l'Aube).

Dastoli, V. (1999): 'L'Europe entre Démocratie Virtuelle et Citoyenneté Parti-cipative: l'Expérience du Forum Permanent de la Société Civile', in J.-C. Boual (ed.) *Vers une Société Civile Européenne* (La Tour d'Aigues: Editions de l'Aube).

Economic and Social Committee (2001): *The ESC: A Bridge between Europe and Civil Society,* ESC-2001–004–EN.

Economic and Social Committee (2000a): *Opinion of the Economic and Social Committee on the Commission discussion paper 'The Commission and non-governmental organizations: building a stronger partnership' (COM(2000) 11 final)*, CES 811/2000, 13 July.

Economic and Social Committee (2000b): *The Civil Society Organized at European Level: Proceedings of the First Convention,* ESC-2000–012-EN.

Economic and Social Committee (1999a): *Avis sur 'La transparence et la participation de la société civile aux 'négociations du millénaire' dans le cadre de l'Organisation mondiale du commerce'*, CES 946/99, 20 October.

Economic and Social Committee (1999b): *Opinion on 'The Role and Contribution of Civil Society Organizations in the Building of Europe'*, CES 851/99, 22 September.

Ehrenberg, J. (1999): *Civil Society: The Critical History of an Idea* (New York, London: New York University Press).

European Commission (2002): *Towards sustainable trade*, Process guidelines, http://www.europa.eu.int/comm/trade/csc/dcs_proc.htm, March.

European Commission (2001a): *European Governance*, White Paper, COM(2001) 428, 25 July.

European Commission (2001b): *'On Certain Arrangements for the Debate on the Future of the European Union'*, Commission Communication, COM(2001) 178 final, 25 April.

European Commission (2000a): *Dialogue on Europe: The Challenges of Institu-tional Reform*, Memorandum, http://www.europa.eu.int/comm/igc2000/dialogue/index_en.htm, 15 February.

European Commission (2000b): *Dialogue on Europe: Questions and Answers on Dialogue on Europe*, http://www.europa.eu.int/comm/igc2000/dialogue/index_en.htm, 18 January.

European Commission (2000c): *White Paper on European Governance, 'Enhan-cing democracy in the European Union'*, Work Programme, SEC(2000) 154/7 final, 11 October.

European Commission (2000d): *Adapting the Institutions to Make Success of Enlargement,* Commission Opinion in Accordance with Article 48 of the Treaty on European Union on the Calling of a Conference of Representatives of the Governments of the Member States to Amend the Treaties, COM (2000) 34 final, 26 January .

European Commission (2000e): *The Commission and Non-Governmental Organi-zations: Building a Stronger Partnership*, Commission discussion paper, COM(2000) 11 final, 18 January.

European Commission (1999a): *Speech by President of the European Commis-sion Romano Prodi to the European Parliament,* Speech/99/158, 10 November.

European Commission (1999b): *Improving the Effectiveness and the Legitimacy of EU governance*, Forward Studies Unit, Lebessis/Paterson, CdP (99)750.

European Commission (1999c): *Adapting the Institutions to Make Success of Enlargement*, 10 November.

European Council (2001): *Presidency Conclusions*, 14 and 15 December.

Hermann, P. (1998): *Partizipationskulturen in der Europäischen Union: Nichtregierungsorganisationen in den EU-Mitgliedsstaaten* (Rheinfelden: Schäuble).

Reese-Schäfer, W. (2000): *Politische Theorie heute: Neue Tendenzen und Entwicklungen* (München, Wien: Oldenbourg Verlag).

Schimmelfennig, F. (1996): *Legitimate Rule in the European Union: The Academic Debate* (Tübingen: Arbeitspapiere zur Internationalen Politik und Friedensforschung 27).

Smismans, S. (2000): *The European Economic and Social Committee: Towards Deliberative Democracy via a Functional Assembly* (European Integration online Papers 12), http://eiop.or.at/eiop/texte/2000-012a.htm.

Tindemans, L. (1998): 'Dreams Come True, Gradually', in M. Westlake (ed.) *The European Union beyond Amsterdam: New concepts of European integration* (London/New York: Routledge), 130–141.

Warleigh, A. (2001): 'Europeanizing Civil Society: NGOs as Agents of Political Socialization', *Journal of Common Market Studies* 39:4, 619–39.

Chapter 8

The Europeanization of Interest Representation: The Case of United Kingdom Environment Policy

Jenny Fairbrass and Andrew Jordan

INTRODUCTION

For more than 40 years the role played by various actors in shaping the development of the European Union (EU) has been a source of fascination and dispute for scholars in Europe and beyond. The role played by interest groups is particularly contested. Until the 1980s rival versions of International Relations (IR) theory dominated much of the discourse and affected the way in which interest groups were perceived. Neofunctionalism held sway in the 1950s and 1960s but was displaced by intergovernmentalism in the 1970s. Whilst these two schools of thought were unable to agree about which actor (or actors) were responsible for European *integration*, they were broadly in agreement that it was a 'bottom-up' process (i.e., that national level factors and forces created or caused European integration). By the 1980s this IR-led debate had reached an impasse. In the early 1990s EU studies received fresh impetus as it drew in scholars of national and comparative politics. One of the novel research themes that subsequently emerged was the study of the impact of the EU on the member states, i.e. *Europeanization*.

In the space of only a few years scholars have begun to apply the concept of Europeanization to explain several features of the EU. It has been used to study individual member states, compare two or more member states, examine political structures and national policy content, and even national culture (see Jordan 2002; Jordan 2003). In this chapter we seek to add to that literature by examining the Europeanization of interest representation in the EU. Part of the originality of this approach lies in thinking of the changed/changing relations between policy-makers (national and EU) and interest groups as part of a broader process of the Europeanization of national politics. In addition, we advance the debate about interest representation in the EU by analysing the *causal mechanisms* that lie behind the Europeanization of interest group behaviour. In doing so we move beyond the confines of a single discipline (i.e. political science) by employing tools and analytical frameworks drawn from management science.

The precise meaning of the term 'Europeanization' is contested. Some scholars define it as the accumulation of competences at the EU level; others see it as a two-way process in which the 'national' and the 'EU' affect each other simultaneously (Boerzel 2002). However, for the sake of convenience, we restrict ourselves to looking at Europeanization primarily as a 'top-down' process in which the EU has a *progressive impact* on national political arenas. Accordingly Europeanization results in adjustments to domestic institutions, policy-making processes and public policies, and affects the behaviour of and relations between national and subnational state and non-state actors. From among this array of actors, in this chapter we focus on nationally based non-state actors (i.e. environmental interest groups). We concentrate on their objectives and behaviour, the opportunities and threats present in their external political environment, and the extent of their resources. We set out to determine the degree of adaptation (i.e. Europeanization) exhibited by the groups and the reasons for any such modified behaviour. We contend that a (relative) lack of opportunity at one level of governance (e.g., in the national arena) is likely to induce an interest group to seek opportunities at another level (e.g., the EU level). We also anticipate that the degree of Europeanization will reflect a number of factors including, *inter alia,* a group's resources, the weight placed on the groups objectives in relation to achieving certain environmental policy outcomes and the particular policy issue at stake.

Earlier research (Jordan 2002) has examined the Europeanization of United Kingdom (UK) environmental policy over a thirty-year period (*c.* 1970 to 2000). The evidence shows clearly that EU membership has led most noticeably to changes generally in UK environmental policy content, and to a lesser extent to policy style and structures.[1] In this chapter

---

[1] Analysis of the impact of the EU on the content, style and structure of national environmental policy provides a useful framework with which to compare different EU member states. The term 'content' refers to the actual substance and scope of the policy. The manner in which that legal substance is administered is captured by the term 'style'. For example, it has been shown (see Jordan 2002) that as a result of the impact of EU membership that the UK's style of environmental policy mutated from being typically voluntary, flexible, and case-by-case to a formal, explicit and uniform approach based on fixed, legal standards. The word 'structures' refers to the organizations and the part they play in policy making. For example, traditionally in the UK environmental policy was devolved to local bodies in the context of a broad framework set by central government. However, Europeanization appears to have had a centralizing impact on UK environmental policy.

we concentrate specifically on two important strands of EU environ-mental policy, namely biodiversity[2] and land use planning. Our discus-sion revolves around a number of key questions that link together Europeanization and interest representation in the EU. How has EU membership affected the relationship between the national environmen-tal groups and policy-makers at various levels of governance? What impact has the EU had on the interest representation by nationally based environmental groups? What aspects of the interest representation beha-viour of the groups has been Europeanized? Where the behaviour of the groups has been altered in response to the EU, why has this occurred? We consider that such an approach helps to move forward the debate about interest representation in the EU and escapes the sterile confines of the well-worn arguments associated with IR theories.

The remainder of this chapter proceeds as follows. The first section provides some theoretical foundations. The second section outlines the background to our chosen case study, in which we explore the critical characteristics of environmental policy and politics at the national and the EU levels. The third section supplies fresh evidence about the strategies and tactics of environmental interest groups. The final section offers some concluding remarks and looks forward to the next phase of Europeanization research.

THEORIZING EU INTEREST REPRESENTATION
Well-worn Paths

The discussion in this chapter sits at the intersection of two bodies of political science literature. The first is very broadly concerned with theorizing about the EU as a polity. The second focuses directly on interest groups. That said, the two are not discrete bodies of scholarship. Within the first area of work attempts to explain the development of the EU have led academics to scrutinize and evaluate the role of various actors (including interest groups) in the political system and their inter-action with one another. Some of the earliest authors, for example the neofunctionalists (e.g. Haas 1958), predicted that domestic interests would form entities beyond the nation state (i.e. transnational groups) and that they would treat the EU institutions as their main focus of interest, thereby facilitating deeper *integration*. When, in the 1960s, actual events in the EU failed to support these contentions other International Relations approaches (i.e. intergovernmentalism) gained prominence.

---

[2] The term biodiversity refers to the variability among living organisms (i.e. flora and fauna), including the variety within and between species and within and between ecosystems.

The latter make claims for the persistence or resilience of the nation state as the *key* actor in EU policy-making (e.g. Hoffmann 1966 and, more recently, Moravcsik 1998), relegating the Commission to a subordinate role and confining interest groups to a nationally delineated one. However, this framework has also been criticized and has subsequently been rejected by some scholars. In the past decade a number of alternative accounts have come to the fore (e.g. multi-level governance).

In the second area of political science, questions about the role and activities of interest groups within political systems dominate. Much of the work in this field originated in the USA (for example, Almond 1958; Dahl 1956; Olson 1965). Some of it examines interest groups in the context of a single nation state (for example, with regard to the UK, see Grant 2000; Jordan and Richardson 1987) and some of it takes a comparative approach (see for example Wilson 1991; Josselin 1996). Almost inevitably, academic concern with interest groups has turned to examining them in relation to the EU (see, for example, Greenwood, Grote and Ronit 1992; Mazey and Richardson 1993; Greenwood 1997; Greenwood and Aspinwall 1998).

Whilst it is acknowledged that the IR-based theories and approaches have stimulated a very useful debate, we would argue that there is little further to be gained from rehearsing these well-seasoned arguments, apart from pointing out that several of the approaches predict a reorientation in the interest groups' behaviour (e.g. Haas' idea (1958: 16) of a shift in loyalties, political expectations and activities to the regional away from the national centre). As an alternative we propose to advance the debate about interest representation in the EU in two ways. First, by considering a fresh perspective which examines the Europeanization of these activities. Second, by moving beyond the confines of political science to borrow tools and analytical frameworks from management science that are concerned with strategic decision-making.

Fresh Tracks: Europeanization

Currently, there is no all-encompassing 'theory' of Europeanization, or even a consensus about what 'Europeanization' research should focus on (Jordan 2003). However, it is clear that those who study Europeanization are broadly concerned with the so-called 'rebound effect' of European integration on member states, perceiving the latter as the cause (i.e. independent variable) of national-level adaptations. In other words, attention now focuses on the 'top-down' processes at work. In this way, work carried out under the Europeanization banner challenges some of the established theories of integration (see Cowles *et al.* 2001; Jordan 2002). A second body of work that employs the notion of Europeanization centres on the implementation of EU policies. This literature, while initially less theoretical in character, has developed strongly in areas of 'low' politics such as the environment (Jordan 1999) and regional policy. The main concern was to have a clearer understanding of the problems associated with implementation of EU policies at the national level, sparking a discourse about so-called 'implementation deficits'. From the empirical work carried out in this field, theory began to emerge. The analysis suggested that implementation problems arise when there is a mismatch between national and EU administrative structures, legal and policy frameworks and policies, and member states are unwilling to adapt to the EU model (for example, Heritier *et al.* 1996; Knill 1998; Haverland 2000). However, where adaptation on the part of member states to the EU framework does occur, this amounts to Europeanization (Knill and Lenschow 2000). Thirdly, and more recently still, scholars of national politics have adopted the view that it is not possible to study national politics without also considering EU impacts (i.e. Europeanization). Rometsch and Wessels (1996, xiii) believe that national and European political arenas have 'fused' together. The full extent of the EU's impact is now being uncovered by studies, *inter alia*, of national administrative structures (Bulmer and Burch 1998), national policy (Kassim and Menon 1996, 1; Knill 2001), parliamentary and socio-cultural change (Cowles *et al.* 2001).

Nevertheless, the basic meaning of the term Europeanization continues to be contested (see Cole and Drake 1999; Radaelli 2000). For some authors Europeanization is the accretion of decision-making authority at the EU level. Several studies of state–EU relations adopt this definition (e.g. Rehbinder and Stewart 1985; Andersen and Eliassen 1993). It was recently embraced by Cowles *et al.* (2001:2), who define Europeanization as 'the emergence and development at the European level of distinct structures of governance'. The main problem with this particular definition is that it risks equating Europeanization with European integration and confusing the two. Other scholars see Europeanization as a two-way process in which states and the EU affect each other simultaneously (see, for example, Bomberg and Peterson 2000: 6–8; Kassim 2000: 235). While quite clearly the 'national' does affect the 'EU', and vice versa, it is difficult to construct a clear research strategy from such a starting point (where does the analyst start to look for the causes and consequences of change if they are reciprocally interconnected? See Boerzel 2001; Jordan 2002). This is because (using the language of more positivistic social science) a two-way definition of Europeanization lacks a set of dependent and independent variables.

Therefore, for the sake of convenience, it may be more helpful to regard Europeanization as the progressive impact of the EU on national and sub-national actors, structures, legal arrangements and policy-making processes (i.e. a 'top-down' mechanism). Accordingly, Europeanization can be seen as a process through which European integration penetrates and, crucially, *in certain circumstances brings about adjustments to*, domestic institutions, decision-making procedures and public policies (see Ladrech 1994: 69; Meny *et al.* 1996; Rometsch and Wessels 1996). Using this or similar definitions of Europeanization, numerous studies were conducted during the 1990s. Some have examined the Europeanization of single countries (e.g. Jordan 1998; Cole and Drake 1998; V Schmidt 1996). More recent analyses have dealt with two or more countries (e.g. Boerzel 2002). Other analysts have compared the Europeanization of particular aspects of the nation state, such as sub-national government (e.g. Hooghe 1996), administrative structures (e.g. Page and Wouters 1995; Bossaert *et al.* 2001), national parliaments (e.g. Maurer and Wessels 2001) and even national cultures (e.g. Risse 2001).

As part of this expanding interest in Europeanization we use the concept to examine the impact of the EU on interest representation. This is based on the understanding that Europeanization is about the growing impact of the EU on national politics and that the 'EU-effect' on interest groups is part of a wider series of changes at the national level. Crucially, we contend that the Europeanization process has altered the relations between state and non-state, sub-national, national and supranational actors *because* it has modified the opportunities and threats present in their external environment and that this in turn has consequences for their resources, objectives and behaviour.

Tools from Management Science

Management science (Luffman *et al.* 1996: 6) focuses on the strategic management of business organizations (although see Fairbrass 2002 for the application of management science ideas and tools to the strategic behaviour of firms and trade associations). Strategic management can be defined as that set of *decisions* and *actions* that lead to the development of an effective *strategy* (or strategies) to help achieve (corporate) *objectives*. In other words, strategic decisions (see Figure 1) are those which the organization takes to help meet its objectives in the light of its external environment and internal resources.

Figure 1 represents the relationship between the internal and external factors that may impact on an organization's decision making. The external environment, wherein lie potential or actual opportunities and threats, should be monitored as part of the strategic analysis phase of the decision-making process. Simultaneously, the organization should conduct an audit of its internal resources, estimating its strengths and weaknesses in terms of its staffing, funding, location, knowledge, internal

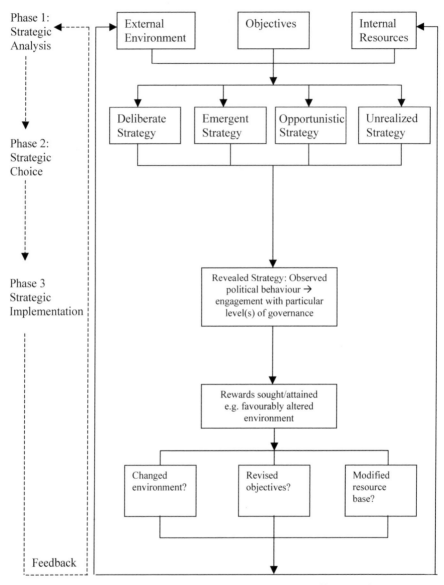

Source: Authors (draws on Johnson and Scholes, 1993:38 and Luffman *et al.* 1996:8 and 33).

Figure 1 Strategic decision making: External and Internal Factors

control systems and other resources. On the basis of these assessments the organization should identify and begin to pursue 'appropriate' objectives. After the strategic analysis phase of the decision-making process has been completed the group makes a strategic choice. This amounts to the selection of a 'deliberate strategy' (i.e. planned) on the part of the group that is designed to meet the group's chosen objectives. However, depending on the nature of the group's external environment (i.e. the degree of stability and complexity) and its ability effectively to manage its internal resources, the group's actual behaviour (i.e. its revealed strategy) may deviate from the one planned. During the third phase of the decision-making process (i.e. during implementation) the organization's revealed strategy may take the form of one of three alternatives: an emergent strategy (i.e. it deviates to some degree from the original plan); an opportunistic strategy (i.e. behaviour which occurs in an *ad hoc* way in response to unexpected circumstances); or an unrealized strategy (i.e. the organization fails to achieve its planned outcomes). In the case of an interest group which chooses to lobby a particular set of policy-makers, be they local, national or supranational, the group's revealed behaviour should lead to securing the desired rewards (e.g. political influence). The outcome may be an altered external environment (e.g. new legislation) and/or revised objectives, and/or a modified resource base (e.g. additional or improved information). At this point the decision-making cycle begins again as the organization takes stock of its new environment, objectives and/or resources.

Employing the above framework, we contend that the Europeanization of UK-based environmental groups can be seen as part of a strategic response to the opportunities created by or encountered in their external environment (i.e. the political opportunities available in the EU policy-making environment). It is also, in part, a reaction to the relative lack of opportunities at the national level (see the background case study section that follows immediately below). In brief, the relative marginalization of environmental groups within the UK political system represents, at least, a lack of opportunity or, more potently, a very significant threat to them. The degree of Europeanization is also likely to reflect, *inter alia,* the groups' organizational resources and the weight placed on the groups' objectives in relation to achieving certain environmental policy outcomes.

BIODIVERSITY AND LAND USE PLANNING: POLITICAL BACKGROUND

To understand the Europeanization of UK environmental politics in general, and biodiversity and land use planning policy in particular, it is vital to have some understanding of their national and EU context. We divide this background section into two parts: the first deals with the political circumstances of the policies in the EU; the second relates to the UK situation. As the details of these case studies have been set out at length elsewhere (see Jordan 2002) both are only briefly summarized here.

Politics at the EU Level

The EU's agricultural policy has had a deleterious effect on the environment (McCormick 2001: 253). The policy has largely been resistant to reform because of an alliance of farmers, national agricultural ministries and DG-Agriculture amounting to one of the most closed policy communities at the EU level (George 1997:191). This policy community has certainly dominated the 'environmental' decisions relating to biodiversity and land use planning. This is partly because environmental pressure groups have found themselves excluded from the business conducted in the Agricultural Council of Ministers. In addition, the European Commission's DG-Environment, MEPs and even national environmental departments often found themselves watching from the sidelines. Despite these difficulties a range of actors working for similar policy outcomes have combined to produce four substantial pieces of EU legislation in the biodiversity and land-use planning areas. Over a 30 year period (*c.*1970– 2000) a mixture of public pressure and the activities of environmental groups directed towards the European Parliament, in conjunction with a proactive European Commission and a supportive European Court of Justice, have combined to create an extensive biodiversity protection regime. The result was two important biodiversity measures: Directive 79/409/EEC (the Birds Directive[3]) and Directive 92/43/EEC (the Habitats Directive[4]). A similar pattern of interaction between state and non-state actors arose in the sphere of land use planning to produce comparable outcomes: Directive 85/337/EEC (the Environmental Impact Assessment (EIA) Directive[5]) and 2001/42/EC on Strategic Environmental Assessment[6] (SEA). The key point here is that UK environmental groups acted strategically and were able to capitalize on opportunities provided by the EU (e.g. by making partnerships and alliances with the

---

[3] The Birds Directive places a duty on member states to maintain the populations of wild birds subject to ecological, scientific cultural, economic and recreational grounds assisted by designating Special Protection Areas (SPAs).

[4] The Habitats Directive extends the range of protected species by placing an obligation on member states to protect plant and animal species and their habitats. It calls for the creation of Special Areas of Conservation (SACs). Under the Habitats Directive member states are required to: avoid deterioration of sites; carry out appropriate assessments of any plans or projects that might damage protected sites; provide compensatory measures as necessary.

[5] The EIA Directive was adopted in 1985 and provides for a system of assessment prior to consent being granted to projects that are considered to have significant impacts upon the environment.

[6] The SEA Directive was adopted in 2001 and requires that an environmental assessment is carried out with regard to plans and programmes (i.e. those proposed by local and national authorities which affect *inter alia* town and country planning and land use) which are likely to have significant effects on the environment.

Commission, Parliament and European environmental groups) and to counteract some of the threats encountered at the national and EU levels (e.g. powerful counter pressure-groups).

The UK Political Context

The pattern of power relationships found at the EU level is replicated in the national arena. In the UK a tightly integrated agricultural policy community of interests (Cox *et al.* 1986:183–184; Smith 1993: 101–103), centring on the Ministry of Agriculture, Fisheries and Food (MAFF) and the National Farmers' Union (NFU), dominated the management of the countryside. The agricultural sector was formally exempt from land-use planning controls initiated in the post-war period. In theory, national biodiversity policy could have constrained agricultural practices but in practice it did not. Those controls that were adopted were mostly of a voluntary nature. UK-based environmental groups active in the area of nature conservation and land-use planning, such as the Royal Society for the Protection of Birds (RSPB), WWF (World Wide Fund for Nature) and Council for the Protection of Rural England (CPRE), were almost entirely excluded from the key decisions, as indeed were powerful land-owning interests such as the Countryside Landowners Association (CLA), and even the Department of the Environment (DoE)[7] itself (i.e. the central government department responsible for the environment). In strategic decision-making terms the UK political arena presented the environmental groups with few or limited political opportunities and posed considerable threats to the achievement of their desired policy outcomes.

THE EUROPEANIZATION OF ENVIRONMENTAL GROUPS

Returning to issues raised in earlier sections, we explore the strategies and behaviour of the surveyed environmental groups. We begin by looking at the issue of organizational resources and then examine the evidence about *who* the UK environmental groups targeted, *how* and *when*. Finally, we scrutinize *why* the groups behaved in the ways that they did.

Organizational Resources

Strategically, the range of options open to the interest groups seeking to exploit political opportunities and mitigate the impact of threats is partly contingent on organizational resources. Clearly, any interest group will require 'sufficient' resources in order to attempt to carry out interest

---

[7] The DoE was renamed the DETR in 1997 and then restructured in 2000 to become DEFRA.

representation in an 'effective manner'. These are likely to include, *inter alia,* adequate funds, staff, location, knowledge, reputation or status, and skill at alliance building. Conversely, 'inadequate' resources are likely to frustrate the realization of a group's policy objectives. This point is highlighted by a nature conservation campaigner employed jointly by the RSPB and the WWF, who said that

> '...you could take the policy battleground and probably set out a number of battle strategies that every campaign ought to follow ... there are a number of broad targets and issues ... these are the buttons you have got to hit ... you decide quite how important they are and prioritize them according to the weight that they can bring to what you are trying to achieve ... you have got a number of skirmishes that you may or may not want to get involved with ... *your time and resources will determine which battles you get involved with* ... which ones you do or don't care about ... which ones are flagship battles ... but all the time, in theory, you are moving towards a particular end result ... but you don't necessarily know what that is because things are changing all the time ... the institutions change, the power bases change, the staff changes ... ' (Hepburn 2000, emphasis added).

The size of the group, measured in staff terms, is a significant factor. For example, the RSPB is described (Pritchard 2000) as being both small enough to be well co-ordinated but also large enough to be an effective organization at the national and/or European level. In contrast, a smaller environmental group such as the Marine Conservation Society (MCS), which in the 1980s employed about three or four members of staff, was too small to lobby Brussels directly. The consequences of being a relatively small organization are summed up as follows:

> '... at that time, as a pretty small organization, they [MCS] certainly weren't going off to the European Commission and doing things at that level ... [we] didn't have the capacity to do that, so we were typical of an NGO that finds a piece of legislation coming out of Europe and then thinking what do we think of this ... how can we influence it? How would we like it to develop? We had no part in saying there should be a habitats directive in the European Union ... ' (Gubbay 2000).

Targets

There are several potential policy-making targets for (environmental) groups. These include, *inter alia,* the public, the media, national government officials and EU-level policy makers. Evidence collected from the groups surveyed reveals that they prioritized their targets. At the national level (within the UK government), the DoE was seen as the most important target (Hatton 2000; Gubbay 2000; Pritchard 2000), although access was also sought to (and not denied by) MAFF, the DTI and the territorial offices within the UK, such as the Scottish Office. In addition to contact with national-level policy-makers, access was sought and gained to EU-level institutions. Again, the groups prioritized their activities and tended to devote more effort to establishing and maintaining relations with the European Commission, rather than the other EU institutions. Within the Commission DG Environment was the most sought after target (Pritchard 2000), although some resources were also expended in developing relations with the DGs responsible for agriculture, fisheries, transport, the EU budget and regional policy (Papazoglou 2000). Amongst the other EU institutions, the groups selectively sought access to particular MEPs within the European Parliament. The groups tended to focus on those MEPs who had shown a personal commitment to environmental issues or who played a significant role in the European Parliament's Environment Committee (Hatton 2000; Hepburn 2000; Papazoglou 2000). The environmental groups (Hepburn 2000) placed less value on contact with the Economic and Social Committee (EcoSoc).

For several of the environmental groups access (albeit indirect access) to the ECJ has played an extremely important role in shaping EU biodiversity and land-use planning policy. A range of groups supported the Commission or UK courts in legal action against member states (the UK included) that had failed to comply with the adopted Birds, Habitats and/or EIA Directives. For the RSPB, for example, the decision to pursue legal action via the ECJ was a 'strategic decision' (Pritchard 2000), taken at the Board level, because of the degree of commitment of resources required by such an action. This approach was seen by the respondent as part of a long-term strategy in which,

'as the directives mature then the main centre will be focused on the law and the courts ... [in order] to create new bridgeheads' (Pritchard 2000).

In effect, a 'cost-benefit analysis' was conducted before the RSPB had recourse to the ECJ (over Lappel Bank[8]). This was partly because the

---

[8] In the *Lappel Bank* case, which was brought against the British government by the RSPB, the ECJ ruled that the British government had been wrong to exclude an area of land from an SPA to allow development of a nearby port. Again, the Court supported a much more maximal interpretation of EC law than Britain had anticipated or been prepared to accept.

group anticipated an adverse reaction from the UK government. In the event there was a backlash (i.e. the UK Government's vigorous campaign to dilute the Habitats Directive) after the Leybucht Dykes[9] ruling (Pritchard 2000). Similarly, the WWF also made a calculated decision to exploit legal channels, via EU institutions, against the UK Government. This action was described in the following terms,

'... we [WWF] do, very often, consciously think about what we do ... every time we [make] a complaint...about a particular site or about transposition, we know that we want the Commission to put pressure on the UK government [because] they [the Commission] weren't in a position, without the information, to do anything about it ... ' (Hatton 2000).

Similarly, the CPRE reports a successful strategy of exploiting EU institutions and legislation to discipline the UK government:

'There have been more complaints to the European Commission about the failure to implement the [EIA] Directive than any other piece of European legislation. This is partly because EIA is a new process, providing many new 'hooks' on which compliance can be judged, and partly because its timing and importance opened many campaigners' eyes generally to the opportunities presented by lobbying in Europe. Many of the *causes célèbres* of the 1980s and 1990s, including the M3 extension through Twyford Down and the Newbury bypass, were the subject of complaints to the European Commission over alleged failures in the EIA process.' (Reynolds 1998: 241).

Groups confirmed that contact with national officials was extremely important, as were their relationships with EU institutions. The overall strategy adopted by many of the groups is typified by the campaign strategy of the RSPB and the WWF in connection with Habitats Directive (see Figure 2).

Figure 2 shows the actual targets selected. The diagram highlights the extent to which the campaigners made contact with all the major EU-level institutions (i.e. the Parliament, the Commission, the Council of Ministers and the Economic and Social Committee) *and* national level

---

[9] In the *Leybucht* case the ECJ rejected the Commission's argument that the protection of SPAs was an absolute duty other than when there were risks to human life. But it also rejected the German government's demand for a wide margin of discretion when identifying SPAs. Many member states were so alarmed by the ECJ ruling that they worked to secure amendments. The Habitats Directive responds to these by permitting states to take social and economic factors into account when managing SPAs.

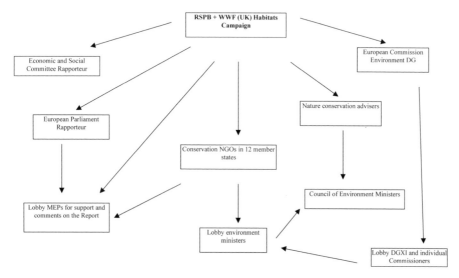

Figure 2 The Habitats Directive campaign strategy of the RSPB and WWF
Source: Hepburn 2000.

administrators and officials. What is striking about the campaign is both its breadth and its highly selective character. The campaign was co-ordinated across the EU: nationally based conservation groups targeted their own national officials as part of a unified approach. It also focused on particular policy-makers such the European Parliament Rapporteur or individual Commissioners. The leading campaigner stated that

> '[his] intention was to ensure that [he] did not neglect any of the targets or routes [shown in Figure 2]. To do so might incur the risk of defeat or opposition' (Hepburn 2000).

Another campaigner reported (Gubbay 2000) that there tended to be an 'ebb and flow' between national government and the Commission. Groups have continued to seek access to national officials because they recognize the value of the latter as important determinants of EU policy (at the policy-decision stage of the policy cycle in the Council of Ministers). Nevertheless, despite establishing and working to strengthen their relations with national policy-makers, it was clear from the respondents that they regarded their access to EU institutions as more valuable under certain conditions. Such circumstances included policy blockages at the national level and/or implementation failure (i.e., where there was a lack of political opportunities at the national level). When the national executives (e.g. the UK Government) hindered or obstructed the development of biodiversity and land-use planning policy, the environmental groups sought and gained access to EU institutions because the latter would be prepared to pursue common policy objectives (i.e. shared objectives with the interest groups). For example, by monitoring implementation at the national level and reporting implementation deficiencies or failure to the Commission, the groups found that legal action could compel non-compliant states to conform to the Directives. In this way, by allying themselves with EU-level policy-makers, the groups achieve more favourable outcomes than those realized by relying on their relations with national officials.

The following reasons for seeking and gaining access to EU-level policy-makers were proffered by the environmental groups. First, environmental groups found several of the EU-level access points to be more receptive and welcoming than some national venues. This receptivity could be accounted for by, for example, the Commission's relative 'understaffing' and its need for data, which the groups can supply (are keen to supply). In addition, EU institutions (particularly the Commission) needs to secure political support for their agenda in the face of opposition from member state national executives. Moreover, the groups are clearly aware which institutions are responsible for drafting legislative measures and recognize the need for early involvement in the policy-formation process: hence, the groups' strategy to develop good relations with the Commission. They also know which public bodies have responsibility for implementation. This reinforces their need to have good access to the Commission, and to a lesser extent (given the difference in legal clout), the national statutory bodies in these two policy areas.

Routes and Partners

The empirical evidence shows that the UK-based groups sought and gained access to EU-level policy-makers via one or more of three potential conduits: the 'direct' route, the 'national' route, and the 'European' route (see Grant 1989; Bennett 1997 and 1999; Fairbrass 2002). They established direct contact with EU officials, placed some reliance on lobbying via the national executive and operated via European groupings. There is evidence that smaller UK-based groups, which are relatively poorly resourced, such as the Marine Conservation Society, have worked to influence biodiversity policy via a wider UK grouping, namely WildLife and Countryside Link (Gubbay 2000). At the national–EU level interface there were ample examples of national groups co-operating to access EU policy-makers to shape EU policy. The RSPB worked with and through the Brussels-based BirdLife International. The RSPB was also part of a more heterogeneous grouping lobbying for biodiversity protection that included the Council for the Protection of

Rural England (CPRE), WWF and WildLife Trust (Hepburn 2000). WWF's Brussels offices host the European Habitats Forum, which is another example of a wider grouping. It is clear that environmental groups have been able to work collectively, despite having a variety of aims and approaches (Hepburn 2000). The groups are careful not to undermine each other and will actively support one another where they are able to do so. For example, WWF supported the Greenpeace action in the UK High Court in 1999 (Hatton 2000).

Timing and Contact Patterns

It is evident from the interviews conducted with the environmental groups and the policy-makers that the environmentalists sought out and gained access to policy-makers at all stages in the policy cycle. The actual pattern of activities (Gubbay 2000) tended to reflect the importance of the policy phases (i.e. the policy stage would determine access target and the need for contact). It was suggested that it was very important to try to participate in the policy process at the very beginning (if it was possible to find out what was going on), since directives would be very difficult to 'undo' at a later stage. There is evidence that groups were able to establish close relations with the Commission at early stages of the policy cycle in relation to the Birds and the Habitats Directives. In the latter case the RSPB worked with two very senior officials of DG Environment during the period when the Habitats Directive was being drafted. The RSPB advised on the structure of the proposal (Hepburn 2000). It was reported (Hatton 2000) that, once the Habitats Directive had been agreed, the main focus of activity returned to the national level (because of transposition and implementation issues).

Over the course of time, a period of 20 to 30 years, the environmental groups have been able to establish good working relations with both national and EU- level policy-makers. Whilst the environmental groups have clearly valued such relations with national bodies, it is at the EU level that the groups have made most impact in terms of policy development. The environmental groups have succeeded in acquiring a reputation for supplying reliable information, and this has led the Commission to seek the groups' advice and technical expertise. For example, even UK DoE officials (Salmon 2000) recognized that the environmental groups have played a leading (expert) role in the recent Moderation Process associated with the Habitats Directive. Previously, by supplying implementation failure data to the Commission, environmental groups ensured several ECJ court cases have produced favourable outcomes (from the point of view of the environmentalists). In addition, both pivotal MEPs on the Environment Committee and Commission officials have relied on the expert advice from groups such as the RSPB in order to draft legislation. However, the relationship between the groups and EU institutions is not always free from conflict. Some groups have a more confrontational style than others. For example, a number of groups, such as WWF, have acted as litigants against the Commission itself (Hatton 2000).

Behaving Strategically: Opportunities and Threats

Campaign officers from several of the UK-based interest groups spoke about the groups' activities in strategic terms. For example, one senior staff member said that they carried out a careful monitoring of the political process and had worked at 'relationship and credibility building' (Pritchard 2000). He also stated that the lobbying approach of his group was 'subtle, indirect, take[s] a very long-term view [and] is strategic'. He described the whole process as being akin to 'putting bricks into an edifice' (Pritchard 2000), implying careful attention to detail. Groups such as the RSPB looked for the 'long term pay-off' (Pritchard 2000). That is to say that they would engage in lobbying about proposed legislation in the short term but were also careful to maintain a longer-term perspective.

Other respondents alluded to the opportunities and threats present at the national and EU levels. One commented (Hatton 2000) that the WWF-UK had thought that the proposed Habitats Directive was 'very important [and saw the Habitats Directive as] a good opportunity to get new primary legislation [in the UK]'. Another pointed to the significance of threats (opponents). She observed that

'[Birdlife International is] up against huge lobby groups – not just the hunters, in the case of the birds directive. We have to think of others like farmers. We have to think of landowners in general [and] industries. All [of] these huge interest groups [would] face problems by the implementation of the directives...we would never stand a chance of winning right now [if we were to try to get a new directive or rewrite the two existing ones]'. (Papazoglou 2000).

Again the significance of the connections between resources, objectives and the external environment (allies and opponents) is revealed in the following observation

'we really focused in, because of *time constraints*, on those where we had political connections, *established connections* and where we thought the action was going on. If there had been any *sniff of a problem* at Commissioner level, within any one of the other DGs that we thought we could do something about [we would act]. We knew about what was happening in DG XIV [where there were threats/opposition] but we just didn't think we had a locus there, to do anything about it ... and DG XI people [were] basically saying "they are not going to change their minds". *So, that was a battle we decided not to fight'*. (Hepburn 2000, emphasis added).

CONCLUDING THOUGHTS

The evidence collected and presented here concerning UK-based environmental groups suggests that they exist within a changed and changing political environment. In part, this unstable, dynamic environment has been caused by wider political changes, in particular in the development of the EU's competence in biodiversity and land-use planning policy. In a top-down sense the EU has to varying degrees impacted on UK environmental policy. Most discernibly, policy content has been Europeanized; to a lesser degree so have its structures and its style (Jordan 2002). As part of that broad transformation of UK environmental politics, the relations between the (sub)national non-state actors and policy makers at the national and EU level have been affected. Rather than relying primarily or solely on lobbying national level targets in order to secure their objectives, where the UK environmental groups possessed sufficient resources they have sought directly to exploit opportunities created by the EU system (by working with or through the Commission, the Parliament or the ECJ). Where they lacked the staff, funding or other resources to act alone they have joined or formed partnerships with larger entities (i.e. European groups such as Birdlife International) and have worked in a less direct fashion to try to influence (national and EU) policy. This modified behaviour is in part a result of the recognition by the groups that they faced serious threats or lack of opportunities within the national (and EU) arena. The UK-based environmental groups had previously encountered opposition and relatively closed interest mediation channels in the national arena (i.e. threats in strategic decision-making terms) because biodiversity and land-use planning policy had been dominated by a national (and European-wide) agricultural policy community that effectively marginalized 'green' interests.

The evidence clearly shows that UK-based environmental groups have adapted their interest representation behaviour in the EU. Using management science tools our analysis reveals the causal mechanisms at work. The surveyed groups have taken strategic decisions about how to try to influence environmental policy. Their objective – broadly, to extend environmental protection at the national level – was assessed in the light of potential external threats and opportunities presented at the national and EU levels, and the actions they carried out reflected their internal resource base. The UK environmental groups modified their choice of targets, routes, partners and the timing of their activities to place greater emphasis on targeting EU-level policy makers and using European-wide channels of representation.

At first sight, this might be taken to be evidence to support neo-functionalist theory. However, we contend that the altered behaviour exhibited by the UK environmental groups amounts to 'Europeaniza-tion' at work rather than neo-functionalism because predictions based on the latter would lead us to expect that national interest processes and structures would be *replaced* by supranational ones. Alternatively, the concept of Europeanization would lead us to anticipate a *mutation* of national structures and processes, which, indeed, appears to be the case according to our investigation of environmental policy and UK-based interest groups.

In contrast to the rather moribund, IR-dominated debate which has foundered over issues such as which actor plays the decisive role in European integration, employing the concept of Europeanization allows us to conceive of a more complex interplay between the 'national' and the 'supranational' and to escape the intellectual quagmire where the EU is seen as a product of bottom-up (i.e. member state driven) processes. By examining European integration through the Europeanization lens we can discern that it is a top-down process too. In this way, scholars can begin to capture the richness and intricacy of EU policy-making. The challenge now is to extend this work to encompass other member states and other policy sectors (as has been carried out in comparing UK and French industrial policy: see Fairbrass 2002) to discover whether there are common patterns across sectors and states.

REFERENCES

Almond, G. (1958): 'A comparative study of Interest Groups and the political process', *American Political Review,* 52, 270–82.

Andersen, S. S. and Eliassen, K. A. (eds) (1993): *Making policy in Europe: the Europeification of national policy making,* (London: Sage).

Bennett, R. (1999): 'Influence in Brussels: Exploring the choice of Direct Representation', *Political Studies,* 47:2, 240–257.

Bennett, R. J. (1997): 'The impact of European Economic Integration on Business Associations: The UK Case', *West European Politics,* 20:3, 61–90.

Boerzel, T. (2001): '*Pace Setting, Foot Dragging and Fence Setting: Member State Responses to Europeanization'.* Paper to EUSA conference, Madison, May 2001.

Boerzel, T. (2002): *States and Regions in the European Union* (Cambridge: Cambridge University Press).

Bomberg, E. and Peterson, J. (2000): '*Policy Transfer and Europeanization: Passing the Heineken Test? Queens Papers on Europeanization',* No 2/2000 (University of Belfast: Belfast).

Bossaert, D., *et al.* (2001): *'Civil Services in the Europe of the Fifteen'* (Maastricht: EIPA).

Bulmer, S. and Burch, M. (1998): 'Organizing for Europe', *Public Administration,* 76: 601–628.

Cole, A and Drake, H (2000): 'The Europeanization of the French Polity: Continuity, Change, and Adaptation', *Journal of European Public Policy,* 7:1, 26–43.

Cowles, M. G., Caporaso, J., and Risse, T. (eds) (2001): *Transforming Europe* (Ithaca, NY: Cornell University Press).

Cox, C., Lowe, P., and Winter, M. (eds) (1986): 'Agriculture and Conservation in Britain: a Policy Community Under Siege', in C. Cox, P. Lowe and M. Winter, *Agriculture: People and Policies* (London; Allen and Unwin).

Dahl, R. A. (1956): *Preface to Democratic Theory* (Chicago, Ill: Chicago University Press).

Fairbrass, J. (2002): *Business Interests: Strategic Engagement with the EU Policy Process,* Unpublished PhD Thesis, University of Essex.

George, S. (1997): *Politics and Policy in the European Union* (Oxford: Oxford University Press).

Grant, W. (2000): *Pressure Groups and British Politics* (Basingstoke: Macmillan).

Grant, W. (1989): *Pressure Groups, Politics and Democracy in Britain* (Hemel Hempstead: Phillip Allen).

Greenwood, J. (1997): *Representing Interests in the European Union* (Basingstoke: Macmillan).

Greenwood, J. and Aspinwall, M. (1998): *Collective Action in the European Union* (London: Routledge).

Greenwood, J., Grote, J. and Ronit, K. (1992): *Organized Interests and the European Community* (London: Sage).

Gubbay, S. (2000): Interview with author. 4 July, Ross on Wye.

Haas, E. (1958): *The Uniting of Europe* (Stanford: Stanford University Press).

Hatton, C. (2000): Interview with author. 26 July, Godalming.

Haverland, M. (2000) 'National Adaptation to European Integration: The Importance of Institutional Veto Points', *Journal of Public Policy,* 20:1, 83–103.

Hepburn, I. (2000): Interview with author. 18 July, Redgrave, Norfolk.

Héritier, A., *et al.* (1996): *Ringing the Changes* (Berlin: De Gruyter).

Hoffmann, S. (1966): 'Obstinate or Obsolete: the fate of the nation state and the case of Western Europe', *Daedalus,* 95, 862–915.

Hooghe, L. (1996): 'Europe with the regions? Regional Representation in the European Union', *Publius,* 26, 73–91.

Johnson, G. and Scholes, K. (1993): *Exploring Corporate Strategy* (London: Prentice-Hall).

Jordan, A. G. and Richardson, J. J. (1987): *Government and Pressure Groups in Britain* (Oxford: Clarendon Press).

Jordan, A. J. (1998): 'The Impact on UK Environmental Administration', in P. Lowe and S. Ward (eds) *British Environmental Policy and Europe: Politics And Policy In Transition* (London: Routledge).

Jordan, A. J. (1999): 'The Implementation of EU Environmental Policy: A Policy Problem Without a Political Solution?' *Environment and Planning C (Government and Policy),* 17:1, 69–90.

Jordan, A. J. (2002): *The Europeanization of British Environmental Policy: A Departmental Perspective* (Basingstoke: Palgrave).

Jordan, A. J. (2003): 'The Europeanization of UK Government and Policy: A Departmental Perspective', *British Journal of Political Science* (in press).

Josselin, D. (1996): 'Domestic Policy Networks and European Negotiations: Evidence from British and French Financial Services', *Journal of European Public Policy*, 3:3, 297–317.

Kassim, H (2000): 'The National Coordination of EU Policy', in H. Kassim, B. G. Peters and V. Wright (eds) *The National Coordination of EU Policy: The Domestic Level* (Oxford: OUP).

Kassim, H. and Menon, A. (eds) (1996): *The European Union and National Industrial Policy* (London: Routledge).

Knill, C. (1998): 'European Policies: The Impact of National Administrative Traditions', *Journal of Public Policy*, 18, 1–28.

Knill, C. (2001): *The Europeanization of National Administrations* (Cambridge: Cambridge University Press).

Knill, C. and Lenschow, A. (eds) (2000): *Implementing EU Environmental Policy* (Manchester: Manchester University Press).

Ladrech, R. (1994): 'Europeanization of Domestic Politics and Institutions: France', *Journal of Common Market Studies*, 32:1 69–98.

Luffman, G., Lea, E., Sanderson, S. and Kenny, B. (1996): *Strategic Management* (Oxford: Blackwell).

Maurer, A. and Wessels, W. (eds) (2001): *National Parliaments on their Way to Europe: Losers or Latecomers?* (Baden Baden: Nomos).

Mazey, S. and Richardson, J. J. (eds) (1993): *Lobbying in the European Community* (Oxford: OUP).

McCormick, J. (2001): *Environmental Policy in the European Union* (Basingstoke: Palgrave).

Mény, Y., Muller, P. and Quermonne, J. L. (eds) (1996): *Adjusting to Europe* (London: Routledge).

Moravcsik, A. (1998): *The Choice for Europe* (Ithaca NY: Cornell University Press).

Olson, M. (1965): *The Logic of Collective Action* (Cambridge, Mass: Harvard University Press).

Page, E. and Wouters, A. (1995): ' The Europeanization of National Bureaucracies?', in J. Pierre (ed.) *Bureaucracy in the Modern State*, (Aldershot: Edward Elgar).

Papazoglou, C. (2000): Interview with author. 23 August, Brussels.

Pritchard, D. (2000): Interview with author. 1 June, Sandy, Beds.

Radaelli, C. (2000): 'Whither Europeanization?', *EiOP online working paper series*, 4, 8 (http://eiop.or.at/eiop/).

Rehbinder, E. and Stewart, R. (1985): *Integration Through Law, Volume II: Environmental Protection Policy*,(Berlin: Walter de Gruyter).

Reynolds, F. (1998): 'Environmental Planning', in P. Lowe and S. Ward (eds) *British Environmental Policy and Europe* (London: Routledge).

Risse, T. (2001): 'A European Identity?', in M. Cowles, J. Caporaso, and T. Risse (eds) *Transforming Europe* (Ithaca: Cornell University Press).

Rometsch, D. and Wessels, W. (eds) (1996): *The European Union and Member States. Towards Institutional Fusion?* (Manchester: Manchester University Press).

Schmidt, V. A. (1996): 'Loosening the Ties that Bind: The Impact of European Integration on French Government and its Relationship to Business', *Journal of Common Market Studies*, 34: 2, 223–254.

Smith, M. (1993): *Pressure, Power, and Policy* (Hemel Hempstead: Harvester Wheatsheaf).

Wilson K (1991): *Interest Groups* (Oxford: Basil Blackwell).

Chapter 9

Coming to Terms with European Union Lobbying: The Central and Eastern European Experience

Nieves Pérez-Solórzano Borragán

INTRODUCTION

Interest representation is at the core of the democratic experience: its intensity and wealth have grown during the past two decades. The traditional normative frameworks for the study of interest politics (namely, *inter alia,* pluralism, corporatism and policy networks) were initially employed to analyse interest politics at the national level. Their testing grounds were nation-states that were the products of decades of liberal democracy. Three developments have challenged these meso-level approaches: the process of European integration, the transformation in the Central and Eastern European Countries (CEEC) post-1989 and the process of Europeanization of domestic policy domains.

Firstly, European integration and the role of interest groups in the European Union (EU) policy process directly challenge the traditional frameworks for the study of interest politics (see Michalowitz, this volume). While interest groups may be motivated by the same incentives both at the EU and national level (i.e. the opportunity to influence policy), at the EU level the interplay between interest groups and other policy actors takes place within the complex context of the European polity, which is

'compounded by a plurality of highly interrelated "bodies politic" [while] the transnational entity remains in limbo between a system of democratic governments and a democratic system of government' (Chryssochoou 1996: 778).

Hence, as Haas observes,

'interest groups and political parties organize beyond the national level in order to function more effectively as decision makers *vis-à-vis* the separate national governments or the central authority and [if] they define their interests in terms larger than those of the separate nation state from which they originate' (Haas 1958: 11–12).

Secondly, since 1989 the CEEC have experienced a rapid and profound process of transformation, which challenges both regime transition theory[1] and, more importantly for this chapter, the traditional approaches to the study of interest politics. The role of interest groups in this dynamic environment deviates from that normally expected to be found in mature democratic systems. The transition from communism has created democratic and plural conditions and thus the impetus required for the development of interest groups. This has resulted in the multiplication of interest groups and the emergence of institutionalized channels for interest representation in the CEEC. The spectrum of groups emerging there is similar to that found in traditional liberal democracies (Willets 1982: 2–9). However, the rules of the game for interest articulation that have evolved in the 'West' during lengthy periods of political stability are neither clearly defined nor commonly understood in the post-communist context.

Thirdly, the prospect of the EU's eastward enlargement offers a third level for the assessment of the traditional paradigms of studying interest politics in the context of Europeanization. With membership negotiations well under way, emerging interest groups from the CEEC demand a more active role in the European arena through transnational networking. It is this third level of analysis (i.e. the EU) on which this chapter will focus. By assessing the experience of the Central and Eastern European Offices of Representation (CEORs) in Brussels, this chapter analyses the impact of the EU's forthcoming eastward enlargement on the arena for

---

[1] See *inter alia* Ekiert, G. (1991): 'Democratization Processes in East Central Europe: A Theoretical Reconsideration', *British Journal of Political Science* 21:3; Lewis, P. (1997): 'Theories of Democratization and Patterns of Regime Change in Eastern Europe', *Journal of Communist Studies and Transition Politics* 13:1, 4–25; Linz, J. and Stepan, A. (1996): *Problems of Democratic Transition and Consolidation: South Europe, South America and Post-Communist Europe* (Baltimore: Johns Hopkins University Press); O'Donnell G. and Schmitter, P. (1986): *Transitions from Authoritarian Rule: Tentative Conclusions from Uncertain Democracies* (Baltimore: Johns Hopkins University Press); Pridham, G. (1984): 'Comparative Perspectives on the New Mediterranean Democracies: A Model of Regime Transition?', *West European Politics*, 7:2, 1–29; Rustow, D. (1970): 'Transitions to Democracy: Towards a Dynamic Model', *Comparative Politics*, 2:3.

EU interest representation.[2] With the exception of a handful of contributions (Dakowska 2001; Fink-Hafner 1994, 1997, 1998; Pérez-Solórzano Borragán 1998, 2001a, 2001b, 2002; and Saurugger 2000), the relationship between organized interests from the CEEC and the EU lobbying process and the implications of future EU membership for civil society dynamics, organized interest aggregation, and representation in the CEEC have been neglected by the specialized literature. This chapter aims to help fill this vacuum.

Ten of the 13 candidate countries have some kind of physical presence in Brussels other than their permanent national representation to the EU. Since 1989 the number has increased and nowadays there are 27 offices of interest representation from the candidate countries operating in Brussels. They account for less than 2% of the Brussels-based lobbying community (NIROC 2000 and author's own calculations). Their experience reflects the interaction between two parallel processes: Europeanization and socialization. Firstly, the Europeanization of Central and Eastern European interest representation is not understood as synonymous with convergence or imitation (Cole and Drake 2000: 27). Rather, Europeanization occurs as a process of informal integration that flows parallel to and beyond EU activity, clearly influencing the patterns of interest group development in the CEEC. The presence of the CEORs in Brussels and their attempt to find their advocacy cluster (i.e. their space for interest representation and policy influence) in an overcrowded European lobbying arena is clear evidence of this. Secondly, the simultaneous process of socialization of Central and Eastern European interests and their EU counterparts occurs in parallel to, and as a result of, the increasing Europeanization of interest representation. The transnational activity of interest groups from the CEEC and their exposure to the EU lobbying environment permits an exchange of norms and 'ways of doing'. This process presents Euro-interest groups with new challenges in terms of identifying suitable partners, adapting organizational structures and defining strategies and interests. While benefiting from access to EU-level opportunity structures for interest representation, Central and Eastern European interests must face the costs of adapting to the EU lobbying environment, against the background of a fuzzy domestic arena for interest intermediation.

---

[2] There are 13 countries currently negotiating their accession to the EU, namely, Bulgaria, Cyprus, the Czech Republic, Estonia, Hungary, Latvia, Lithuania, Malta, Poland, Romania, Slovakia, Slovenia and Turkey. This chapter is concerned only with the experience of the candidate countries from Central and Eastern Europe and not with that of the Mediterranean countries (Malta, Cyprus and Turkey) or the Baltic republics (Estonia, Latvia and Lithuania).

In order to analyse both processes, Europeanization and socialization, in the light of the CEORs' experience in Brussels, this chapter will be divided into four sections. The first section will assess the domestic *milieu* for interest representation in the CEEC. The second section will revise the concept of Europeanization in order to establish its appropriateness as a framework for the analysis of the CEORs' presence in Brussels and the impact of their EU experience at the domestic level. Section three will illustrate the socialization and interaction between Euro-interest groups and their Central and Eastern European associates in the context of the challenges faced by the former and the adaptational pressures experienced by the latter. The final section will draw a number of conclusions about the impact of the forthcoming enlargement on influence and interest representation in the European Union.

A FUZZY DOMESTIC ENVIRONMENT

The articulation of interests in the former socialist countries is constrained by the 'dense and complex institutional legacy' of the previous political and economic order that still shapes expectations and patterns of conduct (Nielsen *et al.* 1995: 4). It is within this framework that the strategic choices regarding interest articulation and consultative politics in the CEEC are being made. Hence, one Hungarian Member of Parliament argues that,

> 'while all the economic and social conditions of a market economy are in place, regulations and the public recognition of what Western Europe calls lobbying are still lacking' (G. Molnar, as quoted by Csonka 2001).

Typically, corporatist tripartite arrangements constitute the environment for interest intermediation in the new democracies. They have played an essential role in fostering social dialogue and negotiation between social partners in the CEEC (see *inter alia* Ágh, Szarvas and Vaas 1995; Ágh and Ilonszki 1996; Economic and Social Committee 2000). Yet, as Wiesenthal argues (1996: 55), tripartite arrangements are the result of the prevalence of political parties over any other actor and the response to the need for more deliberative policy-making practices in the newly democratized countries. Lobbying is most evident at parliamentary level. Interest organizations are in regular contact with Members of Parliament (MPs) in order to persuade them to include their views on their proposed amendments. These contacts, however, are not always regulated and exhibit a very informal nature. Access to MPs depends on the contacts that members of interest organizations have managed to forge with them (see *inter alia* Daku 1995, Kovács 1995 and Patzelt 1996).

In the CEEC the incentives for collective action clash with decades of communist atomization and mistrust. Nagle and Mahr observe that in the CEEC

'the metamorphosis from latent to organized interest group for members of the growing underclass [...] has not yet occurred' (Nagle and Mahr 1999:127).

At present, the citizens of those countries have not yet fully formed their subjective class identities. The inability to formulate these identities affects interest group membership. Socio-psychological explanations claim that

'it is only when people feel in control of their lives that they will venture out to play an active role in the wider society' (Padgett 2000:12).

It was expected that with the transition to democracy, civic culture and social capital would emerge in post-communist societies. However, this process has been limited by the influence of the communist legacy that destroyed the private space, eliminated trust and developed an élite-led public sphere. In sum, as Padgett maintains,

'communism prevented the development of the social and organiza-tional skills that constitute social capital, leaving a legacy of "civilizational incompetence", which is the antithesis of civic culture' (*ibid*: 14).

While Central and Eastern Europeans are beginning to articulate their interests, the communist legacy of passivity remains. In this context an effective system of interest articulation is yet to develop. Rational choice (Olson 1971) offers a more positive outlook in trying to assess collective action in post-communist societies. Owing to the absence of identity-securing mechanisms and the delayed development of a civic culture, group mobilization 'becomes over-dependent on the provision of selective membership incentives' (Padgett 2000:16). These incentives are based not only on economic gain, but also, most importantly, on the relatively little investment required to set up organizational structures which were operational before 1989 (Pérez-Solórzano Borragán 2001b and 2002). This approach, however, reflects only the case of sectoral interests, such as business organizations.

The nature of interest groups in Central and Eastern Europe is often unclear. According to several Eurogroups, it is not certain whether they represent truly pluralist interests. For instance, in 1996 the Committee of Agricultural Organizations in the European Union (COPA-COGECA) undertook a comprehensive study in order to identify future discussion partners and potential future members of the European organization (Kellner 2000). According to the assistant to the Secretary-General of the Union of Industrial and Employers' Confederations of Europe (UNICE),

'The situation of employers' federations in Central and Eastern Europe is quite fluid and quite diversified [...] There are federations which are very strong already [...] and others that are maybe weaker for all sorts of different reasons [...] There is not as yet a single voice for business' (Isabella 2000).

Basing themselves on their experience, the wider European associations affirm that the most obvious candidates for key jobs in Central and Eastern European interest groups are generally those who were associated with the communist state. Thus, one never knows whom s/he is addressing and whether s/he is really committed to democratic and economic changes, since many of the experts in senior managerial positions have not been able yet to adapt their mental framework to the new situation. The leadership and direction of many organizations has been 'weakened' since those appointed are mainly technical experts who held similar positions during the Communist regime. The path-dependent permanence of old forms of interest mediation, exemplified in the revitalization of old networks and old behavioural patterns, is delaying the emergence of a fully fledged system of interest representation (Nielsen *et al.* 1995: 29–30). In the same manner, confusion regarding the nature and identity of interest groups is compounded by the fact that not all interests within one sector belong to the same umbrella organization. Most importantly, there have been instances when organizations representing similar interests have not managed to create a common front and even question each other's legitimacy, while decision makers try to come to terms with the variety of groups (Pérez-Solórzano Borragán 2001b and 2002).

Finally, the rules of the game for interest articulation that have evolved in Western democracies during long periods of stability are neither clearly defined nor properly understood in the CEEC. Hence, there is a lack of understanding about what lobbying is and the possibilities it offers. There is also a need for a change in mentality and behavioural patterns. Even business groups, which are considered to be the avant-garde of sectoral interest representation in the CEEC, have difficulties in knowing when to lobby: how to keep track of the legislative agenda and become more proactive; how to maintain good links with the civil service; how to articulate cohesive and convincing arguments; when to contact Parliament; and how to strike coalitions with partners in the sector. In sum, they are still in the process of learning how to lobby (Pérez-Solórzano Borragán 2001b and 2002).

EUROPEANIZATION

The concept of Europeanization has traditionally been used in order to assess the impact of EU governance on the member states' domestic environment. Ladrech defines the term as

'an incremental process reorienting the direction and shape of politics to the degree that EC political and economic dynamics become part of the organizational logic of national politics and policy-making' (Ladrech 1994: 70).

Cole and Drake (2000: 27) focus on the mechanisms of Europeanization and define the process as 'an independent variable, a form of emulative policy transfer, a smokescreen for domestic reform and an imaginary constraint'. Knill and Lehmkuhl (1999) identify two effects of Europeanization on the domestic setting: the alteration of domestic opportunity structures with certain domestic actors benefiting over others; and the alteration of beliefs and expectations of domestic actors leading to changes in cognition and preference formation. Radaelli (2000) offers an overarching approach to Europeanization incorporating both its mechanisms and effects. He describes it as:

'a process of construction, diffusion and institutionalization of rules, procedures, paradigms, styles, ways of doing and shared beliefs and norms, formal and informal, defined and consolidated first in the decision-making process of the EU and then incorporated in the logic discourses, identities, political structure and policies at the domestic level' (Radaelli 2000).

This rather limited and inward-looking use of the concept has been challenged by the eastern enlargement of the EU. The candidate countries' experience shows that Europeanization is not self-contained and limited only to the EU member states. Indeed, as Pridham argues, the effects of Europeanization are more easily identifiable in the candidate countries than in the member states because they are more recent, extensive and abrupt (Pridham 2001: 51–52). The variation in the literature on the 'eastward' dimension of Europeanization reflects, as in the case of the more 'inward' approach discussed above, differences in focus. Hence Grabbe perceives Europeanization as 'the impact of the EU accession process on national patterns of governance' in the CEEC (Grabbe 2001: 1014), while in their study of the Europeanization of CEEC's executives Lippert *et al.* maintain that Europeanization

'is about the resources in time, personnel and money directed by current and future members states towards the EU level' (Lippert *et al.* 2001: 980).

Ágh offers an additional dimension by stating that, although a precondition for the accession to the EU, Europeanization

'has to be accompanied by the emergence of public support for integration as tested ultimately in a referendum' (Ágh 1999: 839).

There are a number of qualitative differences between the traditional use of the term and its application to the CEEC. Unlike the other alternative approaches to Europeanization reproduced above, Grabbe elaborates further in her analysis and highlights the significance of the EU's conditionality principle[3] as a Europeanizing force in the applicant countries. She argues that

'The EU accession process is pushing the applicant countries towards greater convergence with particular institutional models than has occurred within the existing EU' (Grabbe 2001: 1014).

Grabbe identifies five Europeanizing mechanisms that illustrate the Europeanization of the candidate countries, namely:

(a) Gate-keeping: the EU determines when each candidate is ready to progress to the next stage towards accession.
(b) Benchmarking and monitoring: the EU ranks the candidates' overall progress, benchmarking in particular policy areas and providing examples of best practice.
(c) Models: the EU provides legislative and institutional templates.
(d) Aid and technical assistance which make the EU the largest external source of aid for the CEEC.
(e) Advice and twinning aimed at helping the CEEC to comply with membership requirements by learning from EU member states experiences in adapting to EU legislation. (*ibid.* 1019–1024)

The rapid speed of adjustment, the openness to EU influence, the breadth of the EU's agenda in CEEC and the asymmetrical relationship in favour of the EU complete the list of qualitative differences which make Central and Eastern European Europeanization distinctive from previous

---

[3] The conditionality principle refers to the accession conditions that apply to all candidate countries. These were outlined by the 1993 Copenhagen Council and include: stability of institutions guaranteeing democracy, the rule of law, human rights and respect for and protection of minorities; the existence of a functioning market economy; the ability to take on the obligations of membership including adherence to the aims of political, economic and monetary union; the creation of the conditions for their integration through the adjustment of their administrative structures.

examples (*ibid.* and 1014–1016).[4] These factors highlight the top-down direction of the process and the Europeanization paradox identified by Ágh. He argues that the (governmental, party and business) élites are much more interested in European integration than the masses. Consequently,

'the more the masses of the well-articulated Western societies are involved through their interest organization in the decision-making process concerning ECE (East and Central European) extension, the more this enlargement process slows down or even comes to a temporary halt [...] A similar Europeanization paradox can also be observed in the ECE states, although the organized interests so far have acted less vehemently than those in the West, and even their activity has been less intensive than would have been expected' (Ágh 1999:850).

The Logic of Collective Action at the EU Level

There are a number of incentives that explain the increasing presence of Central and Eastern European interests in Brussels. The first obvious incentive is the possibility of actively participating in the enlargement process by making sure that their concerns are being voiced at the core of the EU decision-making machinery. As Figure 1[5] illustrates, about 40% of the companies surveyed in 2001 regard EU lobbying as a 'very important' aspect of their representation activities. Within that group, the majority of companies rated lobbying at the domestic level higher than lobbying in Brussels. On the other hand, about 52% of the companies polled believe EU lobbying not to be very important. More significantly, despite the degree of importance awarded to EU lobbying, for almost 45% of the companies surveyed, lobbying in Brussels makes more sense than lobbying at the domestic level.

European networking provides candidate countries' interest groups with a source of trust and legitimization both in the national and supranational arenas (Fink-Hafner 1997: 135). Admissions to (or even close contacts with) European interest groups are presented in the domestic arena as proof of their maturity, respectability and 'European-ness'. In the words of the Vice-President of the Chamber of Commerce and Industry of Slovenia,

---

[4] Lippert, Umbach and Wessels take a chronological approach and identify five incremental stages of Europeanization that are linked to the evolution of the CEECs' relations with the EU since 1988 (Lippert, Umbach and Wessels 2001: 985–1001).

[5] The empirical data emanates from the CAPE 2001 Survey on corporate readiness for the EU Single Market in the ten candidate countries of Central Europe, namely Bulgaria, the Czech Republic, Estonia, Hungary, Latvia, Lithuania, Poland, Romania, Slovakia and Slovenia. Through the respective national chambers of commerce and industry, 1,658 of the more than 3,000 companies contacted participated in the survey.

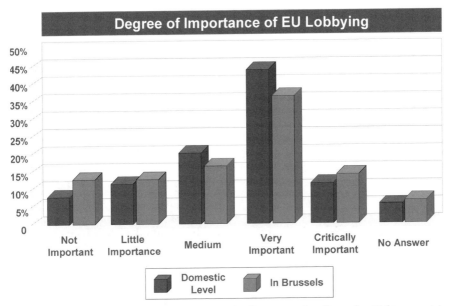

Figure 1 Source: Eurochambres and SBRA, *Corporate Readiness for Enlargement in Central Europe*, 2001.

'We believe that [the Slovenian Business and Research Association] is going to be a step forward in acquiring and getting a *qualified*, even more *reliable*, and what is important, *independent* source of information for our business community' (Stantič 2000, emphasis added).

Moreover, as will be argued later in this chapter, collective action at the domestic level has become over-dependent on the provision of selective membership incentives, whilst securing an effective access to the European arena promotes the emergence of professionals specialized in EU matters who could subsequently provide the domestic constituencies with expertise in exchange for trust. Thus, the establishment of liaison offices in Brussels and membership of Eurogroups can strengthen the position of the groups' entrepreneurs and provide benefits to their membership through the promotion of new economic ventures and immediate access to EU-related information.

However, access to the EU *loci* of power in order to influence policy outcomes does not appear to be a priority. For instance, the Hungarian and Polish Research and Development liaison offices and the Slovenian Business and Research Association (SBRA) were created in order to manage co-operation within the 5th EU Framework Research Programme. In addition, the relationship between the Association of European Chambers of Commerce and Industry (EUROCHAMBRES) and

UNICE with their Central and Eastern European counterparts is focused on the exchange of expertise and training programmes.

The explanation for this state of affairs can be found in the distinctiveness of the eastward approach to Europeanization. EU member states are both producers and consumers of Europeanization, hence influencing the EU decision-making process is a priority for EU interests, as such action is likely to have an impact on the final policy or legislative output. However, as result of their asymmetric relationship with the EU, the candidate countries are affected by the outcome of Europeanization but cannot participate in the decision-making process. In other words, although the candidate countries need to converge toward the benchmark of the *acquis communautaire,* they are not involved in the initial drafting of legislation within the European Commission. Nor are they represented when decisions are made in the Council of Ministers and the European Parliament. Hence, by default, accessing EU institutions permits information gathering but does not enable the candidate countries to shape legislation (Cizelj 2002).

Thirdly, interest groups in the CEEC lack experience of lobbying within a liberal regime. However, through their interaction with their EU counterparts (via membership of Eurogroups) they can benefit from the experience of their Western European colleagues. In fact, interest groups from Central and Eastern Europe operating in Brussels expect to make full use of the knowledge that their counterparts have about the EU decision-making process and how to influence it (Cizelj 2000). According to the permanent Slovak delegate to UNICE, her organization became a member of UNICE in order to become more active at the European level,

'With this status, we can participate in a UNICE policy committee, where we have access to important information about what is [happening] at the European level, in the European Commission' (Hudobova 2000).

Moreover, Central and Eastern European 'lobbyists' working in Brussels regard themselves as 'conveyor belts', transferring the knowledge and experience acquired on consultative politics for the development of a more participative political culture in their countries of origin (Cizelj 2000; Fink-Hafner 2000).

Finally, even the most remote possibility of interest groups from the CEEC being able to bypass their national executives in the representation of their sectoral interests becomes a powerful incentive. As Figure 2 shows, the communication between national governments and the business

Assessment of Government's Negotiating Position	No of Answers
Information we obtain is from the media, it is rather general, we had no influence on positions taken	1113
We have very little information on negotiations	189
We are informed on conditions for accession, but they are causing concern for our company	184
We were consulted on negotiating position, we know the results achieved so far and we shall not have major problems over full compliance with EU regulations	80
Don't know	57

Figure 2 Source: Eurochambres and SBRA, *Corporate Readiness for Enlargement in Central Europe*, 2001. This table shows the views of 1,658 companies on the negotiating positions of their governments in view of their forthcoming EU membership. 'We' refers to the companies surveyed. Their sectors of activity ranged from agriculture and fishing to manufacturing, wholesale and retail trade, real estate, health and social work, and transport.

sector on enlargement-related issues is limited. Sixty-seven per cent of the respondents maintain that their main source of information on their governments' negotiating position in view of the accession is the media. In the context of business interests' access to policy making at the domestic level it is worrying to observe that over 3% of the companies surveyed do not know anything at all about their government's negotiating position. These results indicate that the business community in the candidate countries is far from being fully involved in discussion regarding accession to the EU.

Figure 2 proves that the above-mentioned incentives have not translated into real influence on EU-related policy outcomes at the domestic level, despite the fact that groups seek to participate actively in any domestic debate regarding the EU. This domestic route entails strengthening contacts with national governments and parliaments. However, as recent research has shown, the slow Europeanization of government structures and parliaments has delayed the expansion of such contacts (Ágh 1999; Lippert *et al.* 2001). In the case of the Hungarian Parliament, the most arduous demands of domestic and party politics absorb the attention of MPs; hence EU-related affairs are not a priority. Even in the second parliament (1994–96) two proposals submitted to the Parliament by the Committee on European Integration Affairs in order to debate European integration matters were rejected (Czaga 1996: 7). The executive administers the policies concerning Hungary's accession to the EU almost exclusively. In the case of the Polish *Sejm*, the committees lack a stable membership and strong leadership, limiting their ability to actively participate in the decision making regarding Europe (Olson *et al.* 1998). As argued by Waller (1994: 24),

> 'in changing political systems, parliamentary structures tend to have only weak links to organized interests in society.'

The Slovenian case is an exception to this state of affairs. The Slovenian negotiating team for the accession process meets regularly with the SBRA, which is the office for interest representation in Brussels. What makes this case very interesting is the fact that the SBRA provides the Slovenian negotiating team with evidence about the degree of compliance of member states with those aspects of the *acquis communautaire* that are going to be discussed as part of the accession chapters. The logic of influence is not based on shaping the government's opinion but on providing the negotiating team with useful information in order to strengthen its stand vis-à-vis the EU (Cizelj 2002). In the case of the Czech Republic a selection of companies that belong to the Czech Economic Chamber meet together regularly with representatives of the Czech government, public administration, politicians and independent experts directly involved in the accession process to the EU:

> 'They openly discuss and exchange opinions with those who draft legislation and are involved in the Czech Republic preparations for EU accession' (Economic Chamber of the Czech Republic, http://www.komora.cz/en/euroclub.html).

The CEORs' Brussels Experience

The Central and Eastern European community for interest representation is growing in Brussels. Yet they still account for less than 2% of the Brussels-based lobbying community.

Figure 3 shows that the status and representation arrangements of these offices from Central and Eastern European Countries are varied and loose. Most offices represent business interests, while others perform a wider function as research and development offices, public relations bureaux or cultural ambassadors. This is a reflection of the heterogeneity of their clientele and the recent development of interest-group activities and legislation in their countries of origin.

The main tasks performed by the CEORs are similar to those performed by their counterparts from the EU member states: (i) to inform

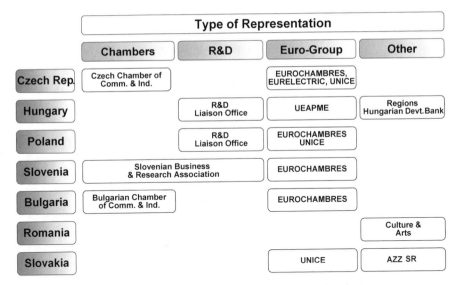

Figure 3 Comm. & Ind. refers to Chamber of Commerce and Industry.
R&D refers to liaison offices for Research and Development.
Eurogroup refers to membership of a sectoral Eurogroup.
Other refers to additional categories such as regional offices.
The AZZ SR is the Federation of Employers' Associations of the Slovak Republic.

their members about EU legislation, funding opportunities and relevant developments in EU member states; (ii) to represent their members in large European associations; (iii) to provide members with specific services on request; (iv) to raise their members' profile at the European level; and (v) to design training seminars for their members in order to increase their awareness of the enlargement process. For instance, the Brussels office of the Polish Chamber of Commerce, the KIG Euro-consulting,[6] not only offered information and services concerning the EU and business integration to its members but also regularly informed the Polish government on the attitude of Polish entrepreneurs to EU membership (*Poland AM* 2000a).

Figure 4 identifies the lobbying objectives of the business sector in the CEEC in view of the enlargement. Companies were asked to specify whether those lobbying objectives should be taken care of at the domestic level or in Brussels. The results offer an interesting insight into the short-term planning of business interest in the candidate countries. Their lobbying does not appear to prioritize the immediate application of the *acquis communautaire* (namely, derogations, transitional periods and concessions for pre-accession) but learning how to interact with

---

[6] Established in January 2000.

Lobbying Objectives (Percentage)				
Objectives	Domestic Level		In Brussels	
	No	Yes	No	Yes
Derogations	78.3	21.7	84.8	15.2
Transitional Periods	72.1	27.9	79.7	20.3
Concessions for Pre-Accession	65.9	34.1	70.9	29.1
Financial & Technical Assistance	23.4	76.6	37.4	62.6
Assistance in dealing with EU Institutions	39.4	60.6	47.1	52.9
Influence in EU Institutions	64.4	35.6	63.8	36.2
Influencing Member States	69.7	30.3	70.7	29.3
Other	80.4	19.6	88.7	11.3

Figure 4   Source: Eurochambres and SBRA, *Corporate Readiness for Enlargement in Central Europe*, 2001.

EU institutions while securing technical assistance. Influencing the EU institutions and member states is only a priority for about 30% of the respondents at the domestic level and at the Brussels level. This could be interpreted as yet another consequence of the candidate countries' consumer status vis-à-vis Europeanization or as clear evidence of the general lack of awareness of the EU policy process.

SOCIALIZATION

In addition to opening offices in Brussels, the supranational route includes membership and close contacts with European interest groups (Fink-Hafner 1997: 135). To improve their European profile, a number of interest groups from the candidate countries have gained some type of associated or affiliated membership of experienced Eurogroups such as the European Association for Consumer Protection (BEUC), COPA-COGECA, EUROCHAMBRES, the European Confederation of Iron and Steel Industries (EUROFER), the European Trade Union Confederation (ETUC) and UNICE, among others. Sectoral co-operation provides the newcomers with the possibility of benefiting from the experience that these groups have acquired over the years, their communication networks and contacts, and from their knowledge of the EU policy process. As will be argued below, this new type of partnership constitutes a tremendous challenge for both parties.

It is not easy for Euro-interest groups to identify reliable counterparts in the candidate countries. Moreover, the expansion of membership to such a varied group of newcomers provokes important internal organizational difficulties and policy dilemmas. Eurogroups must adapt their operative structures to a larger membership whose demands and interests may conflict with those of existing members (see *inter alia* Daugbjerg 1997: 27–28; Benedictis and Padoan 1993). As a result, policy dilemmas will need to be solved in order to safeguard the group's cohesion (i.e. the balanced allocation of European and sectional identity with regard to the interests of the candidate countries) and to maintain credibility vis-à-vis the EU institutions. Eurogroups are confronted with a club enlargement problem[7] very similar to that faced by the EU's member states in view of the eastward enlargement. Indeed, Eurogroups seem jealously to guard their EU identity above their sectoral identity. They are ready to transfer some of their sectoral information to the newcomers including (i) events concerning individual EU policy areas and EU member states; (ii) the structure of European institutions and legislative procedures within the EU; (iii) reports elaborated by their analytical units; (iv) expert knowledge on the harmonization of laws; (v) potential European sources to co-finance projects in candidate countries (Fink-Hafner 1994: 229). Eurogroups are not so eager to share their access to the *loci* of power with their Central and Eastern European counterparts. In this sense, if any co-operation towards the creation of a policy community between Eurogroups and Central and Eastern European interest groups is to be created, it would be based on the former enjoying their access to the 'inner circle' of interest groups contacted by the Commission while the Central and Eastern European groups would have to remain on the periphery of the policy-making process, at least until accession took place. Finally, given the generally acknowledged 'disharmony' in the structure of Eurogroups, the eventual incorporation of new members could potentially be disruptive (for discussion on the Eurogroup's weakness see, *inter alia,* Greenwood *et al.* 1993; Greenwood 2002a and 2002b; McLaughlin, Jordan and Maloney 1993).

Euro-interest groups need to balance the advantages of conferring affiliated or full membership on the newcomers against the rather inconvenient reality of having to share their club good (i.e. influence,

---

[7] Club Theory deals with the problems related to the establishment of voluntary associations for the production of excludable public goods. Literally, if the costs of production of a particular good are too high, individuals (potential consumers of the good) may be animated to associate – form a club – and to share the production costs. In order to eliminate the possibility of free riding (for the good produced is virtually public), the club excludes non-members from the use of the good produced.

networks and contacts, human resources, offices) with several new members which, although offering an extremely important insight into their countries' political and socio-economic environments, may not be able to produce an input which is valuable enough. The fear of possible free-riding attitudes (Olson 1971) on the side of the newcomers is compelling Eurogroups to adopt a very cautious attitude. It is not surprising that the German Chamber of Trade and Commerce (DIHT) expressed in the 'Europa 2000 Plus' of April 2000 its members' reservations about the rapid EU enlargement to the East, arguing that none of the countries of the former communist bloc would be ready before 2004. The report maintains that the optimal accession time for Poland will be 2005 and for the Czech Republic 2006, since 'quality is more important than speed' (*Poland AM* 2000b).

For Central and Eastern European interests contact with EU counterparts brings a number of adaptational pressures. They need rapidly and effectively to learn and adapt to the basic rules of the European game while making sure that their own interests are not diluted in the general interest of the wider organization. Since they have been granted only associated or affiliated membership their ability to influence the agenda of the European associations is limited, despite the fact that they pay membership fees. Additionally, most European associations would only allow one member per country. This presents problems at the domestic level when there are several associations that represent the same sectoral interest. Despite the opportunity structures offered by European associations, to date there is no clear evidence of the direct impact of Central and Eastern European interest groups in the enlargement negotiations. Representatives of a number of Central and Eastern European offices acknowledge that they can only play an auxiliary but still important role in the process of accession negotiations by offering an additional interface between the EU and their countries of origin (Cizelj 2000; Iteto 2000; Pálmay 2000).

The conditions for the fulfilment of their advocacy tasks reflect the extent of the adaptational pressures faced by Central and Eastern European interests. The CEORs lack sufficient human and financial resources. For example, the staff of the SBRA[8] comprises only seven employees. Considering that the SBRA aims to encourage co-operation in the domains of business and research between Slovenia, the EU and its member states, to support members of the Association in their preparation for EU membership and to become the representative and mediator of its members in European associations and informal networks, its human resources are overburdened from the start.

---

[8] SBRA was created on 12 May 1999.

The access of Central and Eastern European interest groups to European institutions, although effective as information-gathering mechanisms, are limited by their reliance on Eurogroups. Eastern- and Western-specific modes of political exchange interact with EU-level opportunity structures which permit or block access to interest representation. As has been argued earlier in this chapter, through their membership of Eurogroups Central and Eastern European interests can have access to very influential contacts. Yet the Eurogroups' protection of their EU identity over their sectoral identity limits the CEORs' action repertoires: the transnational activities of Central and Eastern European interest groups evidence a peculiar model of interest group politics, where the exchange and ownership of information are more important than the actual impact on policy-making.

Crucially, the evidence of transnational co-operation *between* partners from candidate countries is more promising. The first attempts towards closer networking and co-operation among CEORs started only in 1999 with the organization of a conference on 'Candidate Country Interest Representation in Brussels' under the aegis of the SBRA. The result of this first attempt was the creation in 2000 of the Network of Interest Representation Offices from Candidate Countries (NIROC).[9] NIROC's impact has so far been limited to the sharing of know-how. In December 2000, under the aegis of EUROCHAMBRES' CAPE Programme,[10] NIROC members met for a two-day seminar to reassess their strategies

---

[9] NIROC co-ordinates the activities of the Association of Agricultural Co-operatives & Companies in the Czech Republic (AACC), the AB Consultancy & Investment Services, the Federation of Employers' Associations of the Slovak Republic (AZZZ SR), the Czech Power Company CEZ, the Turkish Progressive Workers Union (DISK), the Eastern Poland Euro-Office, the Representation of the Regions of Hungary, the Economic Development Foundation (IKV), the Hungarian Office for Research and Development (HunOR), the Hungarian Handicraft & Small & Medium Sized Enterprises (IPOSZ), the Representation of Turkish Textile and Ready-Made Garment Exporters Association (ITKIB), the Malta Business Bureau (MBB), the Hungarian Development Bank Ltd Brussels Representative Office, the Euro-Polish Representation of Economic and Regional Organizations and the Slovenian Business & Research Association (SBRA), Confederation of Industry of the Czech Republic – Brussels Bureau, Union of Chambers of Turkey, Turkish Small Business Organization (TSBO), TUGiAD, Turkish Business, Industry and Employers' Association (TUSIAD-TISK).

[10] CAPE is the Chambers' Accession Programme for Eastern Europe. This two-year (2000–2002) programme consists of two complementary components: CAPE I aimed at strengthening the Central European chambers and CAPE II aimed at preparing the Central European chambers to support their enterprises to adjust to the *acquis communautaire*. CAPE is the result of a joint effort by EUROCHAMBRES and its Central and Eastern European partners. Both parties have co-operated in the drawing up of the programme and will implement it together as part of the ongoing Europeanizing effect that their partnership is producing at the national level.

while exchanging views of their experience of lobbying in Brussels. This and similar events are being repeated regularly not only in Brussels but also in each of the national capitals. This trend clearly suggests the end of the *solo* approach to lobbying in Brussels. This individualistic approach to Brussels has been the norm in the negotiating strategies of the governments from the CEEC which, instead of creating a common front to defend their interests before the EU, limit their co-ordinated activity to the exchange of information (Lippert 1994: 122).

CONCLUSIONS

This chapter has analysed the effect of the enlargement on interest intermediation structures in Europe. The experience of the CEORs in Brussels reveals that Europeanization and socialization are two processes occurring in parallel to and beyond EU activities. As a result of Europeanization the EU has become the arena for the effective representation and promotion of Central and Eastern European interests. Europeanization occurs as a process of emulation (Jacoby 2001:172–174) and formal and informal integration. Secondly, socialization reflects the interaction between EU and Central and Eastern European interests. The presence of the CEORs in Brussels is clear evidence of both Europeanization and socialization.

The impact of both processes in the candidate countries and in the EU arena for interest intermediation has been assessed. The systemic change in the CEEC has resulted in the multiplication of interest groups and interest representation bodies, despite the absence of strongly institutionalized channels for the interaction between policy actors in the post-communist context and their relative inexperience of the lobbying game. Whilst at the domestic level sectoral interest groups seek to influence policy outcomes in relation to EU accession, the opportunity structures available at the European level have not translated into clear evidence of the direct impact of Central and Eastern European interest groups in the enlargement negotiations. There is little evidence of their effectiveness in relation to policy outputs. As a result of the pressures generated by the prospect of EU accession, Central and Eastern European interests are trying to find their advocacy cluster in an overcrowded European lobbying arena. The challenges of adapting to the EU model of interest intermediation reveal the weakness of the domestic environments in the CEEC and the constraints of the EU model of interest representation. As a result the extension of Eurogroup membership to Central and Eastern European interests provokes important internal organizational difficulties and policy dilemmas that will need to be solved in order to safeguard the group's cohesion (i.e. the balanced allocation of European and sectional identity with regard to the interests of the candidate countries) and to maintain credibility vis-à-vis the EU institutions. Eastern- and Western-specific modes of political exchange interact with EU-level opportunity structures which permit or block access to interest representation. The EU's decision-making procedures are complex and involve several institutions simultaneously. Consequently, influencing policy-making requires a thorough knowledge of such procedures and an understanding of the Brussels lobbying scene. Otherwise the impact on shaping policies and decisions would be limited.

Access to European institutions may be effective as an information-gathering mechanism for CEORs' but, as discussed previously in this chapter, effective impact on policy making is limited by reliance on Eurogroups. Eurogroups' protection of their EU identity over their sectoral identity limits the CEORs action repertoires: the transnational activities of Central and Eastern European interest groups evidence a peculiar model of interest-group politics, where the exchange and ownership of information are more important than the actual impact on policy making. It could be argued that this is just an interim situation that will change after accession. As such, the transnational activities of Central and Eastern European interest groups constitute an 'indirect' strategy for the construction of a local 'civil society of interests'.

The challenges faced by the CEORs in Brussels illustrate the differences in the political cultures of Eastern and Western Europe. As a representative from COPA-COGECA has put it:

'with all respect to history, social, economic and political changes in the different CEEC there can be big differences in the representativity of those organizations in terms of numbers and quality' (Kellner 2000).

The increasingly supranational experience of Central and Eastern European interest groups provides a useful ground for comparative approaches in the study of interest politics. The increasing Europeanization of interest politics in the CEEC and the ongoing socialization of actors through interaction between Eurogroups and their Eastern European partners offers a dynamic laboratory for the analysis of new processes and trends within the context of interest group politics in Europe.

REFERENCES

Ágh, A. (1999): 'Europeanization of Policy-Making in East Central Europe: the Hungarian Approach to EU Accession', *Journal of European Public Policy* 6:5, 839–854.

Ágh, A. and Ilonszki, G. (eds) (1996): *Parliaments and Organized Interest: The Second Steps* (Budapest: Hungarian Centre for Democracy Studies).

Ágh, A. and Kurtán, S. (eds) (1995): *Democratization and Europeanization in Hungary: The First Parliament (1990–1994)* (Budapest: Hungarian Centre for Democracy Studies).

Ágh, A, Szarvas, L. and Vaas, L. (1995): 'The Europeanization of Hungarian Polity', in A. Ágh and S. Kurtán (eds) *Democratization and Europeanization in Hungary: The First Parliament (1990–1994)* (Budapest: Hungarian Centre for Democracy Studies).

Benedictis, L. and Padoan, P.C. (1993): *Europe between East and South* (Kluwer Academic Publishers: The Netherlands).

Chryssochoou, D.N. (1996): 'Europe's Could-Be Demos: Recasting the Debate', *West European Politics*, 19:4.

Cizelj, B. (2000): 'Paper presented to the Conference on Candidate Country Interest Representation in Brussels', in B. Cizelj and G. Vanhaeverbeke (eds) *Candidate Country Interest Representation in Brussels Conference Proceedings* (Brussels: SBRA).

Cole, A. and Drake, H. (2000): 'The Europeanization of the French Polity: Continuity, Change and Adaptation', *Journal of European Public Policy* 7:1, 26–43.

Corporate Readiness for Enlargement in Central Europe. A Company Survey on the State of Preparations for the Single Market, (Brussels).

Csonka, A. (2001): 'MPs, Lobbyists, Companies Push for Lobby Law', *Budapest Business Journal*, March 26.

Czaga, P. (1996): *The Role of East Central European Parliaments in the European Integration* (Budapest: Budapest Papers on Democratic Transition, No. 186).

Dakowska, D. (2001): *Comment Approcher le Rôle des Fondations Politiques dans la Politique Étrangère Allemande? L'exemple de la Pologne dans les Années 1989–1999*, Working Paper No. 5 (Berlin: Centre Marc Bloch).

Daku, M. (1995): 'Office Staff and Experts Involved in the Work of the Committees of the First Parliament', in A. Ágh, and S. Kurtán (eds) *Democratization and Europeanization in Hungary: The First Parliament (1990–1994)* (Budapest: Hungarian Centre for Democracy Studies).

Daugbjerg, C. (1997): *Farmers' Influence on East-West Integration in Europe: Policy Networks and Power* (South Jutland University Press: Working Papers on European Integration and Regime Formation No. 9).

Economic and Social Committee (2000): *Opinion of the Economic and Social Committee on 'Hungary on the Road to Accession'*, REX/023, Brussels, 1 March.

Economic Chamber of the Czech Republic, http://www.komora.cz/en/euroclub.html

Ekiert, G. (1991): 'Democratization Processes in East Central Europe: A Theoretical Reconsideration', *British Journal of Political Science* 21:3.

EUROCHAMBRES and SBRA (2000): *Training Seminar on Interest Representation towards the European Union* Brussels, 14–16 December.

Fink-Hafner, D. (1994): 'Promotion of Slovenian Interest in the European Interest Group Arena' *Journal of International Relations* 1, 2:4, 217–233.

Fink-Hafner, D. (1997): 'The Role of Interest Organization in the Europeanization of Slovenian Policy-Making', *Journal of International Relations* 4:1–4, 130–147.

Fink-Hafner, D. (1998): 'Organized Interests in the Policy-Making Process in Slovenia', *Journal of European Public Policy* 5:2, 285–302.

Fink-Hafner, D. (2000): 'Paper presented to the Conference on Candidate Country Interest Representation in Brussels', in B. Cizelj and G. Vanhaeverbeke (eds) *Candidate Country Interest Representation in Brussels. Conference Proceedings* (Brussels: SBRA).

Grabbe, H. (2001): 'How Does Europeanization Affect CEE Governance? Conditionality, Diffusion and Diversity', *Journal of European Public Policy* 8: 6, 1013–1031.

Greenwood, J. (2002a): *Inside EU Business Associations* (Basingstoke: Palgrave).

Greenwood, J. (ed.) (2002b): *The Effectiveness of EU Business Associations* (Basingstoke: Palgrave).

Greenwood, J., Strangward, L. and Stancich, L. (1999): 'The Capacities of Euro Groups in the Integration Process', *Political Studies* XLVII, 127–138.

Haas, E. (1958): *The Uniting of Europe – Political, Social and Economic Forces 1950–1957* (Stanford: Stanford University Press).

Hauser, J. Jessop, B. and Nielsen, K. (1995): *Strategic Choice and Path Dependency in Post-Socialism. Institutional Dynamics in the Transformation Process* (Aldershot: Edward Elgar).

Hudobova, L. (2000): 'Paper presented to the Conference on Candidate Country Interest Representation in Brussels', in B. Cizelj and G. Vanhaeverbeke (eds) *Candidate Country Interest Representation in Brussels. Conference Proceedings* (Brussels: SBRA).

Iteto, A. (2000): Interview with author, Budapest, 13 April.

Pálmay, F. (2000): Interview with author, Budapest, 13 April.

Isabella, M. (2000): 'Paper presented to the Conference on Candidate Country Interest Representation in Brussels', in B. Cizelj and G. Vanhaeverbeke (eds) *Candidate Country Interest Representation in Brussels. Conference Proceedings* (Brussels: SBRA).

Jacoby, W. (2001): 'Tutors and Pupils: International Organizations, Central European Elites, and Western Models', *Governance* 14:2, 169–200.

Kellner, H. (2000): 'Paper presented to the Conference on Candidate Country Interest Representation in Brussels', in B. Cizelj and G. Vanhaeverbeke (eds) *Candidate Country Interest Representation in Brussels. Conference Proceedings* (Brussels: SBRA).

Knill, C. and Lehmkuhl, D. (1999): 'How Europe Matters: Different Mechanisms of Europeanization', *European Integration Online Papers (EioP)* 3:7.

Kovács, J. (1995): 'The Involvement of Interest Organizations in Legislation and in Committee Work', in A. Ágh, and S. Kurtán (eds) *Democratization and Europeanization in Hungary: The First Parliament (1990–1994)* (Budapest: Hungarian Centre for Democracy Studies) pp. 129–134.

Ladrech, R. (1994): 'Europeanization of Domestic Politics and Institutions: the Case of France' *Journal of Common Market Studies* 32:1, 69–88.

Lewis, P. (1997): 'Theories of Democratization and Patterns of Regime Change in Eastern Europe', *Journal of Communist Studies and Transition Politics* 13:1, 4–25.

Linz, J. and Stepan, A. (1996): *Problems of Democratic Transition and Consolidation: South Europe, South America and Post-Communist Europe* (Baltimore: Johns Hopkins University Press).

Lippert, B., Umbach, G. and Wessels W. (2001) 'Europeanization of the CEE Executives: EU Membership Negotiations as a Shaping Power', *Journal of European Public Policy* 8:6, 980–1012.

Lippert, B. (1994): 'The Europe Agreements: Beyond Eurocratic Language', *The International Spectator* 29:1, 109–126.

McLaughlin, A.M., Jordan, A.G. and Maloney, W. (1993): 'Corporate Lobbying in the European Community', *Journal of Common Market Studies*, 31, 191, 212.

Nagle, J.D. and Mahr, A. (1999): *Democracy and Democratization* (London: Sage).

Nielsen, K., Jessop, B. and Hausner, J. (1995): 'Institutional Change in Post-socialism', in J. Hausner, B. Jessop, and K. Nielsen *Strategic Choice and Path Dependency in Post-Socialism. Institutional Dynamics in the Transformation Process* (Aldershot: Edward Elgar).

NIROC (2000): *Presentation Brochure*, Brussels.

O'Donnell, G. and Schmitter, P. (1986) *Transitions from Authoritarian Rule: Tentative Conclusions from Uncertain Democracies* (Baltimore: Johns Hopkins University Press).

Olson, D.M., Van Der Meer-Krok-Paszkowska, A., Simon, M.D. and Jack-iewicz, I. (1998): 'Committees in the Post-Communist Polish Sejm: Structure, Activity and Members', *The Journal of Legislative Studies* 4:1, 101–123.

Olson, M. (1971): *The Logic of Collective Action: Public Goods and the Theory of Groups* (Cambridge: Harvard University Press).

Padgett, S. (2000): *Organizing Democracy in Eastern Germany. Interest Groups in Post-Communist Society* (Cambridge: Cambridge University Press).

Patzelt, W.J. (1996): 'Members of Parliament and Interest Groups: Findings from East Germany', in A. Ágh, and G. Ilonszki (eds) *Parliaments and Organized Interest: The Second Steps* (Budapest: Hungarian Centre for Democracy Studies).

Pérez-Solórzano Borragán, N. (1998): *Assessment of Central and Eastern European Interests' Representation at the European Union Level*, Working Paper Series No. 36 (Brussels: College of Europe and European Interuniversity Press).

Pérez-Solórzano Borragán, N. (2001a): 'Organized Interests in Central and Eastern Europe. Towards Gradual Europeanization?', *Politique Européenne* 3: January, 61–85.

Pérez-Solórzano Borragán, N. (2001b): *Interest Politics in the Light of the EU's Eastward Enlargement. Rethinking Europeanization and Network Building in the Business Sector* (University of Exeter: PhD Thesis, unpublished).

Pérez-Solórzano Borragán, N. (2002): 'The Impact of EU Membership on Interest Politics in Central and Eastern Europe', *ESRC One Europe or Several? Civic Working Paper 2002/1*.

Poland, A.M. (2000a): 'KIG Euroconsulting to Help Polish Entrepreneurs Acclimate to EU Economy', January, 31.

Poland, A.M. (2000b): 'Europa 2000 Plus: German Businessmen Sceptical about Enlarging EU', April 26.

Pridham, G. (1984): 'Comparative Perspectives on the New Mediterranean Democracies: A Model of Regime Transition?', *West European Politics*, 7:2, 1–29.

Pridham, G. (2001): 'EU Accession and Domestic Politics: Policy Consensus and Interactive Dynamics in Central and Eastern Europe', *Perspectives on European Politics and Society* 1:1, 49–74.

Radaelli, C. (2000): 'Whither Europeanization? Concept Stretching and Substantive Change', *European Integration on line Papers (EioP)* 4:8.

Rustow, D. (1970): 'Transitions to Democracy: Towards a Dynamic Model' *Comparative Politics* 2:3.

Saurugger, S. (2000): 'Co-operation and/or Competition? Nuclear Energy and the Eastern Enlargement of the European Union', *Paper presented to the ECPR Joint Session*, Copenhagen, April 14–19.

Stantič, C. (2000): 'Paper presented to the Conference on Candidate Country Interest Representation in Brussels', in B. Cizelj and G. Vanhaeverbeke (eds) *Candidate Country Interest Representation in Brussels. Conference Proceedings* (Brussels: SBRA).

Waller, M. (1994): 'Political Actors and Political Roles in East-Central Europe', in M. Waller and M. Myant (eds) *Parties, Trade Unions and Society in East-Central Europe* (London: Frank Cass).

Waller, M. and Myant, M. (1994): *Parties, Trade Unions and Society in East-Central Europe* (London: Frank Cass).

Wiesenthal, H. (1996): 'Organized Interests in Contemporary East Central Europe: Theoretical Perspectives and Tentative Hypotheses', in A. Ágh and G. Ilonszki (eds) *Parliaments and Organized Interests: The Second Steps* (Budapest: Hungarian Centre for Democracy Studies).

Willets, P. (1982): *Pressure Groups in the Global System* (London: Frances Pinter).

Yancey, M. and Siegel, M. (1994): 'The Non-profit Sector in East Central Europe', *Transnational Associations* 1, 23–41.

Chapter 10

Regulating Satellite Television: A Failure of European Union Governance?

Campbell McPherson[1]

INTRODUCTION

It is axiomatic that all new technologies invoke issues of governance. This was certainly the case when, during the 1980s, developments in satellite television technology resulted in the signal (footprint) from a geostationary satellite[2] delivering good-quality signals to a larger surface area than that of any single European state. Historically, it had been relatively easy to listen to trans-frontier radio within Europe, but because of its physical properties, trans-frontier television reception had generally been limited to the border area. By contrast, direct to home (DTH) satellite television technology was quintessentially pan-European. This technical innovation meant that a broadcaster could be in any state in 'line-of-sight'[3] with the satellite, or the signal could be 'piggy-backed'[4] around the globe from one satellite to another. Programming recipients might be beyond the frontiers of the state for which the transmission was intended. Consequently, broadcasters could be within or beyond the jurisdiction of a single European state, or indeed the European Union (EU) itself, and as a result this new policy area was subject to international law.

---

[1] This chapter draws on years of research carried out by the author, including interviews with various actors whose identities must remain secret. For this reason the indication of sources given here does not follow the standard format of the book.

[2] The broadcasting satellite was in space on the Clarke Belt. This is a point *c.* 36,000 km in space at which the rotational speed of a satellite is equal to that of the earth. Consequently, the satellite appears to be always above the same point on the earth's surface (geostationary orbit) and can thus be relied upon to transmit to that area of the earth.

[3] 'Line of sight': i.e., the satellite is located at a position above the earth's surface where signals can reach it directly and programmes can be beamed to that part of the earth's surface.

[4] 'Piggy-backed', i.e. the signal is relayed around the globe from one satellite to another until it reaches a satellite located in a 'line-of-sight' position for the area for which the signal is intended.

The development of DTH satellite television technology during the 1980s paralleled that of the EU's[5] Single European Market (SEM) programme: the new technological medium both complemented and was symbolic of this project. Crucially, the combination of political rhetoric, advertising promoting the SEM and genuine misunderstandings about the nature of the new technology resulted in a popular belief that DTH services would be freely available. It was assumed that local subscribers, advertisers or a state licence fee would pay for broadcasts systems. This attitude was supported by the reality that the majority of early broadcasts were available in a non-encrypted format and accompanied by much initial company publicity. At the same time, as part of the attempts to revitalize the 'common market', DTH soon became enmeshed with attempts to revive the European electronics industry through the development of a prototype high-definition television system (Thatcher 1997; Fraser 1997). Clearly, all of these issues had, and continue to have, political, economic and regulatory implications.

In the first instance, the technological innovations required new technical standards. The new technology also raised several other important governance and economic issues. Among the potential challenges faced by the EU were the following: the need for regulation of pan-EU DTH broadcasting; a sound relationship between member states, non-member states and business organizations; the creation of a pan-EU market; the role to be played by the EU in a new technological environment linked to a (potentially) multi-billion Euro industry; and the strengthening of a European identity. In response, the Commission moved quickly to frame new legal measures, in the shape of Directive 98/84/EEC, on the Protection of Encrypted Services (which was due to be transposed into national law by May 2000). This directive exhorted member states to prevent any acts which might limit the freedom of movement and trade in television programmes or which might create dominant market positions (European Commission 1984). The interest representation process (i.e., the behaviour, the motivation and the relationship between the actors) that surrounded the development and implementation of this directive forms the core of this chapter. The directive is examined in its own right and in the context of the EU's White Paper on Governance (European Commission 2001a).

COMPANIES, PIRATES AND GOVERNANCE FAILURE

Partly as a result of the conflict between some of the key actors involved, the chance to create an SEM in Satellite DTH (a SEMSAT) (McPherson and Twomey 1994) was missed during the 1990s (see Box 1 for the key

---

[5] For simplicity EU is used throughout this chapter despite the obvious inaccuracy.

actors). Rights owners (generally American film companies) had resisted the integrationist logic of the new technology by insisting on selling rights on a traditional national or sub-national basis. They feared that a SEMSAT would result in the development of powerful pan-European broadcasters with market power to match that of major rights owners. Free-to-air transmissions were continued by state broadcasters such as France's TV5 and some commercial stations such as Germany's Sat 1, but these had limited market appeal compared to encrypted channels such as BSkyB (United Kingdom—UK), TV 1000 (Scandinavia) and Telepi (Italy) whose attraction lay in newly released films, key sporting

Box 1 Key Actors in the DTH Environment Early–Mid 1990s and Their Relationship to technology		
Formal and Semi Formal Extra-European Actors	Formal European Actors	Informal European Actors
• **Rights owners** (especially US Motion Pictures Association) make films • **United States Government** assists in copyright protection	• **Rights owners** make films and other programmes • **European content providers** sell films / programmes to broadcasters. • **Broadcasters** use satellite to broadcast programmes to customers • **Company Security or External content Security** protects programmes against unauthorized viewing using **encryption systems linked to a smart card.** Digital encryption systems use not only smart cards but also **Conditional Access Modules (CAMs)** which are basically microcomputers inserted into the satellite receiver. These make encryption more secure. • **Federation Against Copyright Theft (FACT), AEPOC** and other groups formed to counter piracy • **European Governments** primarily supportive of national broadcasters. • **European Commission** • **European Parliament** • **Consumers** who have a legal right to receive programmes in their home territory. • **Small and medium satellite equipment retailers** who rely upon piracy to generate market demand.	• **Pirates** who make money by penetrating encryption systems and providing reception cards without paying broadcasters or other parties. • **Hackers** penetrate encryption systems as a hobby. They often then release this information to pirates or to the internet. • **Moles** work for Company Security, Broadcasters etc. They sell codes to pirates. • **Out-of-market consumers** as potential customers. These are individuals who cannot legally purchase a programme because of their geographical location 'out-of-market'.

events and regular pornographic films. Several such companies further consolidated their domestic audience base and attracted viewers in areas such as the UK, especially given the latter's conservative content regime.

The result was a confusing situation in which DTH programmes could be received across national frontiers, whilst content providers and their security systems used increasingly sophisticated encryption technology (See Box 2) to try to ensure that only legitimate subscribers, with authorized decoders, could actually gain access to transmissions. Consequently, even a company such as BSkyB, which utilizes relatively effective security systems, issued more than eleven variants of its Videocrypt smart card during the 1980s and 1990s in order to protect its broadcasts.

The diversity of rights enforcement cultures within the EU and European Economic Area caused difficulties for broadcasters, especially as it coincided with the SEM's emphasis on frontier transparency. Hence, whilst countries such as Norway, the UK and France were noted for strict enforcement, Germany and Italy were perceived as having flourishing pirate markets with, in the case of the former, substantial trans-frontier seepage of goods (Lowe 1998). Broadcast protection was further complicated by national legal systems that did not recognize economic loss and interest (*locus standi*) by companies refusing to sell subscriptions within their national jurisdiction. This rendered civil and criminal anti-piracy actions difficult, if not impossible (European Commission 1997:5). The problems were exacerbated by certain struggling companies facilitating piracy in order to benefit from the additional income:

'Their internal security systems leak like hell. Do you know how much a major management key change is worth now? [...] About £250,000! What would you do for that? A lot of people would kill' (M 1998).

Box 2 Encryption Trends: UK and Mainland Europe. Selected Years 1992 – 99			
Month/Year	No. Channels	% UK Not Encrypted	% Elsewhere Europe Not Encrypted
Nov. 1992	186	13%	61%
July 1994	194	32%	64%
July 1996	254	20%	59%
June 1998	237	5%	49%
Sept. 1999	230	5%	32%
Information based on channel listings in *What Satellite TV*, WV Publications London. Dates as per month.			

Such unofficial income helped resolve the difficulties some companies faced in trying to expand their market against a background of increasing pressure from rights owners (Non-attributable Source (NAB) 2 2000; NAB 3). A fine balancing act was also required of the encryption providers who needed an environment in which they appeared to be successful (their fees depended upon this), but not so successful as to destroy the pirate industry whose existence provided a future for their services. Certainly, most anti-piracy measures were known by pirates beforehand (McPherson unpublished research 1995–2002), an issue which has now found its way into the courts, with allegations that at least one large company was actively assisting the pirates (*What Satellite TV* 2002: 8). The EU's failure to establish an appropriate governance system thus both damaged its own policy initiatives in relation to the integration process and indirectly fostered a new criminality.

The resultant reliance upon increasingly sophisticated encryption systems resulted in the creation of fortified DTH markets with diverse encryption modes (see box 3). The Commission itself was critical of such developments (European Commission 1995 and 1999), but its failure to act can be perceived as a critical governance issue in establishing an appropriate technical regime and indicated weakness in the face of corporate power. This pattern reoccurred at the decade's end with the

---

Box 3 CAM Encryption Systems and Main Market Orientation in Autumn 1999

Cam Encryption	Main Market Orientation
CONAX	Scandinavia
CRYPTOWORKS	Austria, Switzerland and Central European States
IRDETO	Germany and Italy
MEDIAGUARD	France and Spain
NAGRAVISION	Spain
POWERVU	United States Armed Forces Radio and Television and US Bloomberg-owned channels
VIACCESS	France
VIDEOGUARD	United Kingdom

introduction of digital encryption systems and was further reinforced by the Balkanization of the European market through the use of regionally linked conditional access modules (CAMs), essential for the reception of encrypted programming. Despite such measures and the increasing sophistication of encryption systems themselves, broadcasters were horrified to discover their continued vulnerability:

'The hackers are incredible. They get together on the internet around one or two in the morning and crack a problem in an hour that my people cannot crack in a week. I wish I could motivate my staff in the same way' (NAB 2 2000).

Broadcasters thus came to see the development of a punitive legal framework as essential (McPherson 1999). It should be noted at this juncture that broadcasters had earlier considered a directive controlling the movement of both CAMs and receivers. This option was abandoned because of earlier European Court of Justice (ECJ) judgments determining that television broadcasting was a service, and therefore subject to free movement under Article 59 of the Treaty of Rome (*Saachi and Bond van Adverteerders and others v The State of the Netherlands* ECJ 155/73) and that any measures, including state sanctions, taken to control the movement of goods and services had to be 'proportional' (*Bela-Muhle v Grows-Farm* ECJ 114/76, *R. v Intervention Board for Agricultural Produce* ECJ 181/84). Having abandoned this option, much commercial pressure was brought on manufacturers to limit their distribution in favour of particular companies and geographical areas.

Such behaviour was potentially embarrassing for the Commission. In its official discourse the Commission insisted that there should be no interference with the free movement of CAMS (Directive 98/84/EEC Article 4), though exceptions were possible on the grounds of policy, security, and health (European Commission 1997: 6). In addition to these policy failures, both broadcasters and the Commission must have been wary of potential criticism that DTH markets were essentially monopolistic in nature, as the Commission itself had already noted (European Commission 1994). For broadcasters the task of transforming EU policy was therefore a delicate one that was made more complex by their own history of disregarding EU legislation (McPherson 2000a).

REPRESENTATION: AGENDA SETTING

'There is no such thing as a good pirate. All piracy involves theft from a company' (BSkyB 1998)

'...this is probably a business which should not exist. I am here simply because of the stupidity of the law in preventing people enjoying themselves' (M 1998).

Official sources represent the draft Directive 98/84/EEC as originating in the Council Of Europe's 'Recommendation on the legal protection of encrypted television services' (COE 1991, cited in European Commission 1997: 4). However, both official and unofficial sources (NABs 1, 2, 3, M, S; varying dates 1997–2000) suggest that the catalyst was the broadcasters' realization that digital technology would not provide the expected improvements in encryption security. By the late 1990s digital television was something of a 'sacred cow' for EU policy makers, both because of its immediate technological and economic potentials and because of its connections with the internet and thence with small and medium industries, the information society and other key policies (European Commission 1997: 1). The linkage of DTH piracy with digital's wider economic and technical significance virtually guaranteed broadcasters free access to the Commission.

This policy shift reflects the enormous tensions created by the contradictions inherent in DTH's pan-European technology, corporate policy and market demand. The EU policy process had to be mobilized in this process because of the inappropriateness, or indifference, of national legislation. National criminal and civil legislation offered some protection against domestic infringement of DTH rights and other encrypted services such as cable television. However, by activating the European dimension companies effectively established a claim to economic interest, even when such an objective economic interest did not exist, effectively criminalizing individuals who afforded access to programmes, which providers refused to supply. The absurdity of this position, and the dubious behaviour of some companies, required that DTH piracy be resolved through legislation addressing a wider issue. Companies were therefore careful to establish a connection between legislation resolving problems created by corporate interests and DTH to a wider policy agenda focusing on the economic future of digital technology. This ploy effectively enveloped a wider, and arguably more justified, policy initiative that effectively guaranteed unfettered access to the Commission and Parliament because of their interest in 'things digital'. At a formal level, official Commission discourse (European Commission 1999, Proceedings 1998: 10–15, 25–28, 46–48) utilized corporate arguments in stressing the economic and technological significance of developments in digital technology.

This mobilization by broadcasters, and the associated mid-1990s intensification of representation at the level of both Commission and

Parliament, coincided with improvements in co-operation and intelligence activities between the companies, and the establishment of AEPOC (Association Européenne pour la Protection des Oeuvres et Services Cryptés) by rights owners and content providers as a European level actor. AEPOC stressed the 'economic harm' argument during consultations on the proposed directive (European Commission 1997: 5). Piracy was portrayed as a serious threat to company profitability and part of a wider criminal onslaught on intellectual property. Estimates of corporate losses ranged from *c.* 240 million ECUs (claimed by AEPOC in submissions to the Commission in 1996) to €1,300 million in 2000 (NAB 2 2000). Significantly, the Commission not only accepted this position, but also further expanded it in an emphasis upon the 'after-sales service' element of the market (European Commission 1997: 5). This may be evidence of the characterization of a typical Commission official as 'a very lonely [person] with a blank piece of paper wondering what to put on it' (Hull 1993: 83). The economic argument also served both to overcome cultural differences towards piracy (Zetterholm 1994: Kapteyn 1996) and consequently mobilized national law enforcement agencies to fit a European DTH mould (European Commission 1997: 7) shaped by the companies.

Sources (NABs 1, 2, 3, and S) identify specific companies in the lobbying process. BSkyB and Canal + were seen as some of the most dynamic actors who obtained substantial assistance and support from their governments in the Council of Ministers. Unofficially, company sources (NAB 4) concede this proactivity and, in the case of Britain and France at least, identify a date as early as 1992 in the mobilization of their national administrations to instigate Commission action. This date coincides with the introduction of new French anti-piracy legislation (Levi 2000). Italy's Telepi and Stream became active later and appear to have recruited the Amato and Prodi governments. Italian pirate sources suggest that internal politics may have been significant at an earlier stage in limiting the enthusiasm of the Berlusconi government for measures that would have served the financial interests of his media competitors. It should be noted however that, despite the approval of new legislation in France and Italy (Levi 2000: 65), police involvement was largely restricted to some French action against Canal + piracy.

REPRESENTATION: AVOIDING COUNTER-MOBILIZATION

Directive 98/84/EEC was thus almost unanimously represented by the Commission, companies and national governments as a measure intended to protect broadcasters and other users of encrypted communications from the 'evils of piracy'. Its transposition into national law amounted to a sea change in EU policy, which had historically focused on the DTH's integrationist potential. It is interesting to note the extent to which the European Parliament (EP) was taken on board. Both the Council of Ministers and the Internal Market Commissioner, Mario Monti, felt obliged to oppose draconian proposals (European Parliament 1998a) emanating from the Parliament's Rapporteur Georgious Anastassopoulos (EEP Greece), such as making possession of unauthorized reception equipment a criminal offence (as under Italian and Finnish legislation). There was a concern that such measures might be perceived as both a barrier to trade and excessively illiberal.

The tempo of policy formation consequently quickened with discussion on 'Europe's Way to the Information Society' (European Commission 1994), resulting in consultations with 'interested parties' during 1995 (European Commission 1997: 1) and the circulation during 1996 of the Green Paper on the 'Legal Protection of Encrypted Services' (European Commission 1997: 1). The initial proposal was formalized in July 1997. The first comments were received from the European Parliament in April 1998 and the full legislative process was completed between 15 April 1998 and 20 November 1998 (European Parliament 1998b: 2–5). The speed of legislation lends further credibility to claims that legislation was a response to a growing crisis in digital encryption. Directive 98/84/EEC can thus be seen as a classical recapturing of a new technology's potential (Webster 1991) by established economic actors (rights owners in this case). This replacement policy focused on the same politico-social, technological and economic advantages of digital as had been identified earlier, but now stressed the significance of encryption and digital technology and the importance of the corporation as technology gate-keeper within secured markets.

Speedy consideration and the determined focus on the claims of economic loss also reduced the risk of a wider debate that might have revealed flaws in the entire philosophical and legal basis for action. Such a debate might have encouraged a reaction against legislation intended to protect what were widely perceived to be overpriced and monopolistic DTH companies. Such sentiments were reinforced by attitudes similar to American free-market radicalism in their opposition to film, video and music rights payments. These had been clearly expressed in the letter pages of popular satellite TV publications during the 1980s and 1990s, and were reflected in high subscriber churn rates (McPherson 2000a). McPherson (*ibid*: 105) found that some 3.5 million households had an economic interest in the continuation of piracy (having invested thousands of euros in reception equipment and pirate cards) and were likely to oppose legislation. There was, thus, the potential for a popular reaction against the proposed legislation, if the skills existed to mobilize a disorganized and geographically diffuse sectoral interest. Mobilization of the economic argument was therefore accompanied by the 'politics of stealth' in hurrying through the legislation with minimal widespread discussion. This occurred against a background of public indifference to, or even support for, and financial involvement with, piracy which the Commission had tacitly recognized in its draft Directive (European Commission 1997: 5).

Significantly, because of fears about possible distortion of the SEM, the Commission baulked at demands from broadcasters and the European Parliament that grey imports be brought within the scope of the Directive (NAB 1 2000). However, substantial legal and commercial pressure was applied to stop such imports, much of it in the form of threatening solicitor's letters or threats that supplies of all equipment would be terminated.

'These people (i.e. solicitors representing Irdeto Mindport) are really pissing me off. I only want to sell 'legit' equipment and run an honest business and then they threaten me with a court order. I get the cards legally, but then get told the Irdeto CAMs are illegal' (Z 2000).

At the European Audiovisual Conference[6] in Birmingham in 1998 Working Group 4 had considered the issues of technical and content protection, but there was no public reference to Directive 98/84/EEC in the Proceedings at any point, simply a recommendation that

'the European Community and its Member States should continue their efforts on all fronts to combat piracy' (Proceedings 1998: 25–26).

This was typical of the level of public exposure that the Directive received. The Commission claimed to have consulted with 'interested parties' (European Commission 1997: 1), a claim repeated by the British Department of Trade and Industry (DTI) and Patent Office (Patent Office 1999). The reality was that 'interested parties' constituted companies of the stature of those invited to Birmingham (i.e. large, 'legitimate' business organizations). Companies connected with the pirate

---

[6] Official discourse and policy coordination were highly focused around the European Audiovisual Conference in Birmingham in April 1998, which brought together invited guests from broadcasting, electronics, entertainment and encryption companies, national government and the Commission. At Birmingham the dichotomy between public discourse and actual developments is starkly reflected in Rupert Murdoch's proclamation that News Corporation is "...about change and progress, not about protectionism through legislation and cronyism." (Proceedings 1998:57) – contemporaneously, BSkyB was a vocal advocate of the directive.

industry were not invited (Patent Office 1999). This lack of consultation reflects a cultural perspective which saw pirates as 'fair game', even though their activities were generally legal within member states. The comments of one British DTI official reflects this outlook:

'With the legislation in place we will really be able to get them (i.e. the pirates)' (NAB 1 1998).

When asked about consultations with the pirate sector, the European Parliament Rapporteur's office commented '[w]e hadn't thought about that. Is that a serious issue?' (EP 1998a). There appeared to be no consideration that the fate of legitimate businesses employing many thousands of individuals across the EU was at stake (McPherson 2000a, 2000b, and 2000c).

The ability of the pirate industry to engage in any form of representation was greatly reduced by the nature of the industry itself. The largest UK retailer selling pirate cards employed around 20 staff in 1999, whilst the vast majority employed one or two staff with a mixture of technical, installation, and sales skills. These small companies were extremely constrained in time and in their skills range, whilst their focus was on technical, short-term solutions to urgent problems such as equipment failure and changes in encryption. They knew nothing about the European Commission or its web sites, had not been invited to Birmingham, and when information did exist an absence of human resources to monitor and understand this environment was undoubtedly exacerbated by an unwillingness to circulate information which would detrimentally impact on sales. The cumulative effect of such structural weaknesses, information deprivation and exclusion from the policy process is clearly revealed in a survey conducted after the Directive's approval by the Council of Ministers in November 1998 (see Box 4).

Such factors do not provide a full explanation of the information deprivation process. One hacker was sufficiently informed to both locate the Commission's web site containing details of the proposed legislation and to place his critique of it on the internet in the form of a letter to then Commission President Santer. The letter, which was also mailed, received no reply (Kuhn 1999). This was consistent with the experience of the present author, who found that obtaining information from the Commission, European Parliament and southern member states effectively impossible, though communication flows from the European Parliament's London Office, the British DTI and northern European states were generally good. Regardless of the precise cause of a substantial 'democratic deficit' in the consultation process, the final outcome in governance terms is shown in Box 5.

Box 4 Knowledge of Directive 98/84 in November 1998	
Nature of Knowledge	Number of Companies
Knew precise details of the Directive	0
Knew some details of the Directive	5
Knew of planned implementation date	0
Had no knowledge of Directive	56
Had no knowledge of Directive but had heard about 'something happening'	83
Refused to discuss issue/hung up	3
Other reactions	3
Contacts based upon advertising placed in national magazine 'What Satellite' WV Publications, London, autumn 1998 and other known sources. This urvey covered all of the major satellite retail companies at the time.	

AFTERMATH: IMPLICATIONS FOR IMPLEMENTATION?

'I've been waiting for this new law [the EU anti-piracy Directive]. I have a family and don't intend to spend time inside (prison) ... I have ideas for new work' (M 2000).

Member states were required to ensure the Directive's implementation by May 2000, though most anticipated this deadline. However, no major increase in police action occurred until the summer of 2000 when the Italian police, for example, transmuted themselves from inert to dynamic actors, (Levi 2000: 65) with multiple arrests in various cities and the closure of more than ten internet sites. Italian pirate sources linked this increasing activity to the growing interest by News Corporation in Italy's Stream broadcasting and the News Corporation-British Government-Italian Government-Commission axis embodied in the close personal relations between Messrs Murdoch, Blair and Prodi.

The Directive obliged member states to introduce criminal sanctions which 'shall be effective, deterrent and proportional to the potential impact of the infringing activity within one year of the approval of the Directive' (Art. 5), and makes it an offence to 'import, install or replace for commercial purposes an illicit device' (Art. 3b). Further, it strikes at the possibility of providing 'code information through the telephone, and other electronic means such as the internet, by making illegal the use of

Box 5 General Issues and Response		
Issue	Potential Governance Response	Actual response
Technical potential for pan-EU DTH broadcasting	• Establishment of appropriate technical standards.	• Market fragmentation based on company-controlled technology
Potential creation of pan-EU market	• Legislation supporting pan-European company development. • Legislation changing copyright regimes. • Legislation establishing pan-European franchise network for subscription sales.	• Re-establishment of national and regional markets and regimes. • Directive largely terminates activities providing trans-frontier reception.
EU's governance capacity in a new (potentially multi-billion Euro) industry and power *vis-à-vis* governance and enforcement capacity	• Appropriate European legislative framework and enforcement capacity.	• Legislative framework largely perpetuates national dimension. • Predominance of corporate interests.
Potential strengthening of European-dimension (growth of European identity/embryonic policy catalyst)	• Legislation as in above provides 'spillover'.	• Disillusionment with EU results from EU policy failure.

commercial communications to promote illicit devices' (Art. 3c). By making their actions a criminal offence with potential imprisonment as a penalty, individuals have been obliged either to leave the industry or to become more deeply involved with what is now a criminal act. The motivation of those remaining is clearly not unrelated to the value of a protected market. One encryption system alone protected an estimated market of $1,500 million in 2000 (NAB 2 2000), and obtaining only a small percentile of such a market might be tempting to some. Legislation thus both raised the stakes and accelerated and deepened levels of criminal activity and involvement in previously legitimate businesses.

DIRECTIVE 98/84/EEC AND THE WHITE PAPER ON GOVERNANCE: LESSONS LEARNT?

One of the repeated complaints by British pirates and viewers *post-factum* was that the broadcasters had not been required to carry information concerning the proposed legislative changes during their programming. Consequently, it was repeatedly observed that those most directly affected by Directive 98/84/EEC were totally excluded from what purported to be a meaningful consultation process. Sentiments were expressed that the exercise was essentially conspiratorial and that the

EU's 'policy decision point' (Richardson 1996: 282) had been reached behind closed doors. This process was perceived as constituting a clear aberration from British consultation systems which usually contain relatively sophisticated systems of prior notice of change and appeals to semi- or fully autonomous bodies such as the Independent Broadcasting Authority. The resultant perception was that, if this was European consultation, it was poorer than the British process.

At this juncture it may be observed that experience of Directive 98/84/EEC indicates that, if the EU wishes to achieve an element of democratic legitimacy in its governance, it must become both *more focused* and *more populist* in its policy formulation. There is little direct recognition of this in the 2001 Governance White Paper (European Commission 2001a), though a tacit identification of the issue can be found in the commitment to minimum consultation standards and more guarantees of the openness and representativity of the organizations consulted (*ibid*: 4; see also Goehring, this volume). However, the resultant governance model is based upon formal information flows through *organized* sectoral interests (*ibid*: 6): 'civic society' groups such as churches and religious communities (*ibid*: 14) and official European institutions such as the Economic and Social Committee and Committee of the Regions (*ibid*: 15). From a Commission perspective input by 2,500 organizations and people (*ibid*: 9) is a major achievement, though extrapolating from that figure to a participation base of some 500,000 (European Commission 2001b: 4) assumes some highly effective internal consultation. The White Paper envisages further 'democratization' of the consultation process, improved by the use of specific internet sites that provide access to proposed EU legislation and the existing legal framework. However, such formalized systems had, and continue to have, little congruity with the DTH's European consumer base of *c*.34 million. Though national markets vary significantly in size and composition, the UK was not atypical in that the main consumer base for early DTH services was among low-income groups, although this profile changed somewhat after the introduction of digital transmissions. Such consumers generally possess relatively low levels of political sophistication and influence.

There was a widespread misconception when DTH technology was introduced that consumers would be able to watch whatever they wanted. This belief was partly founded on the idea that the EU's SEM programme would permit such open access. Interestingly, the EU was not perceived primarily as having failed in governance terms, but in its role as a provider of goods and services. Given this focus on the delivery of economic welfare, the concept of 'consumer-citizen' seems more appropriate than that of a 'citizen' who is also a 'consumer'. Commission legitimacy was dramatically reduced in this context by perceptions that it had:

- 'failed to deliver' during the 1990s with the MAC technical programme;
- failed in developing public access to DTH television;
- conspired with major broadcasters in the passing of Directive 98/84/EEC. The details were unknown, but the effect was clearly felt in loss of programming;
- assisted broadcasting companies in the maintenance of national monopolies.

Inherent in these perceptions was a belief that the EU had supported policies which were 'unfair' and which ran contrary to concepts of 'reasonableness' and 'custom'. Fundamentally, experience of DTH technology had the effect of reducing embryonic support for, and confidence in, the EU as a market access actor and as an arena in which representation could be made. The White Paper acknowledges such a crisis of legitimacy and that

'Member States do not communicate well about what the Union is doing [. . .] Brussels is too easily blamed [. . .] for difficult decisions' (European Commission 2001a: 7).

However, as already noted, the response was to associate this with issues of citizenship and communication flow between formal actors. The Commission's White Paper consultation focus thus remains firmly elitist in orientation. References to on-line contact with the public (European Commission 2001b: 4) are essentially internet-focused and rely upon contact with interest groups. Periodical e-mailing of a letter to a database of 1,500 subscribers (*ibid*: 14) leaves doubts about the representative nature of the consultation.

Such a model is inappropriate, given the nature of contemporary Europe. Box 6 indicates the *potential* for Commission communication through a functionally focused 'end user' communication approach rather than the White Paper's unfocused methodology. Indeed, a focusing on national groups as policy gatekeepers to resolve issues of European legitimacy and quality of governance may be somewhat paradoxical: some writers already consider the EU to be populated by 'dense networks of experts' (Pierson 1996: 133).

Such weaknesses are significant in the context of the White Paper's lament over the lack of appreciation for, and contentment with, EU-level action, the failure to recognize the benefits of EU policy, and the tendency for blame to be unfairly apportioned to the Commission (European Commission 2001a: 7 and 8). However, the Commission's response to this is one of identifying a greater role for official and unofficial national groups (*ibid*: 9) on the basis that this will add value

Box 6 Immediate efficacy of Various Consultation/Information Strategies (using DTH as an Example)

End User DTH	Targeted advertising on DTH channels. Potential 100% of users.
Through Church Groups*	Italy 45% of adult population Netherlands 35% United Kingdom 27% France 21% former West Germany 14%
Through Trade Unions†	Italy 65% of working population Netherlands 33.8% United Kingdom 33% France 28.9% Germany (Both former East and West) 24.3%

* Figures refer to early 1990s. Source: University of Michigan, Ann Arbor 1997. *Study Identifies Worldwide Rates of Religiosity and Church Attendance* www.umich.edu/newsinfo/Releases/1997.

† Figures refer to mid–late 1990s. Source: International Labour Organization World Employment Report 1996–97. ILO Geneva. ISBN 92-2-1103331-5.

to national policies. This expectation starkly reveals weaknesses in the White Paper's focus. The latter identifies the importance of the way policy makers use expert advice (*ibid*: 33) in the governance process, but fails to acknowledge that such expertise may be highly diffuse and that expertise is embodied in interests whose objectives may be contrary to either the objective national and/or European good. Inherent in this is the dilemma faced by the EU when trying to improve the quality of its governance in a world in which specialist knowledge and new technology directly impact on, and is perceived as important by, the citizen.

In this context the Commission's identified shortage of expertise and personnel (Peterson and Bomberg 1999) may explain its reliance upon 'expert' opinion from interests which, as already noted, have a long history of failing to observe EU law. Directive 98/84/EEC illustrates the dangers inherent in relying upon traditional, recognized, nationally constituted experts. Central to the DTH case was the existence of groups of nationally based 'experts' (as defined by the existence of specialized knowledge and skills). One expert group was composed of broadcasters and the owners of rights to television programmes. The other expert group consisted of 'the pirates'. The latter's 'illegitimate expertise' lay in knowledge of encryption, access to equipment through the grey market and complex webs of information and support patterns which interfaced with consumers, equipment manufacturers and broadcasting companies themselves. Whilst the White Paper cites the need for greater effective involvement of national actors in the shaping, application and enforcement of Community rules and programmes (European Commission 2001b: 34), experience from the DTH sector, including the thwarting of EU technical standards and some highly dubious behaviour in relation to Articles 81 and 82, powerfully indicates the need for a much-increased range of European specialists with a dedicated function to serve the European interest and consider the European dimension.

Consultation in relation to Directive 98/84/EEC did essentially follow a pattern similar to the one set out in the Commission's 'consultation model' (European Commission 2001a: 16). Nevertheless, in the case of this Directive, the consultation procedure failed to involve the numerous interested 'experts' labelled 'pirates'. They may not have been part of large companies or established pressure groups, but they were not illegal nor economically disinterested bystanders. Micro companies and Small and Medium Sized Enterprises (SMEs) were consistently ignored in the consultancy process despite their employment of many thousands across the EU. This exclusion from the policy networks has been identified as pivotal to much of the EU's decision-making process (Peterson 1995; Richardson 1996) and is starkly demonstrated in the list of consulted parties published by the British government (Patent Office 1999).

The creation of this outsider status was clearly associated with perceptions of legitimacy and runs counter to the consensual approach, especially in technical issues, historically associated with the Commission (Rhodes 1997: 7). In conversations both British and Commission officials repeatedly used expressions such as 'get', 'hit', or 'punish' in relation to the 'pirate outsiders' even before the end of the consultation period and before their activities became unlawful. It is interesting to note the clear 'gatekeeper' role of such officials and their focus upon the unlawfulness of 'pirate' behaviour. No account was taken, nor interest indicated, in the repeated contravention of EU legislation by major corporations.

CONCLUSION

The link between a relatively obscure and rather technical Directive and the issue of European governance may not be immediately apparent. However, the evidence indicates that Directive 98/84/EEC resulted from problems in constructing a governance framework in the DTH satellite television industry and that the directive was part of a series of responses in which major economic interests engaged in policy frustration, redirection and capture. The case study also reveals that national legislation had the potential to resolve other encryption protection issues: EU level legislation was therefore not necessary. The application of an EU Directive to DTH represents the mobilization of EU competence that amounts to the solution of 'corporate difficulties' arising from 'technological advances'. The Directive could, therefore, be viewed as an example of the colonization and mobilization of the European legislative process in order to protect the interests of 'big business'. Directive 98/84/EEC also exposed significant shortcomings in the EU's governance process: there is little evidence that policy proposals contained in the White Paper will prevent a repetition of such shortcomings.

The evolution of Directive 98/84/EEC thus represented the end of a transmogrification in EU DTH policy. Early EU 'open skies' policies had proclaimed the politico-social, technological and economic advantages of trans-frontier broadcasting and partly served the interests of the electronics industry (Bangemann 1992). However, this policy ran counter to the economic interests of rights owners, who were likely to be better served by the continuation of relatively weak and fragmented national and regional broadcasting markets. The EU's role in this process of transformation is crucial. Having failed to develop the potential of a SEMSAT, the Commission has been involved in a legislative process characterized by haste and opacity with which the intended targets of the legislation were incapable of engaging. This process lacked the transparency of consultation that, ideally, would be an essential element of a democratic process. The inability to obtain information, and the haste and closed nature of the process, all indicate that the Commission and European Parliament had been captured by large companies with their seductive discourse of economic loss and threat to digital technology. It lends further support to claims from the pirate industry that large companies were fearful of the consequences of a public debate on DTH broadcasting. From the perspective of the pirate industry the feeling was that the Commission, the Parliament, some large companies and some national governments were intent on destroying them – a fear reinforced by the terminology used by officials.

The policy-making process that surrounded Directive 98/84/EEC also points to serious flaws in the White Paper on Governance. Specifically, the document consistently fails to recognize significant socio-technical changes. When it does so, it comes to what might be considered erroneous conclusions. For example, whilst the White Paper identifies the importance of organizations in the mobilization of civil society, its reliance upon traditional organizations such as churches and trade unions (European Commission 2001a: 14 and 15) produces a consultation model which *may* have been historically relevant, but which disregards a contemporary focus on both technological participation by individuals (e.g. through inter-active digital services) and the importance of SMEs (as employers and significant actors in the life of local communities). The White Paper also perpetuates the (excessive) reliance on experts and organized interests that resulted in seizure of the policy agenda in the case of Directive 98/84/EEC. Hence, the Commission confuses 'openness' (*ibid*: 10) with effective communication. Whilst 'good governance' involves open information flow, as noted earlier, this is not synonymous with effective communication. The latter requires an approach which is both much more 'diffuse' and 'penetrative' to reach 'the person in the street', as opposed to the more politically sophisticated and aware individuals who are generally active participants in the civic society organizations (as envisaged by the White Paper).

Consequently, experience suggests that the consultation process needs to be radically transformed especially in order to identify the interests and needs of the 'end user'. Neglect of the 'consumer' dimension of citizenship, essentially the welfare dimension, risks further alienation of the general public whose support the Commission requires. Further, the evidence suggests that reliance on established expert groups and economic interests does not necessarily serve the 'European project'. Rather, intra- and extra-European economic interests benefit from the Commission's lack of expertise and a comprehensive overview of the economic-technological-political environment. Despite budgetary restrictions and the current focus on subsidiarity, the case of Directive 98/84/EEC indicates that the Commission needs to develop better and more sophisticated intelligence systems. This implies that more, better-qualified staff are needed who are able to identify and address the 'European dimension' before it becomes the domain of 'big business'.

REFERENCES

Bangemann, M. (1992): *Meeting the Global Challenge: Establishing a Successful European Industrial Policy* (London: Kogan Page).

BSkyB (1998): Personal Communication.

Cecchini, P. (1988): *1992 The European Challenge* (Aldershot:Wildwood House).

Council of Europe (1991): *Recommendation No R (91) 14 of the Council of Ministers* (Strasbourg).

European Commission (2001a): *European Governance: A White Paper*, Brussels 25.7. 2001 (COM (2001) 428 final) (Brussels: Commission of the European Communities).

European Commission (2001b): *Consultations Conducted for the Preparation of the White Paper on Democratic European Governance*, SG/8533/01 – EN (Brussels: Commission of the European Communities).

European Commission (1999): *Principles and Guidelines for the Community's Audiovisual Policy in the Digital Age*, Brussels 14. 12. 1999 COM (1999) 657 Final (Brussels: Commission of the European Communities).

European Commission (1997): Proposal for a Directive 9 July 1997, http://www.europa.eu.int.

European Commission (1996): *Information Society Rolling Action Plan*, Brussels COM (96) 607 Final of 16 April.

European Commission (1989): *Directive 89/552/EEC Council Directive on the coordination of certain provisions laid down by law, regulation or administrative action in Member States concerning the pursuit of television broadcasting activities 'Television Without Frontiers'*, Directive OJ L 298 17. 10. 1989 (Brussels: Commission of the European Communities).

European Commission (1984): *'Television Without Frontiers' Green paper on the Establishment of the Common Market for Broadcasting, especially by satellite and cable*, Brussels Com (84) 300 Final 14 June 1984 (Brussels: Commission of the European Communities).

European Commission (1998): *Proceedings of the European Audiovisual Conference,* DG X, Brussels. (Brussels: Commission of the European Communities).

European Parliament (1998a): Personal Communication with assistant to Rapporteur Anastassopulous, 14 September.

European Parliament (1998b): European Parliament Identification of Procedure Tec: T05094 (Brussels: European Parliament).

Fraser, M. W. (1997): 'Television', in H Kassim and A Menon (eds) *The European Union and National Industrial Policy* (London: Routledge).

Kuhn (1999): Personal Communication.

Hull, R. (1993): 'Lobbying the European Community; a view from within', in S. Mazey and J. J. Richardson (eds) *Lobbying in the European Community* (Oxford: Oxford University Press).

Kapteyn, P. (1996): *The Stateless Market* (London: Routledge).

Levi, R. (2000): 'Tempi duri per I pirati', *Satellite Eurosat*, JCE Editorial Group Milan Italy, January, 64–68 (writer's translation).

Lowe, D. (1998): Personal Communication.

M. (1998): Personal Communication.

M. (2000): Personal Communication.

McPherson, C. (2000a): 'Death to the Entrepreneur: an examination of the use of technology and legislation to control programme piracy at the dawn of the digital era', in T. Lees, S. Ralph and J. Langham Brown (eds) *Is Regulation Still an Option in a Digital Universe?* (Chichester: John Wiley).

McPherson, C. (2000b): 'From Grand Policy to Targeted Destruction: Consumers as Victims of EU Satellite Television Policy', *Journal of Business Ethics* 25:2, 129–141.

McPherson, C. (2000c): 'Asymmetrical Information, Poor Knowledge and Satellite Television', *European Business Review* 12:4.

McPherson, C. and Twomey, L. (1994): 'Satellite Broadcasting: A Missed Opportunity for the SEM?', in I. Barnes and L. Davison (eds.) *European Business: Text and Cases* (Oxford: Butterworth Heinemann).

NAB 1 (1998): Personal Communication.

NAB 1 (2000): Personal Communication.

NAB 2 (2000): Personal Communication.

NAB 3: Personal Communication.

NAB 4: Personal Communication.

Patent Office (1999): *Draft Regulatory Impact Assessment: The Conditional Access (Unauthorized Decoders) Regulations 2000.*

Peterson, J. and Bomberg, E. (1999): *Decision Making in the European Union* (Basingstoke: Macmillan).

Peterson, J. (1995): 'Decision-making in the European Union: towards a framework for analysis', *Journal of European Public Policy*, 2:1, 69 – 93.

Richardson, J. J. (1996): 'Eroding EU Policies; Implementing Gaps, Cheating and Re-Steering', in J. J. Richardson (ed.) *European Union: Power and Policy Making* (London: Routledge).

S. (2000): Personal Communication.

Rhodes, R. A. W. (1997): *Understanding Governance; Policy Networks, Governance, Reflectivity and Accountability* (Buckingham: Open University Press).

Thatcher, M. (1997): 'High Technology', in H. Kassim and A. Menon (eds) *The European Union and National Industrial Policy* (London: Routledge).

Webster, A. (1991): *Science Technology and Society* (Basingstoke: Macmillan).

What Satellite TV, May 2002: 8, WV Publications London.

Zetterholm, S. (1994): 'National Culture and European Integration', in S. Zetterholm (Ed.) (London: Berg).

Z. (2000): Personal Communication.

LEGAL CASES

Saachi and Bond van Adverteerders and others v The State of the Netherlands ECJ 155/73.

Bela-Muhle v Grows-Farm ECJ 114/76, *R. v Intervention Board for Agricultural Produce* ECJ 181/84.

Index